The Fus Fixico Letters

ALEXANDER POSEY

The Fus Fixico Letters

A Creek Humorist in Early Oklahoma

EDITED BY

Daniel F. Littlefield, Jr., &
Carol A. Petty Hunter

FOREWORD BY

A. LaVonne Brown Ruoff

ooooo

UNIVERSITY OF OKLAHOMA PRESS

Norman

ISBN 0-8061-3421-6

1   2   3   4   5   6   7   8   9   10

This book is dedicated
to Elizabeth Smith, my mother,
who assisted in my research and traveled
in Indian Territory with me in
search of our Creek friends.
Carol A. Petty Hunter

Contents

List of Illustrations   viii

Foreword   ix

Preface   xiii

Introduction   1

The Fus Fixico Letters   49

Key to Names in the Fus Fixico Letters   267

Notes for the Introduction   271

Headnote Sources   281

Bibliography   285

Index   293

ILLUSTRATIONS
Map:
Indian Territory and
Oklahoma Territory,
1902-1907, page 2

following page 56
Alex Posey
Charles Gibson
Chitto Harjo
George W. Grayson
Green McCurtain
Thomas M. Buffington
Ethan Allen Hitchcock
Clifford L. Jackson
Tams Bixby
J. George Wright
Clarence B. Douglas
Pliny L. Soper

following page 176
Thomas B. Needles
J. Blair Shoenfelt
Clifton R. Breckenridge
Pleasant Porter
Legus C. Perryman
Cornelius E. Foley
Charles J. Bonaparte
Robert L. Owen
Robert L. Williams
Theodore Roosevelt
Alice Mary Robertson
William H. Murray
Charles N. Haskell
J. Fentress Wisdom

Foreword

When the Osage scholar Carol A. Petty Hunter (1937–87) was dying, she asked that I become executor of her manuscript "Alexander Lawrence Posey: The Creek Satirist," which included many of his Fus Fixico letters, selected poems, and journals. As she indicates in her Preface, I had originally suggested that she edit Posey's work, which had long been out of print. Carol had completed a draft of the manuscript and planned to spend at least another year completing the research and polishing the manuscript. Unfortunately, she became too ill to finish the project.

I was delighted when our mutual friend Daniel F. Littlefield, Jr., agreed to finish the edition of Fus Fixico letters, incorporating Carol's research. Carol's family approved his recommendation to omit the journals and selected poems. As his splendid biography *Alex Posey* (1992) demonstrates, Dan possesses the mastery of Creek politics and the knowledge of details of Posey's life essential to the edition. Alex Posey's *Fus Fixico Letters* is a fitting tribute to Carol and Dan's commitment to educating contemporary audiences about early Native American writers whose works have been too long neglected.

Carol's dedication to research on American Indian literature began as a graduate student. After receiving her B.S. degree in economics and education in 1961 and her M.A. degree in English literature in 1972 from Oklahoma State University, Stillwater, she completed her doctorate in American literature at the University of Denver in 1978. Much to the amusement of her family, she turned an old chickenhouse on her mother's property at Ralston, Oklahoma, into a study, where she wrote her dissertation, "Osage Indian Mythology: A Literary Perspective." This study is a testament to her commitment to research in American Indian literature because, like most of us in those days, she had to educate herself in the field.

At the time of her death, Carol was assistant professor of English at the University of Oklahoma. She had also been a visiting professor in the Department of English at the University of California, Los Angeles, and an instructor both in the Department of Humanities, Rose State College, Midwest City, Oklahoma, and at the Institute of American Indian Art, Santa Fe. In addition, she had taught in the public schools of California, Oklahoma, and Bermuda. Among the postdoctoral awards she received were an NEH summer stipend, 1979; Ford Foundation/Newberry Library Fellowship, 1980–81; American Indian Culture and Research Center Fellowship, fall 1983; and a Fulbright scholarship to France, 1985–86.

The 1979 NEH Summer Seminar for College Teachers on American Indian Literature, which I directed, was a turning point for Carol because for the first time she was introduced to early and modern Indian writers and met others who shared her interest in the field. We became close friends during the seminar and worked together until her death. During two of my visits to her family, we did research in the major Oklahoma collections of Indian materials, which made both of us aware of how much there was to be done.

As Carol's dedication makes clear, she was also devoted to her mother and other members of her family. No matter how far we traveled to museums and libraries during my last visit, Carol always made sure that we returned to Ralston in time to prepare supper for her mother.

Carol's major publications include two fine essays on John Joseph Mathews (Osage): "The Historical Content in John Joseph Mathews's Sundown" (*MELUS* 9 [1982]: 61–72) and "The Protagonist as a Mixed Blood in John Joseph Mathews's Novel, *Sundown*" (*American Indian Quarterly* 6 [1982]: 319–37). Carol had planned to write additional studies of his work. She also published an informative interview with Wendy Rose, which originally appeared in *MELUS* 10 (1983): 67–87 and was reprinted in Bo Schöler's *Coyote Was Here* (1984).

After returning from her Fulbright year in France, Carol became very ill with what was eventually diagnosed as pancreatic cancer. After many months of pain, she died on March 12, 1987, and was buried in the family plot in the Osage cemetery at Gray Horse, Oklahoma.

Carol was a gentle, kind, and generous person with an infectious sense of humor. Her family and friends will always miss her. Her death was a genuine loss not only to her family and friends but also to the profession. Her earlier scholarship and this book remind us of the important contributions to the study of American Indian literature she made during her brief postdoctoral career.

A. LAVONNE BROWN RUOFF

University of Illinois at Chicago

Preface

In the history of Oklahoma, Alexander Lawrence Posey is noted as a Creek author who was secretary of the Sequoyah convention in 1905 when the Indian tribes attempted to establish Indian Territory as a separate state. Although he is recognized as a historical figure, Posey is virtually unread as a writer. Yet before 1900, Posey's poems were frequently printed in major newspapers and journals of Indian Territory. After 1900, they continued to be published there and appeared as well in some U.S. publications. After 1902, when Posey purchased the *Indian Journal* and became editor of that weekly newspaper at Eufaula, he achieved national fame among journalists. In addition, he earned a widespread reputation for his political satire, the Fus Fixico letters, which he began in his *Journal* in 1902 and published intermittently until his death.

In 1908 Posey died in a tragic accident while still a young man, and his widow immediately began to collect his works for publication. In 1910 Minnie Posey edited and published a collection of his poems. This rare first edition, which includes a memoir by William Elsey Connelley, sold poorly and has long been out of print. In 1969 a revised, limited edition of this work was printed by the Five Civilized Tribes Heritage Foundation at Muskogee, Oklahoma. However, a number of Posey's poems were excluded from both editions. Mrs. Posey also wanted to collect and publish the Fus Fixico letters but had difficulty finding publishers who were interested. After Posey's death, excerpts from his satire were published only on rare occasions when memorial articles were written by journalists and others who had known Posey. Until now, the Fus Fixico letters have remained uncollected in the archives of journalism.

Posey was one of the earliest American Indian writers of satire and humor and was the best known before Will Rogers. Posey wrote when the Indian nations of Indian Territory were most severely affected by the allotment legislation that dissolved the nations and disrupted the Indians' social, political, and economic structures. He brought his satire and humor to bear on these events through the Fus Fixico letters. Yet Posey's satire represents more than a historical view. The letters mirror life on one of the last frontiers for non-Indian Americans, focusing on social and political events in Indian Territory and depicting its people— Indian, white, and black—some who were to become famous or infamous and others who were practically unknown though no less interesting. Most important, the satire captures the Indian's humor, a characteristic often overlooked by non-Indians.

The initial research for this project began with field trips to McIntosh County and to the Creek Nation capital at Okmulgee, Oklahoma. I believed it was essential to interview Creek people living in communities such as Eufaula, Henryetta, Holdenville, and other rural towns of the old Creek Nation, where Posey had lived and worked to become familiar with the landscape and people. Although the Creeks with whom I visited had heard of Posey, they were not familiar with the content of his writings. Nevertheless, our conversations led to interesting and important resources, and overall, the interviews were invaluable. The Creeks are today, as they were in Posey's time, a hospitable people. And like Creeks of his day, they have a sense of humor not immediately apparent to outsiders. In matters of Creek history and culture, I am more than indebted for their help in the research.

This work was made possible by a postdoctoral fellowship at the American Indian Studies Center and by funds sponsored at the American Studies Research Institute at the University of California, Los Angeles. I want to thank Charlotte Heth, the director of the American Indian Studies Center, and to acknowledge her staff and Anthony Brown. I also want to thank Lenore Stiffarm, research director, whose encouragement led to the completion of the research. I am grateful to LaVonne Brown Ruoff, of the University of Illinois, Chicago, a colleague and friend who suggested and prompted this study, and Kathryn Barrett, for her patience and help in typing my manuscript. I want to mention the curators of the Western History Collections at the University of Oklahoma, who gave me access to the Posey collection, the Thomas Gilcrease Institute of American History and Art, and the archives of journalism at the Oklahoma Historical Society. In addition, I wish to acknowledge Bill Bear and Steve Wilson and their Creek community.

CAROL A. PETTY HUNTER

Carol Hunter's intent was that this collection include not only Posey's Fus Fixico letters but selected poems and his journals as well. She had chosen the selections, written an introduction, and done a large amount of editing.

When I was asked to complete Carol's work, I was engaged in researching and writing a biography of Posey. Because she was my friend and because I shared her belief that contemporary readers should have access to Posey's works, I agreed to undertake the project. I determined, in light of my biographical study, to include only the Fus Fixico letters for the following reasons. First, Posey's journals are readily accessible in the *Chronicles of Oklahoma*, though some errors in transcription mar the printed texts. Second, the limited number of poems that Carol had included represented only a mild sampling of the more than two hundred Posey wrote. On the other hand, Carol had collected and included sixty-four of the seventy-two letters Posey published. Her preface and introduction indicated that she believed — as I do — that the Fus Fixico letters were Posey's most important work. Her introductory matter, the letters, and the notes and annotations that accompanied them constituted more than half of her manuscript. Because the letters have literary and historical value and represent an important development in Indian literary history, I concluded that they could easily stand on their own merits as a separate volume. Thus I revised her sketch of Posey's life in light of my biographical study, which had not been completed at the time she wrote, and reshaped the introductory matter to emphasize the historical and literary contexts for only the Fus Fixico letters. Finally, I drafted headnotes for the letters and completed the annotations that Carol had begun.

The result of our combined efforts is this volume. The Introduction establishes the broad biographical, historical, and literary contexts for the Fus Fixico letters. It is followed by the letters, which are arranged chronologically by date of publication. Each letter or limited sequence of letters — if they deal with a common subject — is preceded by a bibliography and a brief headnote, which give the publication history of each letter and describe the historical circumstances that generated the letter or sequence. Esoteric matters, special terminology, or literary allusions not dealt with in the headnotes are explained in footnotes.

Some textual problems exist. The copy text for each letter is the first available printing. Fortunately, for most letters, the first printing is available. However, because of a lack of extant newspapers, subsequent printings must serve as copy texts for eleven letters. Eight of these eleven letters appeared in Posey's own newspaper; whenever possible, his printing serves as the copy text. For nine letters, first printings exist only as undated newspaper clippings in the Posey scrapbooks at the Thomas Gilcrease Institute of American History and Art; six of the nine appeared in Posey's newspaper. For most of these, approximate dates of publication could be established through content or by reference to subsequent printings. The first printing listed in the bibliography before each headnote indicates the copy text. In addition to his published letters, Posey left a fragment of a letter concerning the death of Yadeka Harjo. Apparently he later rendered the content of the fragment in his poem "Hotgun on the Death of Yadeka Harjo." Both fragment and poem are reprinted in the collection. Finally, there are minor textual problems such as missing lines that are impossible to determine because no subsequent printings are available. These problems are indicated in the notes. Obvious typographical errors have been corrected, as have printers' inconsistencies or omissions regarding quotation marks. However, instances of possibly intentional misspellings for effect remain and are indicated by [*sic*]. Posey's inconsistencies in the spelling of proper names remain.

The help of others was invaluable in this edition. I especially thank Sarah Erwin, librarian at the Thomas Gilcrease Institute of American History and Art, Tulsa, Oklahoma; William Welge and his staff at the Archives and Manuscripts Division of the Oklahoma Historical Society, Oklahoma City; librarians and archivists at the Western History Collections, University of Oklahoma, Norman; librarians at the Bacone College Library, Muskogee, Oklahoma; librarians of the Muskogee Public Library, Muskogee, Oklahoma; Joe Johnson, Posey's grandnephew and mayor of Eufaula; and George Bunny, who translated for me.

DANIEL F. LITTLEFIELD, JR.

Introduction

On October 24, 1902, a letter from one Fus Fixico appeared in the *Indian Journal*, the weekly newspaper at Eufaula, Creek Nation. It began, "Un Hesse Mahhe, Mr. Editor, Toyets Kat: So I will sent you some news to put in this time."[1] The dialect alerted the readers to the type of person the author represented: Fus Fixico was a Creek, possibly a full-blood. For local readers, there was nothing remarkable about the letter's mild humor or its publication, since letters of that type had occasionally appeared in the *Journal* during the preceding months. Readers would not discover for several months more that the author was Alexander Lawrence Posey, the young Creek editor of the *Journal*. By then, a number of Fus Fixico letters had been published, and Posey was well on his way to establishing a reputation as a political humorist.

Posey was, in fact, only one of a number of Indian humorists that Indian Territory produced. From the early days of European settlement on the continent, Indians had demonstrated that they could not only laugh at themselves but also have a good laugh at the expense of the whites.[2] In the late nineteenth century, Indians began to draw on their humor in literary expression, and by the first decade of this century, a number of them in Indian Territory had counted themselves as humorists.[3] The Fus Fixico letters that Posey wrote between 1902 and 1908 made him the best of his contemporaries and one of the best Indian humorists of all time.

Indian Territory and Oklahoma Territory, 1902–1907

Preface

Some textual problems exist. The copy text for each letter is the first available printing. Fortunately, for most letters, the first printing is available. However, because of a lack of extant newspapers, subsequent printings must serve as copy texts for eleven letters. Eight of these eleven letters appeared in Posey's own newspaper; whenever possible, his printing serves as the copy text. For nine letters, first printings exist only as undated newspaper clippings in the Posey scrapbooks at the Thomas Gilcrease Institute of American History and Art; six of the nine appeared in Posey's newspaper. For most of these, approximate dates of publication could be established through content or by reference to subsequent printings. The first printing listed in the bibliography before each headnote indicates the copy text. In addition to his published letters, Posey left a fragment of a letter concerning the death of Yadeka Harjo. Apparently he later rendered the content of the fragment in his poem "Hotgun on the Death of Yadeka Harjo." Both fragment and poem are reprinted in the collection. Finally, there are minor textual problems such as missing lines that are impossible to determine because no subsequent printings are available. These problems are indicated in the notes. Obvious typographical errors have been corrected, as have printers' inconsistencies or omissions regarding quotation marks. However, instances of possibly intentional misspellings for effect remain and are indicated by [*sic*]. Posey's inconsistencies in the spelling of proper names remain.

The help of others was invaluable in this edition. I especially thank Sarah Erwin, librarian at the Thomas Gilcrease Institute of American History and Art, Tulsa, Oklahoma; William Welge and his staff at the Archives and Manuscripts Division of the Oklahoma Historical Society, Oklahoma City; librarians and archivists at

Preface

the Western History Collections, University of Oklahoma, Norman; librarians at the Bacone College Library, Muskogee, Oklahoma; librarians of the Muskogee Public Library, Muskogee, Oklahoma; Joe Johnson, Posey's grandnephew and mayor of Eufaula; and George Bunny, who translated for me.

DANIEL F. LITTLEFIELD, JR.

Introduction

Historical Background

The Fus Fixico letters were a literary reaction to the dramatic transformation of the Indian nations of Indian Territory. They were a response, in part, to the shift in land tenure from common tribal or Indian national title to private ownership. By the time the Fus Fixico letters were begun, the concept of Indian Territory had changed drastically from what it had been in earlier generations. The land mass known as Indian Territory had been the site of resettlement of tribes after their negotiated or forced removal from their traditional homelands, mainly in the Southeast. On the verge of the American Civil War, the peoples known as the Five Civilized Tribes — the Cherokees, Chickasaws, Choctaws, Creeks, and Seminoles — held title to all the lands that now compose the state of Oklahoma, except for the panhandle, a disputed area south of the north fork of the Red River, and a small area east of the Neosho River in the northeast corner, occupied by the Quapaws and Senecas. Drawn into the Americans' civil conflict, the large tribes split in loyalties, and because of Confederate alignment by factions in all tribes, the United States levied strong penalties. In treaties in 1866, their land mass was greatly reduced through cessions of much of the western half of the territory. On those ceded lands, the United States resettled tribes removed from the Southwest, Midwest, Great Plains, and Rocky Mountain regions.

Between 1887 and 1902, when the Fus Fixico letters began, the western half of the territory went from common tribal land titles to private ownership. The General Allotment Act of 1887 provided for the breakup of the common titles and for the allotment of land in severalty to tribal members. The provisions of the act were carried out among the tribes, and in rapid succession, the surplus tribal land, the unassigned lands, and the Cherokee Outlet were opened to non-Indian settlement. After 1890, the region was

3

known as Oklahoma Territory, leaving the lands of the Five Civilized Tribes, the Osages, and the small tribes in the northeastern corner of the territory to compose Indian Territory.

By 1902, allotment was under way in Indian Territory as well. Though the Indian nations of that region had been exempt from the General Allotment Act, Congress had created a commission chaired by Senator Henry L. Dawes to negotiate allotment agreements. The Five Civilized Tribes resisted the arguments of the Dawes Commission until 1897, when the Seminoles made an agreement, and the next year a frustrated Congress passed the Curtis Act, which provided for allotment as a prefatory step to statehood for Indian Territory. This legislation forced the remaining nations to negotiate allotment agreements in order to salvage as much of their land and other resources for their people as possible.

These changes in land tenure were paralleled by social and political changes. The Five Civilized Tribes had been greatly acculturated before the Civil War, having adopted much from the Euro-Americans in such matters as dress, housing, governmental structures, religion, agriculture, and herding. After the war, the acculturation accelerated.[4] Tribes that had not had constitutional governments or public-education systems developed them. The population became more diversified. Intermarriage with people of European descent had been common in some tribes for more than a century. Thus the Indian population varied widely in blood quantum from full-blood to small percentages. Some tribes adopted or gave citizenship to intermarried whites. All of the Five Civilized Tribes had been slaveholders before the Civil War. The treaties of 1866 had required the adoption of former slaves and free blacks and their descendants; only the Chickasaws refused to comply. Each nation had a sizable black population, who participated in the social, political, and economic life of their respective nations in varying degrees, depending on the level of racial animosity among the Indian population. The population of the territory became even more diversified after 1872 when the first railroad was built across it. People from the United States and elsewhere went to the territory in great numbers, some squatting on the Indian public domain and others settling in the American-style towns that sprang up along the railroads.

By the early 1890s it was becoming evident that the nations were losing control of their affairs. The federal government made inroads on their jurisdiction by establishing a system of federal courts. Their lands were overrun by hundreds of thousands of intruders and others who rented farms and rangelands from the Indians. Their governments became less and less effective. After the Curtis Act, the federal authorities assumed increased control while the tribal governments entered a caretaker role during the allotment of land, the closing of tribal affairs, and the preparation for eventual statehood. Citizens of the nations varied widely in their opinions of the changes that were occurring. Some, who called themselves progressives, favored allotment and statehood; at the other end of the scale were those the progressives called conservatives or pullbacks, who resisted change in their national status.

Change was rapid in the Creek Nation, to which Posey belonged. The Creeks had been less acculturated than the Cherokees, Choctaws, and Chickasaws before the Civil War. They had not had a constitution, but in the Reconstruction era they wrote one, providing for a legislative council made up of the House of Kings and the House of Warriors and for other governmental offices filled by popular ballot. The Creeks no longer resisted missionary efforts, as they had before the war. They developed a public-school system. The first railroad to be built through Indian Territory cut through their lands and gave rise to Muskogee, the largest town in the territory, as well as to Wagoner, Checotah, and Eufaula, which Posey called home. The Creek Nation had the largest number of black citizens among the Five Civilized Tribes and provided for their participation in the legislative and administrative affairs of the nation. The Creek population, like that in the other nations, was divided in opinion concerning the changes that occurred in the last twenty-five years of the nineteenth century. Conservative Creeks resisted the change to constitutional government, becoming openly rebellious in the Green Peach War of the early 1880s. After the establishment of the Dawes Commission, they resisted negotiation of allotment and, after the Curtis Act, the allotment process itself. These conservatives, known in later years as the Snake faction, stood at one extreme of Creek opinion. Alexander Posey, who labeled himself a progressive, stood at the other.

Posey's Life: An Overview

Posey's beginnings might appear unlikely for a humorist.[5] He was born on August 3, 1873, in a remote section of the Creek Nation known as the Tulladega Hills, about fifteen miles northwest of Eufaula. His mother was Chickasaw-Creek and a member of Tuskegee tribal town, a membership that devolved to her son. His father was white, but he had been in the Creek Nation since early childhood, spoke Creek fluently, and was a member, probably by adoption, of Broken Arrow tribal town. The younger Posey spent his childhood at the family homestead in the Tulladega Hills and at the Posey ranch at Bald Hill, about ten miles west of Eufaula. Creek was the language of the Posey household, but when the younger Posey reached age fourteen, his father insisted that he speak English and set him on a course of English education that took him to the Creek national boarding school at Eufaula and to the Indian university at Bacone, near Muskogee.

Posey began writing while he was a student at Bacone. While pursuing a curriculum that included readings in both British and American literature, Posey began not only to write but to publish. Though he wrote some prose in the form of orations and Creek legends, his interest was mainly poetry. His tastes inclined to romantic models, and his poetry was, unfortunately, imitative. Nevertheless, he achieved a local reputation as a writer, adopted the persona Chinnubbie Harjo for his poetic voice, and acquired the aspiration to become a writer.

Posey left Bacone in 1894 without taking a degree and pursued his literary career while making a living. In 1895 he was elected to the House of Warriors, the lower chamber of the Creek National Council, as a representative from Tuskegee. Later that year he was appointed superintendent of the Creek Orphan Asylum at Okmulgee. Two years after that he was appointed superintendent of public instruction for the Creek Nation, a position he held until the fall of 1898. During these years he read extensively and wrote prolifically. He also married Minnie Harris, who helped him manage his daily affairs and find time for his literary pursuits. From the fall of 1898 through the summer of 1899, he engaged in writing full time at his home at Stidham and then reentered Creek national service as superintendent of the Creek boarding schools at Eufaula and Wetumka. He left the latter occupation in the summer of 1901, by which time he had produced nearly two hundred poems, many of which he had published but which imitated their models and contained little that was distinctive. After 1901, Posey wrote little poetry. Though a few poems demonstrate his remarkable talents as a poet, his literary reputation rests on his humor, especially the Fus Fixico letters.

Introduction

In 1902 Posey launched his career as a journalist. Early that year he bought the *Indian Journal*, a weekly newspaper at Eufaula. Though Posey had published only a few prose pieces by that time, he turned his literary efforts almost exclusively to prose, particularly to journalism, through which he would establish his reputation as a humorist. He combined humor and news reporting to produce a journalistic style that his readers found engaging. In the fall of 1902 he began to publish the Fus Fixico letters. His reputation soon spread and became national in 1903. That fall, Posey sold the *Indian Journal* to become city editor of the *Muskogee Evening Times*.

Posey interrupted his journalism career in the spring of 1904 when he went to work for the federal bureaucracy, first as a translator and then as a fieldworker for the Creek enrolling division of the Dawes Commission. In the latter capacity, he traveled extensively throughout the Creek Nation, taking testimony to clarify and document the existing tribal rolls and to enroll those Creeks who had failed or refused to be enrolled to receive their land allotments. When the allotment process was completed and the rolls were closed in 1907, Posey was engaged for several months as a real estate agent before resuming the editorship of the *Indian Journal* in April 1908. A few weeks later, on May 27, he drowned.

Because of the Fus Fixico letters, Posey had been well known as a political humorist since 1903. Fus Fixico, or "heartless bird," as some translated it, was an alleged Creek full-blood who wrote in Creek English dialect to Posey, as editor, about events in the full-blood neighborhoods west of Eufaula. Some months after the first letters appeared in October 1902, it became apparent that Fus Fixico was another of Posey's personae, and Posey turned his attention away from the full-bloods' domestic affairs to Creek national issues. As time passed, Fus Fixico became less a commentator and more a reporter of conversations between his friends, especially Hotgun and Tookpafka Micco, who discussed Creek politics, allotment of Creek lands, fraud and graft by officials, the approaching statehood, and the difficulties for some Creeks in adjusting to the changes taking place in their affairs. In the summer of 1903, the letters caught the attention of readers in the United States when Posey focused on a breaking scandal concerning graft by federal officials in Indian Territory. Posey published the Fus Fixico letters in the *Indian Journal* until he sold it in the fall of 1903, continued them briefly in the *Fort Smith Times*, and resumed them on a regular basis in the *Muskogee Evening Times*. After he left the *Times* in the spring of 1904, he published the letters irregularly, mainly in the *Muskogee Phoenix*. He published few letters during the time he worked as a field agent for the Dawes Commission and did not publish them again on a regular basis until he resumed the editorship of the *Indian Journal* shortly before his death in 1908. He published seventy-two letters, by any estimate a sizable body of dialect literature. In addition to their literary significance, they represent the first major excursion into literary humor by an American Indian.

Evolution of the Fus Fixico Letters

That Posey became a humorist is not surprising.[6] As a child, he delighted in perpetrating practical jokes and pulling pranks on family members, neighbors, and hired hands.[7] He carried his propensity for joking into adulthood. One family photograph, for example, shows him peeking from behind a potted plant, and another shows him standing with a watering can in hand and his hair wild, his eyes rolled to one side, looking at a giant flower painted on the backdrop. He teased or scared his workers at the Creek Orphan Asylum, and he engaged in pranks with his father.[8]

His contemporaries liked to attribute his sense of humor to his father's Scot-Irish heritage. Lewis Henderson Posey was known as a jolly fellow, and he was a good storyteller, greatly admired by his son, to whom he told dialect stories even after the younger Posey was an adult.[9] Lewis Posey no doubt fostered wit and humor in his son, but so did Alex Posey's Creek heritage. The Creeks in general exhibited a strong sense of humor and were fond of teasing one another. Like his father, Posey's mother, Nancy, was an accomplished storyteller who told stories to the Posey children. As an adult, Posey enjoyed an easy rapport with his mother's extended families of Tuskegee, Tulmachussee, and Artussee towns. He was especially fond of his cousin John Phillips, who had attended Bacone with Posey and later worked for him at the orphan asylum. Posey enjoyed teasing John, who in return liked to laugh.[10] When Posey became editor of the *Indian Journal* in 1902, he often related humorous anecdotes about family members in his local news columns. Though Posey had used humor in some of his earlier autobiographical sketches as well as in his news reports, he did not find a vehicle to give full vent to his talent until he created Fus Fixico.

The Fus Fixico letters were, on one level, simply an extension of Posey's creative journalistic style. Journalists in Indian Territory, Oklahoma Territory, Texas, Kansas, and Arkansas who received the *Indian Journal* in exchange for their own papers noted a marked difference in its style after Posey became its editor. They commented on its originality: its individuality, terseness, quaintness of expression, and humor. What they referred to was his use of coined words, slang, western expressions, Latin phrases, puns and other plays on words, literary allusions, and understatement in reporting not only insignificant events and odd occurrences but more ordinary local news as well.[11] After Posey had edited the

Journal for six months, the editor of the *Muskogee Daily Phoenix* wrote, "There is a freshness, a crispness, a novelty with each issue that is delightful and entertaining!"[12] And when Posey decided to sell the newspaper in the fall of 1903, the editor of the *Fort Smith Times* glowingly wrote of the way that Posey "mingled humor and philosophy so admirably that what he wrote was readable, agreeable and digestable. All of it smacked of the time and the place, it was a growth of the soil and conditions."[13]

More important than being an outlet for his creative urge, the letters served Posey as editorials. He considered an editorial simply an opinion rendered in a personal essay. Early in his editorship, he declared that his *Journal* was "a newspaper and not an essay." Readers had their own opinions, he said, and to write an editorial would simply add his opinion to theirs.[14] However, Posey was too good a journalist to believe that he could publish a paper without an editorial slant. Historic changes were occurring throughout Indian Territory. In the Creek Nation, the Creek government was in the process of dissolution, allotment was under way, and Creek society was undergoing dramatic changes. Posey had opinions on all of those matters and found ways to let his opinions be known. For example, he followed the common practice of reprinting news reports and editorial comments from other papers and briefly responding to them. He also printed brief statements that varied in length from one sentence to a short paragraph on topics ranging from town boosting to the administration of Indian affairs. During the summer of 1902, he published a series of "Street Interviews" in which older Creeks commented on Creek society, politics, and history.[15] Posey was at his best when he could blend editorial comment and humor. Thus, none of the editorial methods that he used in the spring and summer of 1902 provided the forum that the Fus Fixico letters would provide.

Introduction

By the fall of 1902, the need to find that forum was more apparent than ever. Several issues had begun to take focus: delivery of the Creek allotment deeds, the stirrings of a movement for separate statehood for Indian Territory, and the growing disaffecton of the Snake faction of Creeks. In addition, in the ensuing months, campaigning would begin for the election of the last principal chief of the Creeks to oversee the final dissolution of the Creek government and the settlement of Creek affairs. Posey does not seem to have settled immediately on the persona of Fus Fixico as a vehicle for commentary on these and other topics. Instead, elements of Fus Fixico had antecedents in Posey's writings of both the recent and the distant past.

For at least a decade, Posey had recognized the usefulness of a persona. As a student at Bacone Indian University in 1892 and 1893, he had written four tales about Chinnubbie Harjo, whom he described as a humorist, a "notorious wit and drone" who possessed "every trait common to man, with a strong unnatural leaning to traits characteristic to neither man nor beast." He was a carefree poet and liar, given to whims of kindnes and violence.[16] Though Chinnubbie was prone to violence and cruelty, it was his humorous side that Posey liked. After Posey had firmly established the identity of the mythical hero-wit through the Bacone Indian University Press, he took Chinnubbie's name as his pen name. During the 1893–94 academic year, he used the Chinnubbie persona to report Bacone campus news to the *Indian Journal*. In his reports — usually humorous and often whimsical — Chinnubbie seemed at times on the outside, detached from events going on around him, even occasionally talking about himself in the third person.[17] The reporter who is detached from events, the outsider who could report them with humor, was a key element in the Fus Fixico letters. By 1894, when Posey left Bacone, he had adopted the persona Chinnubbie for his poetry as well as his prose and used it for the rest of his life. It is not surprising, then, that in the fall of 1902, Posey adopted another persona as a vehicle for his editorial views.

The first clear indication of what that persona would be like was a series of letters by Joe Harjo or about his activities, published in the *Indian Journal* during the late summer and early fall of 1902. The common English given name attached to the common Creek warrior class designation as a surname suggests a kind of Everyman of the Creek-Seminole full-blood world of the allotment period. Joe, whose letters reported everyday affairs in his community, was the kind of character Posey sought, but he was too well traveled and too involved in cattle raising. Posey needed an observer who was more on the fringe of the economic system. However, the Joe Harjo letters provided the dialect voice he wanted. One letter said: "Please I sent you news. I was down at Sunday night stomp dance and somebody was stole my winchester and coat and three dollars in money. I aint find him yet. So I will close."[18] The next letter reads: "I will sent you put in news. Mr. Joe Harjo and his brother Johnson Harjo and some friends he have been to Santa Rosa city of Mexico, buying cattle. Mr. Harjo said four car load of cattle be here in Seminole country this week. . . . Him and his brother and friends return north bound train. Joe Harjo of Thruman and brother of Sasakwa. That's all I got news."[19] Two weeks later, the first Fus Fixico letter appeared. Posey's problem, however, had not been simply one of finding a dialect voice but of placing that voice in a credible character.

Posey capitalized on current news about the Snake faction of Creeks who, under the leadership of Chitto Harjo, or Crazy Snake, had resisted the allotment process and had occasionally created excitement, mainly among whites, near Hickory Ground town, where the Snakes assembled. Chitto Harjo had been active in his resistance since the Curtis Act of 1898, but he had received widespread publicity in late 1900 when the Snakes had met at Hickory Ground, established their own government, and declared the old treaties between the United States and the Creek Nation in force. In January 1901, they passed laws aimed at punishing Creeks who took allotments or rented land to non-Creeks, and they set about enforcing their laws. Although they had done little more than deliver stern warnings to their fellow Creeks, white renters in the vicinity became panicked, and rumors of an "uprising" spread. U.S. marshals and the cavalry were called out, and Chitto Harjo and a large number of his followers were arrested and taken to jail at Muskogee. They were later released on the condition that they would behave themselves. Crops were poor in 1901, and late that year the Snakes met to discuss their condition. Once more rumors spread, and early in 1902 the Snakes were arrested again. This time, Chitto Harjo was sent to the federal prison at Leavenworth, Kansas, where he spent several months. Posey reported the events of early 1902 in detail and throughout the rest of 1902 kept the story of the Snakes before his readers.[20]

Starting in the fall of 1902, Fus Fixico reported activities in the Snake settlements at Shell Creek, Proctor, or Weogufky. The political and economic realities that forced the Snakes to the margins of society in the waning years of the Creek Nation would give Fus Fixico and his friends Choela and Hotgun the advantage of distance as observers. Though not a Snake himself, Fus Fixico was privy to conversations among the followers of Chitto Harjo, thus providing the credible character for the dialect voice that Posey had found in Joe Harjo. The first letter read in part: "Well, I hope you and your families is well, but I got very bad cold in my head. I was take my dogs and went possum hunt last night and catch nothing but bad cold. Guess I pull off my coat too quick when I get too hot trying to stay with my dogs. When I rise up this morning my head is almost busted and I can't breathe hardly. I feel like I been in calaboose all night in Eufaula."[21] This letter, which appeared on October 24, was followed by another the next week.

At that time Posey seems not to have settled on Fus Fixico as a persona. A third letter did not appear until November 21. On November 7, a week after the second letter, Posey published some of his local news in dialect. His "Artussee News Notes" column read:

> I will sent you a few words for news.
>
> Well, last Sunday evening while the sun was hang about 4 o'clock high, Lewis Colbert was marry Sarah Phillips at Artusse [*sic*] church house. The wedlock was join by Rev. Johnson J. Phillips, and many people was be present and see it.
>
> That Sunday morning Rev. Watson Washington was preach from Luke, 15:4, about one sheep what the man was lost in his woods. Watson preach big sermon.
>
> We was had good times and lots good things to eat.[22]

Posey may have been having fun rather than experimenting, for Johnson J. Phillips was his mother's brother. But it is interesting that after this piece, he published no more Creek English dialect except in the Fus Fixico letters. After the letters resumed on November 21, they appeared more or less regularly until he sold the *Indian Journal* nearly a year later.

Between the fall of 1902 and summer of 1903, the letters changed subtly but significantly. First, the content changed. The early letters concerned the full-blood community. Fus Fixico reported matters of personal concern — his health, the weather, crops, the disposition of his allotment deed. He also reported on the activities of his friends, especially Choela and Hotgun, and other followers of Chitto Harjo. Early in 1903, however, the focus of the letters shifted to Creek national affairs: activities of the Creek delegation in Washington, potential candidates for the Creek principal chief to be elected in the summer of 1903, allotment policies, and efforts to achieve statehood. Occasionally, there were jabs at President Theodore Roosevelt and Secretary of the Interior Ethan Allen Hitchcock.

Corresponding with these changes in content were changes in the central characters of the letters. Choela, rather than Hotgun, was emerging as the central character in the letters, until his death in early 1903. On March 20, Fus Fixico wrote: "Well, so I was tell you bad news about my old friend Choela. He was gone to be good Injin, like white man say when Injin die. It was look like all old Injins die now and make good Injin that way. Maybe so pretty soon Fus Fixico was make good Injin, too."[23] The focus then shifted to Hotgun, whose responses to current events were reported indirectly (letters 18–21). Tookpafka Micco was also brought into the letters. Then their responses were reported directly, and by the summer of 1903, Fus Fixico had become more or less the recorder of conversations between Hotgun and Tookpafka Micco (letters 22 and following). They added to their circle Wolf Warrior and Kono Harjo, who did little more than listen, smoke, and, like Washington Irving's Nicholas Vedder, grunt their assent to, or displeasure at, their friends' statements.[24] From their position outside the mainstream society to which the newspaper readers belonged, Fus Fixico and his friends could give vent to their satire of that society.

"Este Charte" English

Fus Fixico and his friends couched their satire in what Posey's good friend and fellow Creek writer Charles Gibson claimed was "este charte," or "red man," English. In 1908 Gibson complained about some dialect letters that had appeared in the Checotah paper: "It's the poorest dialect stuff that was ever forced upon the reading public. Don't dodge behind 'Este Charte,' white man, but get up your rot in straight English, if you can write it." He added: "Get from behind 'Este Charte' and wash the paint off your pale face. Take off the turkey feathers. They don't become you."[25]

Posey agreed with Gibson's condemnation of the same writer and criticized others. "Those cigar store Indian dialect stories being published in the Checotah papers and the Hoffman Herald Auxiliary will fool no one who has lived 'six months in the precinct.' Like the wooden aborigine, they are the product of a white man's factory, and bear no resemblance to the real article."[26]

What were the distinguishing features of "este charte" English? Some idea of what Posey and Gibson saw or heard or did not see or hear in the dialect of white writers might be gained by looking at the style of those letters. "Fus Fixico Jr." accused Eufaula of recruiting Posey as editor of the *Indian Journal* to engage his pen in the county seat contest then going on between Checotah and Eufaula. He wrote: "An Hot Gun he say history repeat itself again an I done change my mind since I talked to Alex last week about natural resources, an County Seat. Checotah way ahead of Eufaula in natural resources. She way up high on prairie where get good breath, an when he go to County Seat he see Court House long time fore he get there."[27] "Fus Fixico No. Two" wrote: "Well, so Hot Gun he say battle gettin' hot: County Seat fight. Eufaula give war whoop long time 'go, make heap lot noise like big gun. When smoke clear 'way didn't hit thing. Checotah keep still 'till game get close an' then let gun go off, kill big County Seat Buck."[28] And "Este Charte" wrote about Posey: "I jist read it in Eufaula paper lots of big talk what that Edtor man told it to every body bout that town going to beat it bad this Checotah in the county seat race he say Eufaula going to beat it Checotah slick, like Owl greece. Well, I think it maybe so, that Edtor man dont know all what he is talking bout or of folks he is going to vote on it, on this business and I jist think maybe so, Edtor man he jist talk loud and blow hard like broke wind horse."[29]

The reader's ear need not be too keen to recognize this as "cigar store Indian" or "Tonto" English, which has an unnatural staccato effect that results from dropping the articles. Here too, for example, there is no use of the verb *to be* to determine tense, as in the Fus Fixico letters: "Then he say he was let the future take care of its own self like a calf when it was get too old to suck" or "I was had to go after my plow what Hotgun was let rust so long in his blacksmith shop." There is no use of nominative personal pronouns as reflexives or possessives, as in Fus Fixico's English: "This was sound like humbox che (make ready to eat) and Legus Perryman and Wolf Warrior was get ready to help theyselves" and "Well, so they was not much talk about next chief, and it was look like Creek Injins was lost they grip and they suspenders couldn't hold up they breeches." Neither is there a use of the characteristic expression *maybe so* to indicate conditional action or possibility: "Maybe so next time I write you more news to put in like this one" and "Then Hotgun he say, 'Well, maybe so this time he was smoked out the fox.' "[30] "Este Charte" uses the expression in excess. Whether or not such stylistic features as these were what Posey and Gibson associated with "este charte" English, they are some of the distinguishing features of Posey's style.

Popularity of Fus Fixico
Readers recognized the distinct quality of the Fus Fixico letters, for in the summer of 1903 the letters received wide public atten-

tion. In June, Posey began publishing the *Journal* as a daily as well as a weekly paper. The publishing world found an Indian publisher of a daily newspaper enough of a journalistic oddity to be interesting. After the *Kansas City Journal* ran an article about Posey and his daily, he was besieged by requests for information about himself from reporters for the *St. Louis Post-Dispatch*, the *New York Herald*, and the *New York Tribune*, from the Guilliams Press Syndicate and the Union Bureau of News, and from freelance writers throughout the United States. Articles about him appeared in newspapers and magazines such as the *Philadelphia Ledger, Pittsburgh Leader, Indian's Friend, New York Times, Boston Transcript*, and *Colorado Springs Evening Telegraph*. Editors and others in Indian Territory, Oklahoma Territory, Kansas, Missouri, Iowa, Indiana, Tennessee, Massachusetts, New York, Hawaii, Canada, and England sought copies of his newspaper, his autograph, his photograph, or his biographical information. After this flurry of publicity, the *Kansas City Journal*, expecting his popularity to continue, asked for an autobiographical statement to be used as the need arose.[31]

The *Kansas City Journal* article that had brought Posey's daily to national attention also brought attention to the Fus Fixico letters, which were reprinted by other newspapers. Posey was asked to explain how the persona had evolved, and J. Ojijatekha Brant-Sera, a Mohawk who was arranging a lecture tour by Indians, asked Posey to take his humor to the stage. And newspapers in New York, Philadelphia, and St. Louis asked Posey for a regular contribution of letters.[32]

Posey's popularity was boosted by his focus on Indian Territory affairs as they were affected by federal policy. Of particular interest to outsiders in the summer of 1903 was the widespread allegation that federal officials in Indian Territory, including members of the Dawes Commission, were involved in speculation, graft, and fraud in the sale and lease of Indian lands. Posey's letters followed the public debate on this issue throughout the summer and fall. After that, with only few exceptions, he made the impact of federal policy on the Indian nations the subject of the letters: statehood for Indian Territory, allotment policy, condition of the conservative Indians, bureaucratic ineptness, fraud and other forms of corruption, politicians and political ambition, and capitalism. He presented his satire in a form his readers could easily accept.

Fus Fixico and Contemporary American Dialect Humor

Posey's fellow editors clearly recognized the affinity of the Fus Fixico letters to certain forms of dialect humor currently popular in America. Local and regional publishers had been the first to give the letters notice. After the first letter appeared, the *Denison* (Tex.) *Herald* said: "The Indian Journal publishes an item about a man named Fus Fixico. Must be Republican."[33] After a dozen letters, the *Muskogee Times* editor wrote: "A few more letters to the Indian Journal, and Fus Fixico may, with propriety, be termed the William Allen White of Indian Territory. His letter this week is full of the keenest satire."[34] Shortly thereafter, the *Muskogee Daily Phoenix* said: "We have philosophers in all kinds of dialect. The Irish, Mr. Dooley; the negro, Uncle Remus; the slang of George Ade; the Dutch Yacob Undervider, and even the Norwegeian [*sic*] or the Sweed [*sic*] in Ole Oleson or Yonny Yonson. Not last of all, yet oldest of all, we have the Indian and the disciple is Fus Fixico of Eufaula."[35] The Fus Fixico letters continued to gain attention so that by the spring of 1903, they were commented on by the *Kansas City Star,* and the *Kansas City Times* referred to Fus Fixico as "the Dooley of Indian Territory politics."[36] In early

Introduction

June 1903, the *Muskogee Daily Phoenix* said that Posey was "going to write his name on the literary history of this country in indelible letters. As a paragrapher, poet, and satirist he has demonstrated his right to the title of the country's most brilliant literary Indian genius."[37]

Though Posey had apparently written no Indian dialect before 1902, other dialects had interested him for years. He had written poems in rural white and "cowboy" dialects and had published several prose sketches containing black dialect. In earlier years, he had considered Robert Burns his favorite poet. His friend George Riley Hall did not share his enthusiasm for Burns because of Burns's use of dialect. In an effort to lead Hall to a greater appreciation of Burns, Posey rendered one of his dialect poems in "correct" English and spoiled it.[38] Thus Posey clearly understood the relationship between form and meaning in dialect literature.

Posey's interest in humor was also long-standing. As a student at Bacone, he had read the works of well-known satirists and other humorists: Chaucer, Shakespeare, Gay, Cervantes, Swift, Irving, Lowell, and Holmes. Posey's personal library contained the works not only of most of these writers but also of lesser known and more recent writers such as Jerome K. Jerome and John Kendrick Bangs.[39]

As an avid reader of newspapers from his youth onward, Posey without doubt encountered the dialect works of other American humorists. Though his fellow journalists recognized similarities between his and the American humorists' works, how familiar with them was he? Conclusions might be drawn from the contents of the *Muskogee Phoenix*, the local newspaper during his years at Bacone, where he had access to not only newspapers but other periodicals as well. Like most small-town newspapers of the day, the *Phoenix* used "canned" reprints, added to its home print, to fill out its pages. During the period 1890–94, the *Phoenix* used short humorous filler from *Puck, Judge, Life, Wide Awake, Arkansas Traveler, Texas Siftings*, and other periodicals, much of which was in Irish, Scandinavian, German, and American black and rural white dialects. It reprinted works by well-known dialect humorists, including the Bowser stories by M. Quad (C. B. Lewis), the Gotham stories by Alex E. Sweet, and stories by Tom P. Morgan, who wrote for *Puck*. By the time he left Bacone, Posey had acquired a taste for dialect humor. He subscribed to *Puck, Judge,* and *Truth* and read other popular magazines that published humor, such as *Cosmopolitan.*[40]

That Posey was aware of the works of humorists such as Finley Peter Dunne, George Ade, and C. B. Lewis is undeniable. In addition to his years of habitually reading newspapers and magazines, as editor of the *Indian Journal* in 1902 he was further exposed to contemporary humor through exchange copies of newspapers he received from outside Indian Territory. The *Fort Smith Times*, which reprinted the Fus Fixico letters, regularly carried Lewis's M. Quad sketches. Posey's own *Indian Journal* reprinted filler material frm the *Chicago Tribune, Judge,* and other publications. When Bill Arp (Charles Henry Smith) died in 1903, Posey published a notice of his death. Posey's personal library contained Ade's *Fables in Slang* (1899) and William Patten's edition of *Short Story Classics* (1905), which, though published after Posey began the Fus Fixico letters, contains works by Dunne, Ade, Charles Heber Clark (Max Adeler), and other humorists and reflects Posey's abiding interest in contemporary humor.[41]

The relationship between Posey's work and that of other writers is clearer in some instances than others. For example, Ade's influence is suggested in the form and style of Posey's fables, published in 1901 and 1902. In them are found the concise, economical narrative and the moral of the fabulist. Unlike Ade's fables about the urban dwellers of Chicago in the Gay Nineties, Posey's were beast fables that made use of Creek lore to satirize human foibles. The form of these fables, like Ade's, could have been more strongly influenced by Posey's reading of Aesop and, perhaps to some extent, Joel Chandler Harris.[42]

Fus Fixico and Indian Dialect Humor

Despite comparisons of Posey's humor to that of his American contemporaries, it had more affinities to the work of older generations of humorists reaching back as far as the 1830s and Seba Smith. Since pre–Civil War days, works of American dialect writers had been common fare for Indian Territory readers. Territorial newspapers such as the *Cherokee Advocate*, the *Indian Arrow*, the *Muskogee Phoenix*, and the *Indian Journal*, as well as the *Arkansian* at Fayetteville, Arkansas, and Fort Smith newspapers such as the *Fort Smith New Era* and *Wheeler's Western Independent*, which circulated in Indian Territory, published works by well-known writers: Seba Smith's Jack Downing letters, the writings of Artemus Ward by Charles Farrar Browne, David Ross Locke's Petroleum V. Nasby letters, Charles Henry Smith's Bill Arp pieces, the works of Josh Billings by Henry W. Shaw, Edgar Wilson Nye's Bill Nye stories, and works by Opie Read and other dialect pieces from the *Arkansas Traveler*.[43]

The influence on Posey by these older generations of dialect humorists was probably indirect: many Indian Territory writers imitated these earlier forms and styles. During the 1880s, the decade in which Posey began reading, territorial writers established a tradition of dialect humor that grew in popularity during the next twenty years. Using personae, Indian and non-Indian writers alike produced dialect humor similar to that of Artemus

Ward, Josh Billings, Old Si, and others and published it widely in territory newspapers.

A good example is Unakah (perhaps a corruption of the Cherokee *yonega*, or white person), who produced more than a score of letters between 1878 and 1886 for the *Cherokee Advocate*. Unakah is particularly interesting because his early letters contained none of the dialect that became more pronounced in his letters as time passed. Unakah was a white schoolteacher who was married to Miranda Emmeline, a Cherokee. While he took life easy and she did the work around their home, they debated the "Indian Question," the Cherokee land title, and Cherokee political issues. "Time has been using Miranda Emmeline purty muchly," wrote Unakah in 1884, "and has scratched fearful wrinkles in hur countenance, and has boxt out all of hur frunt teeth, and now when she gets riled as formerle, hur voice has a whistlin' metalik ring to it, the which indicates 'bizziness' every time."[44] Despite this assessment of her, he is at times brought up short and reminded of her value to him. One day, listening to the sound of her mortar and pestle as she pounded corn for *conahany*, he said: "The Kwestion struk me all ov a suddin, (and almost knoct me crank sided with its force.) What cud I ever du without Miranda? And wer she cut off bi ole remorsles time, who wood provid for the Unakah household? Ah! indeed who wood pound the corner-ha-ne then? Who wood git up on the cold winter mornins and bild the fire and prepar the sasafras T. for breakfas?"[45]

Black citizens of Indian Territory were represented by writers such as Ole Si, Abraham Linkum Jones, Joner Slimkins, Cyrus Leondus Blackburn, and Big Creek Scribe. Ole Si was the persona of a Choctaw freedman who was concerned about his status as a citizen of the Choctaw Nation. Cyrus Leondus Blackburn was what was known as a "state" black, a U.S. citizen who was seeking to make Indian Territory his home, and Abraham Linkum Jones, Joner Slimkins, and Big Creek Scribe were Cherokee freedmen. When the Cherokee Nation made a per capita payment in 1885 to only its citizens who were Cherokees by blood, Jones wanted to know what the legal status of the freedman citizen was. He wrote to the *Indian Chieftain* in Vinita: "I has allers counted myself in ez er culid Cher'kee, blackwashed or transmogerfied into er aborigine ob dat tribe by de treaty. Doan de treaty say dat sartin cullid folks shall hab all de rights uv er native Cher'kee and doan de constitution say dat de treaties shall be de supreme law ob de lan'?"[46] There were a number of models from American literature for these writers to draw on, but likely candidates were Old Si and his replacement at the *Atlanta Constitution*, Uncle Remus, whose works had appeared not only in the *Cherokee Advocate* but also in the newspapers of border towns, such as *Wheeler's Western Independent* at Fort Smith, which circulated widely in the Cherokee Nation.[47]

Cherokee personae included Pewter Dick and Skiatook, whose work, like Unakah's, bears marked resemblance to that of American dialect writers. In 1885, Pewter Dick wrote to the editor of the *Indian Chieftain*, "Ive hearn a smart chance about you, some cussin you like blazes and some hollerin hooray and some takin it easy like, jest as the woman did when her husband and the bar fit, caring durned little hoo got licked." Dick wrote about W. A. Phillips, an attorney representing the Cherokee Nation, "I took a good look at him and I cum to this conclusion about him, that it would be much safer to fool with his picter than with him, purty much on the same principle that one would be safer to monkey with the picter of a skunk than with the animal itself."[48] In an 1889 series titled "An Essay on Hosses," Skiatook wrote: "Hosses iz the next thing, at least in my opinion, to the human race. You may call them beasts or you may call them critters, it matters not, because a hoss iz a hoss, whether he be a race hoss or a draft hoss; a circus hoss or a carriage hoss."[49] In style and title, this work is reminiscent of Josh Billings's "Essa on a Muel" and "Hoss Sense."

Such letters, like Unakah's, belong to the crackerbox philosopher tradition. The writers took as their models the "phunny phellows," and as their models had done, they used to advantage the same linguistic devices: misspellings; puns; deviations from standard grammar, punctuation, and usage; and juxtapositions of different levels of usage—in short, any device that might get a laugh. Also, like their models, these Indian Territory humorists varied in the extent of misspelling and other typographical effects. Their dialect, rural background, common sense, and anecdotal style present the facade of the unsophisticated or unlettered Cherokee citizen whose writings often provided sharp insights into the internal affairs of the nation and the usurpation of Cherokee lands by non-Indians, mainly white Americans.[50] Like many American personae, they are ultimately "wise fools." However, the "unliterary pose" adopted by these Cherokee writers does not mask the "substantial literary background" that David B. Kesterson has found to characterize the American "literary comedians."[51] Herein they also differ from Posey, whose Fus Fixico letters reflect his vast knowledge of Western literature and history.

Other Cherokee personae included Choo-noo-lus-ky and Ah-sto-la-ta, the first territorial writers who are known to have written in "este charte" English. In letters to the *Cherokee Telephone* from 1890 through 1893, Cho-noo-lus-ky expressed his concerns and those of his wife, Katie, about such matters as per capita payments, the influx of intruders into the Cherokee Nation, and Cherokee politics. The intruder whites were taking over the land. "Way up Delaware, Cooweescoowee—all lan dun got it white man. White man he make it big fiel—he get it heap cow, heap hoss, eat it dat Cherokee grass. I bin way up Delaware, I see no Injin up dar—look it state—all white mans."[52] Per capita payments made the Cherokees the targets of the whites' greed. "Dat white mans sa I hav purtiest gal dis nation. I guess he want marry him dat gal, git it rite in nation; every time goin get it monie, white mans he tink Injin gal heap purty. Katie she heap mad dat white mans; he say 'I kill it fust white mans fule round my gals."[53] The land issue also concerned Ah-sto-la-ta. "I got it bout 5 aker corn and wheat bout 2 aker, taters and oder tings bout one. Dats all lan can get here." He had seven children and wondered what future they would have because all of the Cherokee land was occupied.[54] In the style of these writers are not only the techniques of the "misspellers" but also the vocabulary, grammatical structures, and syntax that Posey and Gibson later identified as "este charte" English.

The careers of some Indian Territory dialect writers overlapped Posey's. Between 1888 and 1898, Choonstootee of the Cherokee Nation wrote dialect leters for the *Telephone* and the *Arrow* in Tahlequah. Oo-law-nah-stee-sky, also Cherokee, wrote for the *Afton News* in 1895. Choo-noo-lus-ky was revived as Chunul-lun-sky in 1898 and wrote during the next two years for the *Vinita Leader*. During the same period, that paper also contained the dialect letters of Chun-chustie, Kingfisher, Jeem Featherhead, and Too-stoo. Arnawaky, Choonstootee's daughter, wrote for the *Wagoner Record* in 1899, and Mary Jane Bramble wrote in rural white dialect for the *Weekly Indian Chieftain* in Vinita. In 1896 Lee Allen wrote in rural white dialect for the *Muskogee Phoenix* about his neighborhood of Possum Bend in the Cherokee Nation. Through the course of fifteen letters, Allen transformed the title of the series from "The Grindstone Club" into "Possum Bend" and himself from Allen into Josiah Snooper.[55]

The Fus Fixico letters bear certain striking resemblances to these works produced in "este charte" English. The Choonstootee letters, for example, like those of Fus Fixico later, created a community of characters in which the persona moved. Choonstootee and his wife, Aky, their daughter Arnawaky, and her husband, Cicero — a white man from Arkansas — resided in Flint District of the Cherokee Nation, which was beset by many problems: intruding whites and blacks, Texas cattlemen who usurp the range, corrupt politics, railroad land grants, and the double threat of allotment of land and statehood.

Also like Fus Fixico and his friends, Choonstootee is concerned with the changing affairs of his nation. "Stootee," as he calls himself, gets much of his information by rumor and does not know what is meant by ideas such as railroad right-of-way, cowmen, Dawes Commission, deeds, or hop-tea joints. And he is beset by "white mans" who want to rent Cherokee lands or develop his homestead as a railroad townsite. He says, "I tell my wife, A-ky, may be so dat Cow-man, he's got horn, may be so he's got tail like Cow, I dont know." When he hears that the United States has offered the Cherokee Nation eighteen million dollars for the Cherokee Strip, he wants the nation to sell, but Aky argues to hold out; perhaps other whites would give more. "I say, 'Oh no, nobody got so much money. Ateene mill yon doller, hes mose wagen lode.' Aky tell me I like E-jot. She say its more'n 2 wagen lode." Then Stootee wants to know what an "E-jot" (idiot) is. Because Choonstootee's homestead is located on a new railroad, it is prime land for development as a townsite.

One man come my house lass week en tell me: "Stoo-tee, I want make it town site you places. . . ." I ask him, that man, what it is he call it ton sites. I got it "fo sites" en "hine sites" on my guns, but I dont know what tis, "ton sites."

That man he say: "O you let it lail load lay it off town you places, en make it station en you sell heap lots, you sell it lots to whitemans, injuns, nigger, enybody en make it heap money en give it half to lail lodes en you get heap rich."

I tell him that mans: "Maybe so that Cherokee nations hang my neck fi sell him that lots."[56]

An important question is to what extent Posey was aware of this local literary tradition of Indian dialect humor. His long-standing interest in humor and dialect, his voracious appetite for periodical literature, and his deep interest in Creek and Indian Territory affairs from early youth onward make it seem a certainty that he had read some of these writers. They shared common concerns. Choonstootee in many ways typifies the other writers. Like his, their sources of information are often overheard conversations, a newspaper story, or a "white mans" who comes to their houses. Like him, they often air their domestic troubles. Chu-nul-lun-sky's wife, Katie, for instance, is much more decisive than he. She's a "curis wimmens," who "just hate it intruder." Like Choonstoo-tee's humor, that of other writers often turns on a lack of under-standing of bureaucratic language such as "sectionized" land, townsites, and guardianships. They are mystified, amazed, or dis-gusted at the whites' unceasing attempts to take their land, marry their daughters, and involve them in land grafting or politics. In short, the concerns of these writers are in most regards the same as those of Hotgun, Tookpafka Micco, and their friends in the Fus Fixico letters. The reader also notices some striking differences as well: the use of *it* as part of the verb ("make it heap money") and more frequent and exaggerated tricks of spelling ("ateene mill yon dollar"), for example.[57] If nothing else, the Choonstootee letters and others demonstrate that the Fus Fixico letters were not an isolated phenomenon but were part of a continuing Indian literary tradition in dialect humor, a tradition that Posey likely recognized.

He was certainly aware that the Fus Fixico letters were, in fact, only one example — but the foremost example — of literature produced in "este charte" English between 1902 and 1908. During that time Cherokee writers — for example, under the personae Athome, Woochee Ochee, Too Stoo, and Bill Kantfraid — produced dialect letters similar to Fus Fixico's, as did the Creek writer Little Frog. Similarities in tone and style between their works and Posey's are easily recognized. Athome, for example, complained that when he went to file on his allotment, it appeared that the federal bureaucrats were allowing all sorts of non-Cherokees to sign up. As he looked around the land office, he couldn't "see nuthin look like Injun." He wrote, "It looks lik bout 500 peoples, some neger, some white man an' some grafter, some Arkansaw mans but cant fin it shore nuf Injun."[58] Woochee Ochee wrote about the politics of the Cherokee election of 1903 and complained about Gus Ivey, the Cherokee editor of the *Sallisaw Gazette:* "He tell it lie jus lik truth and truth he tell it vicer wurser. Don't lik it much dat man. He too smart — fool it poor Injin all time."[59] Like Woochee Ochee, Too Stoo was concerned about Cherokee politics but also about the possibility that the Cherokee Nation would run out of land to allot to its members. As he told the editor of the *Adair Weekly Ledger,* "Paper she say Dawes commission say no nuff lan Cherokee, she ges give em money, $825 cash injun what she get no lan."[60] Bill Kantfraid (Elias M. Landrum), in a 1906 letter, told how a representative of the government questioned his competency to act as guardian for his own fourteen-year-old son. The bureaucrat told Bill to make bond, which would allow him to keep count of the boy's money, land, and other assets. Kantfraid wrote: "He say can you count it? Flee plus fly how many times make it? She-e-e! I don't know plus. Then he say 'gin all lite you don't make it bond. I send 'way Kansas git um white mans, smart lak ever'thin'. I make him your daddy, dis boy. I tell him yes, mebbeso, smart lak grasshopper — eat it up ever'thin'. Mebbeso raise hell lak Kansas cyclone."[61] Finally, Little Frog, the Creek, overheard white men discussing politics in 1906, debating whether the Creeks would be Democrats or Republicans and what the parties had done respectively for the Indians. Little Frog reported the conversations to his wife: "When I tells my wife this, for He was at home where he lives when I got there, he say now Little Frog, you vote with them demecats, for them beoble will help the Injin, they will help the poor Injin to get his restrictions off a his land, and he can sell som and build a the good house on his homestead, and run for cunstable a his township."[62]

These writers were inheritors of the same Indian literary tradition as Posey, yet in the long history of Indian dialect writing, no other writer achieved the literary success that Posey did. When the Fus Fixico letters appeared on the Indian Territory literary scene, they stood out, as they do today, among the works of Indian dialect humorists.

Literary Achievement of the Fus Fixico Letters

In volume, Posey surpassed the production of any Indian dialect writer before 1902, and he outproduced most who followed him. As a journalist-publisher, he had the ready means to give his letters broader circulation and to popularize them. But his success was not simply a matter of numbers. In addition to the qualities of style, over time he created an engaging persona and a set of characters through whom his humor shines even today.

Fus Fixico, the reporter, was not as averse to change in Creek society as his Snake friends were. Though a full-blood who lived in the full-blood community on Shell Creek, he differed from Hotgun and Choela regarding allotment. He did not entertain any notions of emigrating to Mexico, as they did. Unlike them, he wanted his allotment deed, for he had discovered that the promise of title was good collateral for charging goods at the white mercantile establishments. Though Fus Fixico was only a figment of his creator's imagination, Posey gave him historical substance by promoting his letters. "Fus Fixico, our fullblood literary genius," he wrote one week, "is at his best in this issue." A week later he wrote: "Fus Fixico raps Chief McCurtain over the knuckles this week. Read his letter." And another time he reported that Fus Fixico had been in town that week to appear before the grand jury.[63] Thus Posey created a believable character who represented a type of person that readers might have occasionally encountered coming and going from the mercantile establishments, walking on the streets of Eufaula or Muskogee, lounging about the courthouse, or doing business in the offices of the Indian agent or the Dawes Commission. He would have been seen more often at the busk grounds at Eufaula, Hickory Ground, or Weogufky.

Choela, who was apparently Posey's first choice as a central character for the letters, was also a type of character familiar to his readers, but unlike Fus Fixico, he was based on a real person. This Choela was a member of the House of Kings, the upper chamber of the Creek National Council, and was well known in his neighborhood on Shell Creek as a "medicine man," the kind of "prophet" that Posey had known in his childhood and had described in earlier works such as "The Alabama Prophet" and "Two Famous Prophets."[64] It was this aspect of Choela's life that Posey found interesting. In 1902 he had described Choela as a "doctor of renown" among the full-bloods; his forte was "curing obstinate cases of unrequited love and consumating happy marriages." Fus Fixico attested to the efficacy of Choela's powers in other respects:

Old Choela was sure good doctor. He was just take his grubbing hoe and go out in the woods and dig up lots medicine anywhere. Then he was take his cane and blow in the medicine pot long time and sing little song with it, too, like at busk ground. But he aint want no monkey business round there neither while he was fixing that medicine. If you aint dead yet before he was got through, he make you so well you just want whole lot sofky, right quick or maybe sak-ko-nip-kee.[65]

When Choela died in March 1903, Posey began his article of tribute to the old man as follows: "Choela, the Creek medicine man legislator and one of the unique characters of Fus Fixico's letters, is no more." He then related an anecdote that demonstrated the good character of the old man.[66]

Hotgun, Choela's successor as the central character in the letters, was also a real person, a medicine man. Posey had brought Hotgun to his readers' attention in early 1902 when he reported on the arrest of Chitto Harjo and his Snake followers. Hotgun, it seems, had been at Hickory Ground making medicine for them when the authorities arrived, and he was taken. Posey wrote: "He is a little dried-up, crick necked Indian with long hair. He is a noted mechanical genius among his tribe. He can make anything, from a pocket knife to a first-class residence. He can also knock the bottom out of any preacher's grace by his rare performance on the fiddle. Withal he is a medicine man and a dead-shot when it comes to curing people."[67] Hotgun remained in jail at Muskogee for several weeks. Claiming innocence of the charge of conspiracy and angry because federal officials had cut off his long hair, he threatened to sue the United States for false imprisonment. Hotgun had been a government blacksmith for the Creeks and maintained a shop at his cabin near Weogufky town square, about twenty-five miles west of Eufaula. Posey described him as "an Indian tinkerer of great fame," whose "inventive genius was remarkable. He was a philosopher, carpenter, blacksmith, fiddler, clock maker, worker in metals and maker of medicines."[68] Also known as Mitcka Hiya, Hotgun was a leader of the Snakes and served as their chief in 1906. Though he resisted allotment, the government, without his consent, allotted him the land on which his cabin sat. His wife, however, was allotted land somewhere else, but they neither knew nor cared where it was.[69]

When Hotgun died at age sixty in early 1908, Posey had not published a Fus Fixico letter in a little more than a year and referred to Hotgun and his friends in the past tense, as if the fictional characters had been abandoned. After he became editor of the *Indian Journal* later that spring, however, he revived the letters — and Hotgun — for editorial purposes, just as he had created them in 1902 for the same reason. Posey once wrote: "I do not know what Hotgun thinks of the 'Fus Fixico Letters,' but I imagine he takes kindly to them. His sense of humor is too keen not to appreciate the remarks quoted as coming from him."[70]

Though less is known about Tookpafka Micco, he was also based on a real person. The Tookpafka busk ground was near Proctor, not far from Weogufky, where Hotgun lived. The *micco* was the town leader. Tookpafka Micco was described in 1905 as a prominent citizen and a member of the Creek national Council who had been noted in the Fus Fixico letters. When Tookpafka Micco visited Eufaula in 1908, Posey said that he owned property near Eufaula and described him as "one of the disciples of the Hot Gun school of philosophy." Posey took the occasion to ask him about the relative merits of Eufaula and Checotah as county seats (Checotah was challenging Eufaula for permanent location of the seat), and Tookpafka Micco replied: "Well, so Eufaula was the

Injin's old stomp ground, and all the Injins was feel good to be here. Eufaula was the Injin's first resting place when he come here from Alabama. So the Injin didn't want no new busk ground like Checotah."[71]

Like Fus Fixico, the remaining two members of Hotgun's circle — Wolf Warrior and Kono Harjo — seem not to have been based on historical figures. In some early letters Yaha Tustenuggee (Wolf Warrior) is clearly Posey's good friend George Washington Grayson. But the well-educated mixed-blood Creek translator, public official, and businessman is hardly the type of character Wolf Warrior represents in subsequent letters. Perhaps Wolf Warrior is the only character in the letters besides Hotgun to have an English name because Posey had already identified his Creek name — Yaha Tustenuggee — with Grayson. Like Kono Harjo, Wolf Warrior became part of the quartet after Posey moved from Eufaula to Muskogee in 1903. Though Wolf Warrior and Kono Harjo rarely engage in dialogue, they fill out the scene. They are the quiet full-bloods who listen but say little, and their cabins at times provide the setting for the dialogues between Hotgun and Tookpafka Micco. Though not based on historical figures like their compatriots, they represent a type of individual commonly encountered in the remoter parts of the Creek Nation.

The characters are made more credible by the English they speak. It can be safely assumed that Posey had a keen ear for dialects. Besides English, he spoke Choctaw and the dialects spoken by the Creeks.[72] Though like most dialect writers he stylized some elements of the language, he apparently rendered a dialect familiar to the ears of local readers. Some indication of the effect he sought is suggested by Creeks who spoke or wrote English without humorous intent. Fair samples, for example, can be gleaned from records kept by the clerks of the Creek district courts in the late nineteenth century. In Eufaula district, Posey's home region, in 1890 three men were charged with "mister meaner, for disturbing religious gathering on Christmas 25 Dec 1889 at Artusse Church at night, using profane words," and another man was charged with the theft of some steel traps at "where place call Tullwthlocco Town."[73] Creek children who were just learning English at mission schools also provide interesting examples. A student at Nuyaka Mission school in 1890 wrote: "The black bird haf come back for it has snow" and "I like to run at rabbit with they white tails." Another Nuyaka student wrote in 1891: "His father said to him a wolf might catch you on the prairie you are to much little to go by self" and "Tomorrow my mother going to put the eggs for the hens to lay on till it is hatch."[74] Other linguistic evidence can be gained from Posey's contemporary Creeks, such as the Reverend James Barnett. A preacher at Quassarte Church near Stidham, Barnett was described as a full-blood whose ideas were full of "quaint Indian philosophy." He complained about such matters as Sunday baseball games and whiskey. Of the former he wrote: "The Bible say God made everything on the six days and rest on the seventh. And God said for us to keep this day holy, and he didn't mean't preachers and christian people only but everybody."[75]

In such passages, one hears the rhythms and recognizes the linguistic patterns that Posey stylized in his letters. What Rudolph Flesch has said about Charles Round Low Cloud, the Winnebago writer, might be said of Posey. Regarding American attempts to write English as it was spoken by the foreign-born, especially the Germans, Flesch said, "To write or speak 'correctly broken English' is almost impossible for anyone who isn't born to it." Flesch added that probably no one but an Indian could have written Low Cloud's sentence "The weather is change wind every

half day and person getting catch cold easy." According to Low Cloud's biographers, "The English of his column is written by a Winnebago who for all practical purposes thought and spoke in his native language and who just happened to write in English."[76] Occasionally in the Fus Fixico dialect is a statement that one suspects — or is willing to believe — that only a thinker in Creek could have said in English: "I will sent you put in news"; "That's all I got news"; "Well, it was just stay raining all the time looks like"; and "One Snake lighthorse was be at the dance."

The sources of humor in the letters derive in part from the perspectives of the characters. From their vantage point at the Shell Creek or Weogufky busk ground, the full-bloods are both literally and figuratively distanced from the events hurtling the Creeks toward a new order. They are amazed, amused, and puzzled by the greed, materialism, political ambition, dishonesty, and hypocrisy in the whites, especially the federal bureaucrats, merchants, petty entrepreneurs, and would-be politicians. Yet they recognize the complicity of Indians — even themselves — in the process of change. Though they make fun of Indians who part their hair in the middle and make self-aggrandizing speeches, they can imagine themselves as country editors or political flunkies of the Dawes Commission who smoke fancy cigars and bog down in the plush carpets of special railroad cars. Although they favor Prohibition in Indian Territory, they will take a drink of "bust-head" if they can get it, or of the patent medicine Peruna if they cannot, and they admit that the Indian's vote can be bought for a drink. Though they decry the whites' materialism, they admit that the Indians want tailor-made clothes, drop-stitch stockings, bon-bons, and new buggies. In their satire of the Americans and themselves, they become somewhat jaded and simply accept graft, political chicanery, greed, and political ambition as facts of everyday life in the allotment era. They conclude that the Dawes commissioners are pioneers and that bureaucrats look out for themselves simply because the opportunity for them to do so presents itself.

The characters' apparent lack of a clear understanding of all that is going on contributes to the humor. Sometimes it turns on their lack of understanding of something as complicated as the legalities of the allotment process or as simple as the definition of a county seat. Often it turns on their mispronunciation of names. They apparently do not realize that "Rooster Feather" suggests the cocky little president, that "It's Cocked" hints that the hesitating Interior Department secretary was like a pistol ready to fire but never fired, or that "Booker D. Washingtub" hints at the domestic work that blacks were engaged in at the time. Neither do they realize that their versions of the names of the Dawes commissioners, other petty federal bureaucrats, and local politicians reflect the grasping, avaricious, greedy behavior in which these men were engaged: Tams Big Pie, C. R. Break In rich, J. Gouge Right, J. Bear Sho'amfat, Plenty So Far, Rob It L. Owing, Toms Needs It, Charlie Divide Some, and so. Though the speakers may not realize the implications of these names, the readers do; they are constantly reminded of the quiet simplicity of life at Weogufky in contrast to the hustle and bustle of the steadily approaching — and encroaching — modern technological society.

Much of the humor also derives from the characters' attempts to speak the English language. Apart from the grammatical anomalies of "este charte" English noted above, several other characteristics mark Posey's style. First is a propensity for slang. For instance, Choela's medicine makes Fus Fixico feel "bully," Choela does not like "monkey business" while he is making medicine, and people who take shortcuts are trying to "fudge." Understatement is rampant. One politician they discuss is a Cherokee, but he would rather be a Republican; blacks, they suggest, might want to emigrate to Africa or to Muskogee or Wildcat, two Creek Nation towns with large black populations; and they put "white folks" and "Arkansawyers" into separate categories. Fus Fixico and his friends also have a propensity for metaphor: pie comes to represent graft; the sofky patch, or corn field, Creek allotments; the lightning-rod salesman, materialism; and Bud Weiser, legalized drink. Political maneuvering is described in terms of a poker game or a parody of the Twenty-third Psalm. Common expressions, such as that connecting politics and strange bedfellows, are given new force: "Maybe so politics was not make a stranger sleep with you." Colloquial expressions abound; people "light a shuck" for town, and a political campaign that gains momentun is "96 in the shade." In addition, the Fus Fixico letters are sprinkled with Creek expressions, history, folk beliefs, and traditional tales. In short, in Fus Fixico's and his friends' efforts to assess matters in a foreign language, their assessment becomes a *tour de force* of humorous effects. Yet through it all, they show themselves coping with events while maintaining their dignity as Creeks. Always, the clear logic and common sense of the speakers who are outside the mainstream expose the weaknesses of the social and political systems they discuss.

Fus Fixico's letters are rich in allusions to the Bible, classical history, English and American literature, and current world events. Like the personae of the "phunny phellows" and other American rural humorists, Fus Fixico and his friends may seem too well read and too informed for their historical counterparts or the characters they project, but the "literacy" of the speakers rarely breaks the fictional illusion of the character. Posey successfully substitutes the sofky pot for the cracker barrel. What the scholar C. Carroll Hollis has said in summary about the best of the

American rural humorists applies in a large measure to Posey as well. They were people of "detached critical intelligence" who exhibited "an amused, tolerant, yet critical concern with the quality of American life" and who used their "native shrewdness, homely common sense, and realistic awareness to keep the country from being threatened by the excesses which the national freedom permits." Through their personae, they "surveyed the institutions and concerns of American people to show the disparity between what people thought some institution was supposed to perform and what actually took place, to point out folly of exaggerated concern with some part of life to the neglect of other equally important parts, to ridicule the silly sentimentality of the period."[77] What American rural humorists did for America, Posey did for Indian Territory.

With such literary achievement, why did Posey not gain greater recognition as a humorist? Some blame rests with Posey himself. Twice in his life he had opportunities to reach a wider audience with his writings, and twice he refused. In 1900, at the height of his reputation as a poet, he was urged to submit his poems to eastern publications, but he refused, arguing that he wrote for a local audience and that eastern audiences would not appreciate his local references. In like fashion, in the summer of 1903 at the height of his popularity with Fus Fixico, he was asked to seek a wider readership for the letters by expanding their scope to take in the American national scene. Again he refused, citing his concern for territorial issues and characters and his belief that eastern readers would probably not understand him.[78]

Posey understood a major distinction between himself and the American literary humorists. The "phunny phellows" and other rural humorists before him had for the most part divorced themselves from the local scene and remained independent of any specific locale. Nor did the urban humorists contemporary with Posey depend on locale for their humor. Though Dunne and Ade, for example, set their works in Chicago, it was not Chicago but urban dwelling that provided the source of their humor.[79] Posey, on the other hand, like Indian Territorial humorists before him, turned to his own society for the substance of his writing and, much like the American local colorists, reflected the speech, geography, occupations, politics, and customs of common people of the Indian nations. As the editor of the *Fort Smith Times* had said, Posey's prose smacked of the time and place, a veritable outgrowth of the soil. Many of the Fus Fixico letters were esoteric for most readers outside Indian Territory. They dealt with local events and people, most of them Posey's good friends, family, acquaintances, political allies and enemies, and fellow journalists and bureaucrats, many of whom he liked very much, despite their weaknesses, politics, or complicity in the seamier side of the allotment. The caustic prose in which he attacked others through his journalism is absent from the letters. His relation to many of the objects of his humor might explain the mildness of his satire, or it may be, as Hollis has said, that the humorist has the ability to see "life as it is," to understand "his own and his neighbor's relation to it," and "to focus his consciousness on these social relationships with detachment and without rancor or prejudice or fear."[80]

It could be, however, that Posey thought something else was at work in his humor. When he rejected an expanded audience for his poetry in 1900, he argued that the Indian had difficulty expressing poetic thoughts in English and predicted that for this reason Indian writers like him, whose first language was not English, would never achieve greatness as a poet. Perhaps being Creek had something to do with his reluctance to expand the scope of his letters in 1903. Cross-tribal generalizations and generic statements about "Indians" have their dangers, but what James Welch, the Blackfeet novelist, recently said about Indian humor describes what Posey had done in his letters. Welch described such humor as "based on presenting people in such a way that you're not exactly making fun of them, but you're seeing them for what they are and then you can tease them a little bit. That's a lot of Indian humor — teasing, and some plays on words; Indians are very good at puns."[81] Posey knew well the Creek propensity for joking and teasing, for he engaged in it all of his life. Perhaps he feared that readers outside Indian country might not understand that special relationship between the teaser and the teased.

Time ultimately conspired against Posey. Though dialect humor of the sort Posey wrote was still popular in his day, its popularity was in decline. It now seems more reflective of nineteenth-century than of twentieth-century reading tastes.[82] Also, the historical circumstances that gave rise to Fus Fixico, Hotgun, and Tookpafka Micco passed; after 1907, new politics, new legalities, and new social orders were in place. Posey's untimely death in 1908 prevented the world from seeing how, or if, he would turn his humor on those matters.

The Literary Legacy and Literary Tradition

Posey left a literary legacy, at least among Indian writers on the local level. During his lifetime he had imitators and parodists. A "Mus Nixico" letter, for instance, appeared in the *South McAlester Capital* in 1904, and a "Fus Fixico" letter was published in the *Bartlesville Weekly Examiner* in 1906, replete with plays on names and commentary on Indian Territory and Cherokee affairs, respectively. A "Cold Pistol" letter, an obvious parody of Hot Gun and his friends, appeared in the *Muskogee Daily Phoenix* in 1904.

Then there were "Fus Fixico Jr.," "Fus Fixico No. Two," and "Este Charte" in 1908.[83] After Posey's death, his work strongly influenced other Creek writers such as Tulmochess Yohola, Fus Harjo, Jesse McDermott, Chinnubbie (Thomas E. Moore), and Acee Blue Eagle (A. C. McIntosh), as well as writers from other tribes in Oklahoma. The continuing tradition of Indian dialect literature suggests that in the Indian community, it remained a viable literary form long after it had become unfashionable among non-Indian readers.

As might be expected, Posey's influence was most pronounced on the Creeks. In the summer of 1908, Tulmochess Yohola reported on the debate about the county seat location in Hughes County, just as Fus Fixico had done in McIntosh County that spring. For instance, he said, "[Harry Oxfoot] jist talks it about Holdenville all the time lots big talk maybe so me think Harry Oxfoot has house and lot in Holdenville maybe so he thinks it Holdenville get county seat he sell it house and lot for big price."[84] He continued to report what other local folk had to say about the prospects for their communities.

Jesse McDermott, who worked as an interpreter for the Dawes Commission at the same time that Posey worked there, claimed to have taken Posey as his literary model. He began writing about Creek social characteristics and history in 1909, and the following year he produced a series of dialect works modeled after the Fus Fixico letters, with Tulsa Harjo and George Bear as his equivalent of Hotgun and Tookpafka Micco.[85] In one work, Tulsa Harjo brought up the question of taxes.

George Bear, he was push his hair back; cock his feet way up on fire jam an' was look wise like county judge or may be so county sheriff an' say, That tax was very thing what was make me fight statehood when them political fellers an' them Injins what had they hair part in the middle was make stump speeches all over country and was tell our old renters what had nothing but old gray mule and Johnny Deer plow that statehood was good thing so we ought to had it right now 'cause we was all ready for it.[86]

McDermott was producing dialect humor in this same style as late as 1913.[87]

Another Creek humorist of this era was Fus Harjo. In a 1916 letter, he commented on the refusal of surety bond companies to sign bonds for guardians of Indians and freedmen because the guardians were prone to squander the assets of their wards. He pondered where the crooked white guardians might escape to when they were found out. "Whiteman, he use to be run off Mexico when he got crooked but he can't do it now 'cause Wee-la [Villa], he down there raise smoke like Crazy Snake in 1909 when he was start Smoke Meat Rebellious."[88]

In the 1930s the Creek dialect humor tradition continued with "Sour Sofkee," a regular feature in the *Tulsa World* from late 1937 until early 1941.[89] In more than 150 letters, under the persona Chinnubbie, Thomas E. Moore commented on taxes, modern conveniences, politics, international affairs, Indian traditions, and other topics, sometimes speaking in the voice of his persona and sometimes reporting what Chinnubbie overheard in the conversations of Wooley Fixico and other characters. When the whites complained about taxes, for instance, and said that the government should just give the country back to the Indians, Chinnubbie responded: "You know what Indian say if White man try to give back this country to him? He say, 'Well, you bring it back wild turkeys, buffalo, prairie chicken an' all that kind, then you take away all that income tax stuff, sale tax, old age pension an' WPA projects, then I take my country back an' I run him right! Then nex' time don't you take away from somebody his country if you don't know how to run it.' "[90]

The Creek dialect humor tradition continued. Moore contributed occasional dialect pieces to the *Tulsa World* in the 1960s. Some humorous dialect poetry of the well-known Creek-Pawnee painter Acee Blue Eagle was also published posthumously in that decade.[91] In 1983, Moore collected some of his letters to the *Tulsa World* as well as some of his dialect poetry and published it as *Sour Sofkee* under the pen name William Harjo.

Dialect humor was also popular among writers from other Indian nations, some of whom were clearly influenced by Posey. The humor of Bill Kantfraid (Elias M. Landrum), Posey's Cherokee contemporary, was known for a decade after Posey's death. In his public speeches, Landrum, a member of the Oklahoma state senate, would often switch from his fluent "standard" English to "este charte" English and back to "standard" English with ease.[92] Royal Roger Eubanks, the Cherokee cartoonist, wrote to Posey shortly before the latter's death, proposing that Posey collect his works, which Eubanks would illustrate. In earlier cartoons, Eubanks had used "este charte" English in the captions, and in 1910 he began a series of dialect stories titled "Nights with Uncle Ti-ault-ly."[93] A few years later, Eubanks illustrated a collection for B.N.O. Walker (Hen-toh), a Wyandot, who used dialect not only in his humorous animal tales but in his poetry as well.[94] In the 1920s, Ben Locke, a Choctaw, wrote prose under the pen names Illapotubbe and Kiamitia and also produced, under his own name, what the Chickasaw editor Lee Harkins called "Indian brogue writings."[95]

Other dialect humorists who may have been influenced by Posey are Daniel M. Madrano (Caddo) and Joseph B. Shunatona (Pawnee-Otoe). Madrano's *Heap Big Laugh* (1955) is a mixture of

Indian vaudeville jokes, stand-up comic routines, Poor Lo's almanac, and humorous historical anecdotes, often concerning his character Sidemeat Cholly. For example, "Sidemeat Cholly he been say lately, he shore don't unnerstan' when peoples say necessity is th' mother of invention, but nobody is find out who th' papa is."[96] Madrano attributed some of his stories to Shunatona, who, as the character Skookum, performed his dialect humor routines on stage, radio, and television in the United States and abroad. His *Skookum's Laugh Medicine* (1957) has much in common with Madrano's work. For example, he told the following story:

I got two fren's, and one of it he shore got the bad lucks. Rats been eat-um-up his corn in grainary an' he sure dont like it that way. So he gone seen his white man fren' an' ask him maybeso what he could do. His fren' told him if he feed it the rat traps with yellow laundry soap it's gonna kill-it-off dead all those rats. So he went seen his Indian fren' then, John Turkey Leg, an' he said, "Turkey Leg, you got any them yellow laundry soap?" Turkey Leg, he said. "No, I shore dont got them yellow laundry soap, what for you want 'em?" My fren' told him, so Turkey Leg, he sed, "Well I shore dont got no yellow laundry soap, — but I got WPA soap tho, cause I work WPA now." But my fren, he sed, "Shucks, I dont want no WPA soap, I want yellow laundry soap cause it's gonna kill-it-off dead all them rats." Then Turkey Leg, he said, "Well, WPA soap it aint gonna kill it but it's make it so darn lazy you can ketch-it e-a-s-y and kill-it yourself."[97]

These later generations of writers, whether or not influenced by Posey, demonstrate that dialect humor has been a part of the Indian literary scene for more than a century.

Although dialect has most often been used for humor, writers have used it for other purposes as well. Sometimes dialect is the unaffected, honest style of the writer, such as that found in the news reported by the "Indian Reporter" (Arapaho) for the *Colony*

Courier (1912–15) at Colony, Oklahoma; by Charles Round Low Cloud (Winnebago) for the Black River Falls, Wisconsin, *Banner-Journal* (1931–49); and by Mollie Shepherd (Cheyenne) for the *Kingfisher Free Press* (1964–75) in Oklahoma. Other writers have used dialect in fiction and literary nonfiction. Francis La Flesche used it, for example in the boys' English conversations in *The Middle Five* (1900). John Joseph Mathews (Osage) used it in *Sundown* (1934) in the episode in which the older boys are teasing Chal about being a girl and *Talking to the Moon* (1945) in Mathews's report of his conversations with old Ee-Nah-Apee and with John Abbott in Washington, D.C. Napoleon Kills-in-the-Timber's prayer is in dialect in N. Scott Momaday's novel *House Made of Dawn* (1968), as is the narrative voice in Simon J. Ortiz's "A Story of Ríos and Juan Jesús" (1974).

Though the type of dialect humor found in the Fus Fixico letters has long since gone out of literary fashion, its historical significance is great. It marked a departure from the reflective lyrical poetry and serious prose, most of which was autobiographical, that characterized American Indian literature of the nineteenth century. The Fus Fixico letters represent the best of Indian dialect humor, a literary form that Indian writers found useful for more than a century. Dialect is simply one reflection of the humorous side of life in the Indian community — a side that non-Indians have usually ignored or failed to recognize. It is but one expression of what James Welch has called the "traditional Indian sense of humor that has survived for hundreds of years."[98] Some writers believe that keeping that sense of humor alive through generations has been critical to survival. As the Lakota journalist Tim Giago has written, "As Indians were forced to take their culture and sprituality underground, they also found that in order to keep from going mad, they had to sharpen their sense of humor in order to make the horrible things happening around them more palatable."[99]

Though Posey believed that allotment of lands and statehood were inevitable, he was not blind to their impact on the Indian peoples of Indian Territory. Perhaps his letters made the process "more palatable" to many in the Indian nations. For others, perhaps the letters offered a diversion from the realities of greed, deception, fraud, political arrogance, illegalities, and political chicanery, realities that Angie Debo has described in her study of the allotment period and the making of Oklahoma.[100] Though some of the contexts for Posey's humor have been lost, readers today, with a little editorial help, can find most of the letters not only readable but downright funny. That is the primary reason they should be read.

The Fus Fixico Letters

Letters No.1 and No.2

[Indian Journal, October 24 and 31, 1902, respectively]

The Curtis Act of 1898 made inevitable the allotment of Creek lands. Though individual Creeks began the selection of their allotments in 1899, no formal allotment agreement between the Creek Nation and the United States was reached until 1901. Under that agreement, the secretary of the interior would supply the Creek chief with blank deeds that would be filled out, returned to the secretary for his signature, and sent to the chief once more for his signature before distribution to the Creeks. From late 1901 onward, the local press had taken Chief Pleasant Porter to task for not delivering any deeds.

The delay was caused in part by what Porter and other Creek leaders believed were flaws in the 1901 agreement. They sought to negotiate a supplemental agreement to correct some of the weaknesses. In May 1902, Posey accused them of using the proposed supplemental agreement as an excuse to delay issuing deeds until large land companies could gain a hold on Creek lands. Delay also worked against economic progress, which Posey had personally and editorially embraced. He had written on May 16, "Delay of deeds means delay of progress." Even though a supplemental agreement was reached in June and ratified by the Creeks in July, no deeds had been issued by October, when Posey began the Fus Fixico letters. Meanwhile, some Creeks had made agreements with land dealers who sought title to Creek lands; others, like Fus Fixico, charged goods against the value of their allotments.

Besides broaching the subject of the allotment deeds, the first two letters established Fus Fixico as a correspondent to the *Indian Journal* and placed Choela, a "medicine man" and member of the House of Kings, as his informant among the conservative Creeks.

✍ [No.1]

Un Hesse Mahhe, Mr. Editor, Toyets Kat:[1]

So I will sent you some news to put in this time.

Well, I hope you and your families is well, but I got very bad cold in my head. I was take my dogs and went possum hunt last night and catch nothing but bad cold. Guess I pull off my coat too quick when I get too hot trying to stay with my dogs. When I rise up this morning my head is almost busted and I can't breathe hardly. I feel like I been in calaboose all night in Eufaula.[2]

Well, Hagee was come back from Okmulgee yesterday.[3] He got lots news to tell about Creek council. He says it ain't do nothing but run in debt. He say it will be good thing when we get deeds so we can shut up that old council house if we can't rent it to some mens like the Dawes commission that's got lots a time and money from Washington.[4]

I was to Muskogee last week and buy heap stuff on my land.[5] Them white mens was good to me. Next time I go to Checotah,[6] or maybe Eufaula, and buy stuff the same way.

I was read Charley Gibson's pieces all time. He writes heap good sense too.[7]

Maybe next time I write you more news to put in.

1. "You are my real friend, Mr. Editor" (translation by George Bunny).

2. Eufaula, in present-day McIntosh County, Oklahoma, was on the Missouri, Kansas, and Texas Railroad, thirty-five miles south of Muskogee.

3. Hagee has not been identified. Okmulgee, in present-day Okmulgee County, Oklahoma, was the location of the Creek National Council.

4. The Dawes Commission, established in 1893, oversaw the allotment process.

5. The merchants allowed him to charge goods against the value of his allotment. He indicates that he will repeat the process in other towns. Such activities were reportedly common.

6. Checotah, Eufaula's rival town, was located on the Missouri, Kansas, and Texas Railroad about fifteen miles north of Eufaula.

7. Charles Gibson, a Creek, was a regular contributor to the *Indian Journal*. His column, called "Gibson's Rifle Shots," concerned Creek history, lore, and politics. See also the reference to Gibson at the end of Letter No.2.

✍ [No.2]

Well, so I was got all right again once more. My friend old Choela was give me some physic and make me feel bully like old time. Old Choela was sure good doctor. He was just take his grubbing hoe and go out in the woods and dig up lots medicine anywhere. Then he was take his cane and blow in the medicine pot long time and sing little song with it, too, like at busk ground.[1] But he aint want no monkey business round there neither while he was fixing that medicine. If you aint dead yet before he was got through, he make you so well you just want whole lot sofky, right quick or maybe sak-ko-nip-kee.[2] The medicine what Choela was give you taste good all right too, you bet. 'Taint stink like white man medicine.

Well, them council members was all come home now from Okmulgee. They all bust up last week sometimes. All them was come back on passenger trains, or maybe some was come back in buggies. They was all quit riding horse or maybe wagon like long time ago. Reckon so they was get civilized.

Well, so Tookpafka was stay all night with me when he get back from council this last time.[3] He got heap influence too and make them other Injins vote like he say all time nearly, except them what's got influence over him. Me and him talk long time till about one o'clock I reckon. He was tell me lots thing about Creek council. He says they was elect Mr. A. M. Bassador[4] delegate to see what them Choctaws want, also them Cherokees and Chickasaws, too. When he was come back from there, council meet again about two weeks more and hear what news he was bring back.

Please, you must tell Charley Gibson that I was read what he says in the JOURNAL last week about dozen time. He was told the truth good that time sure enough.

Maybe so next time I write you more news to put in like this one.

1. A busk ground was a tribal town square where the Green Corn Ceremony, known as *posketv*, or busk, was held.

2. Sofky and sak-ko-nip-kee were favorite traditional Creek foods made from pounded corn. Sofky was corn grits cooked in lye water; sak-ko-nip-kee was grits boiled in water, seasoned with grease and salt, and cooked with wild game. Millie Bullett (interview), *Indian-Pioneer History*, Archives and Manuscripts Division, Oklahoma Historical Society, Oklahoma City, 17:309.

3. Tookpafka is probably a forerunner of Tookpafka Micco, a character in later letters. He is not identified as a historical figure. Tookpafka was a tribal town on the Canadian River in present-day Hughes County, Oklahoma. The *micco* was the town leader.

4. A. M. Bassador is Posey's first play on names, for which his letters later became famous. Here he refers to a Creek delegate (or ambassador) sent to the other nations of Indian Territory.

Letter No. 3

[Indian Journal, November 21, 1902]

Although some Creeks like Fus Fixico (and Posey) anxiously waited for their deeds to arrive, most of the so-called Snakes had refused to sign up for allotments. They continued to live where they had, sometimes on lands taken as allotments by other Creeks. The Dawes Commission had arbitrarily assigned allotments to the Snakes, but they refused to recognize the commission's authority.

Under the leadership of Chitto Harjo, or Crazy Snake, the Snakes had steadfastly insisted on the authority of the Treaty of 1832, which guaranteed their lands in Indian Territory, they said, as long as the grass grows and the water flows. After the Curtis Act of 1898, the United States had steadily assumed more control over Creek affairs; the Snakes, however, insisted that the old Creek national laws and government were valid. In the fall of 1900, they had established their own government and in early 1901 sent out their lighthorse policemen to whip Creeks who signed up for allotments, leased lands to whites, or hired whites as laborers. A troop of cavalry was called out, and Chitto Harjo and nearly a hundred of his followers were captured and sent to the federal jail at Muskogee, where two-thirds of them stayed for several weeks without trial. They were at last given long suspended sentences and paroled on their promise of good behavior. In early 1902, they assembled at Hickory Ground again, apparently to discuss their destitution as a result of a poor corn crop during the previous season. U.S. marshals took a number of them to Muskogee, where, once more, they languished in jail without trial. This time, Chitto Harjo and a few of his followers were given jail terms. By the fall of 1902, however, he was back at Hickory Ground, meeting with his followers once more.

✍

Well, so I was not write to you any news to put in for about a month nearly. But I didn't had no time to write. My cotton was bust open so much last two three weeks I was had to pick it out like everything. Guess so I pick out every day about twenty-five pounds or little over, and my wife,[1] he was pick out about fifty pounds maybe.

55

I was raise about two wagons plum full of sofky corn too, and lots of bushels of sweet potatoes, like what the white mens call "nigger chokers" — they wont choke Injins though, 'cause Injins don't eat potatoes that was cooked dry like niggers.[2]

I was raise lots pumpkins and turnips and things like that too. My wife was sliced up the pumpkins and hang it up all 'round the kitchen to dry for Christmas times.

Well, Chitto Harjo and his friend, was all come back from jail and was hold some councils in the woods already. They was make lots big speeches about old times. I think maybe so if they don't quit their monkey business the white man will round them up and put them back in jail for about ten years next time.

Well, one thing I like to know is if Porter was quit trying to issue them deeds.[3] I guess maybe so he was had so many deeds to sign up he was just give out of breath and quit. I think the Creek counsil [*sic*] ought to elect some white man to fix up them deeds for us anyhow. It's too much work for one Injin.

I don't know what I do if I don't get my deed pretty soon. The land buyer say he can't give me but 15c for my land if them deeds don't show up. So you see I was in a bad fix for Christmas times with nothing but sour sofky to make me feel good.[4]

1. In Indian-English dialect, the speaker often does not make gender distinctions with pronouns.

2. Over one-third of Creek citizens were officially listed as Creek freedmen: former slaves of the Creeks or free black residents of the Creek Nation or their descendants. Many citizens listed as Creeks had some African heritage. Creeks tended to distance themselves culturally and racially from the blacks so that by the turn of the century, many, like Posey, held racial views that were comparable to those held by white Americans. As statehood approached, racism against blacks became more blatant.

3. Chief Pleasant Porter.

4. The longer sofky sat after cooking, the more it soured, or fermented.

1. Alex Posey about 1900. Courtesy of
Daniel F. Littlefield, Jr.

2. Charles Gibson, author of "Gibson's Rifle Shots."
From H. F. O'Beirne and E. S. O'Beirne, *The Indian
Territory: Its Chiefs, Legislators, and Leading Men*
(St. Louis: C. B. Woodward Co., 1892).

3. Chitto Harjo, leader of the Creek Snake faction.
Barde Collection, courtesy of the Oklahoma Historical
Society, No. 1201.

4. George W. Grayson, Creek interpreter and
Posey's friend. Courtesy of the Oklahoma Historical
Society, No.648.

5. Green McCurtain, chief of the Choctaws (1902–10).
Courtesy of the Oklahoma Historical Society, No.569.

6. Thomas M. Buffington, chief of the Cherokees
(1899–21903). Courtesy of the Oklahoma Historical
Society, No.99.

7. Ethan Allen Hitchcock, secretary of the interior
(1898–1907). Courtesy of the National Archives.

8. Clifford L. Jackson, railroad attorney and single-state
booster. Courtesy of the Oklahoma Historical Society,
No.2924.

9. Tams Bixby, Dawes Commission chairman (1897–
1905) and commissioner to the Five Civilized Tribes
(1905–7). Courtesy of the Oklahoma Historical
Society, No. 14627.

10. J. George Wright, inspector for Indian Territory (1898–1907). Photograph by Harris & Ewing, Washington, D.C., courtesy of the Oklahoma Historical Society, No. 7737.

11. Clarence B. Douglas, editor of the *Muskogee Phoenix* (1902–7). Courtesy of the Oklahoma Historical Society, No.4432.

12. Pliny L. Soper, seated, U.S. attorney for the
Northern District of Indian Territory (1897–1904).
Barde Collection, courtesy of the Oklahoma
Historical Society, No.4286.

13. Thomas B. Needles, member of the Dawes
Commission. From *Muskogee, Indian Territory*
(Muskogee: John H. N. Tindall Co., 1903).

14. J. Blair Shoenfelt, Indian agent at Muskogee.
From D. C. Gideon, *The Indian Territory* (New York:
Lewis Publishing Co., 1901).

15. Clifton R. Breckenridge, member of the Dawes
Commission. From *Muskogee, Indian Territory*
(Muskogee: John H. N. Tindall Co., 1903).

16. Pleasant Porter, chief of the Creeks (1899–1907).
Photograph by Robertson Studio, Muskogee, Creek
Nation, courtesy of the Oklahoma Historical
Society, No.7720.

17. Legus C. Perryman, former Creek chief and candidate in 1903. Courtesy of Western History Collections, University of Oklahoma, Norman.

18. Cornelius E. Foley, unofficial congressional delegate
from Indian Territory (1903–4). From D. C. Gideon, *The
Indian Territory* (New York: Lewis Publishing Co.,
1901).

19. Charles J. Bonaparte, special investigator of fraud (1903–4). Courtesy of the National Archives.

20. Robert L. Owen, Cherokee attorney and
U.S. senator from Oklahoma (1907–25). Barde
Collection, 19383.141, courtesy of the Oklahoma
Historical Society, No.4322.

21. Robert L. Williams, Democratic national committeeman from Indian Territory (1904). Courtesy of the
Oklahoma Historical Society, No.20123.

The Fus Fixico Letters

Letters No.4 and No.5

[*Indian Journal,* December 12 and December 19, 1902, respectively]

In addition to providing for allotment, the Curtis Act of 1898 had established the eventuality of statehood for Indian Territory. The question
was whether the territory would become a separate state or would merge
with Oklahoma Territory. Many Indian leaders believed the United
States had promised the Indians a separate state and envisioned one
whose political destiny would be controlled by Indians. The Creek chief
Pleasant Porter supported the idea and twice attempted, but failed, in
the fall of 1902 to organize the chiefs of the Cherokees, Choctaws,
Chickasaws, and Seminoles to act. Finally in late November, at the call
of the Choctaw chief Green McCurtain, the leaders met at Eufaula and
drafted resolutions, asking Congress not to annex Indian Territory to
Oklahoma but to give it separate statehood. Posey at first opposed such
a plan, believing that it would thwart economic progress in Indian Territory.

The political and economic changes that were transforming Indian
Territory left Chitto Harjo and the Snakes bewildered. At various times
they maintained a delegation in Washington with instructions to work
for reinstatement of the authority of the Treaty of 1832. In addition to
refusing to participate in allotment, many Snakes reconsidered an old
plan: emigration to Mexico. Shortly after removal in the 1830s, some
Creeks and members of other tribes had gone to Mexico and remained
there. Thus Mexico was considered a political haven by many conservatives of the Creek and other Indian nations. Others reacted differently to
change. Wacache, who lived near Lenna, gave up farming, became a
"prophet," and obtained a large following in his call for a return to the
old ways. Others, like Fus Fixico, who accepted allotment, anxiously
awaited their deeds.

In these letters, Fus Fixico called Theodore Roosevelt "President
Rooster Feather" for the first time and introduced Hotgun. The latter, a
medicine man and follower of Chitto Harjo, had been arrested in early

1902, spent many weeks in the Muskogee jail without trial, and was humiliated by having his long hair cut. He was destined to become the central character of the Fus Fixico letters.

✍ [No.4]

So I will write you some more news to put in like Charley Gibson, while I was got lots a time sitting round the house doing nothing but drink sofky and smoke maybe.

Well, it was just stay raining all the time looks like, and come put near wash all my cotton off in Shell creek.[1] I don't care nohow if it did. It's get too cold to pick cotton in the winter like white folks and take bad cough and die.

Someone tell me the big Injins was had a council in Eufaula, and write long letter for President Rooster Feather to look at it. Guess maybe so it take a heap of stamps to send it. And I hear they was make big bad talk about Oklahoma two days nearly 'cause the white folks wants to give it back to Injins and be good friends.

Well, so I guess when I was go to the postoffice next time I get my deed for Christmas times.

Choela he say he was druther had a ticket to Mexico instead of a deed, and Hotgun he says the same thing too. If Porter don't hurry up maybe they go horse back or 'foot.

I was had some good news to put in about Wacache.[2] He was got to be big prophet and make better medicine than Choela. Lots fullbloods believe him and camp at his house a week, and maybe two weeks some times, before they was come home. Wacache he says he was had a talk with God and knows lots of things like wise mens of old times in the Bible. He says the Creeks was not live right now like before Columbus and Dawes commission. So God was tell him to make medicine for Creeks, and make them wash off in the branch, too, and rub lots sand on their hides and dance stomp dance and play ball game. This way they was get strong and quit renting land to white folks and let the country get wild and have lots game like long time ago.

Well, so the Creek council was make four delegates to Washington.[3] One delegate was get too lonesome with white folks; so, I reckon, council was make three more delegates to stay with him and talk Creek.

Council was knock lots old debts in the head, too, like killing hogs and was rent the old council house and quit like some Injins busted that was had a store out in the country.

So, I guess, I say enough this time.

Cen hesse mahhe, Fus Fixico, ekis ce.[4]

1. Shell Creek, a branch of Mill Creek, joins the latter east of Proctor, a community about twelve miles southwest of Eufaula. Hotgun's home was on Shell Creek.

2. Wacache, a successful farmer, had made news several months earlier when, in protest against the allotment process, he burned his house piece by piece and held a continuous dance around the fire. He began to practice "medicine" and became known as a prophet. He died in 1906. See *Muskogee Democrat*, December 23, 1904, and *Muskogee Times-Democrat*, February 21, 1906.

3. John Goat was one of the delegates; the others have not been identified.

4. "I mean your real friend, Fus Fixico" (translation by George Bunny).

✍ [No.5]

Well, I think was have to make big ark like old Noah and put my families in it if it was keep on raining this way all time. Guess so it rain 'bout forty days and nights, too, already. But I was want no animal in that ark except lots a hog meat and 'bout wagon load of sofky corn and also 'bout hundred bundles of devil shoestrings to pizen fish with maybe.[1] Hotgun he was good etow calafa (carpenter) and he says he show me how to make ark better than what old Noah had. Maybe so Hotgun thinks he could get in and go to

Mexico easy this way, but he was had to look out for himself like me.

Well, reckon so them Injin delegates was all in Washington looking at lots a things to talk 'bout and was drink lots good whiskey instead old sour sofky like at home. One Snake Injin says he was stay at Washington put near six months maybe and had good times. He say Washington was like Saturday in Eufaula all time, but he say he was see no cotton and renters like in Eufaula.[2] He was see nobody but big mens that was not wear overalls and buy things with due bills.[3] He says them big white mens was ride in wagons that didn't had no horses hitched to it neither, and run like down hill all time.[4] But he say he was not had chance to see president and secretary interior and make treaties before he was had to come back busted.

I read in Journal Charley Gibson was go to Gulf a Mexico. He say he was Snake Reporter and maybe so he call council and tell Latah Micco and Chitto Harjo he was find lots good hunting ground cheap.[5]

Wacache was not quit make medicine. He was got lots water to make it in, too. Limbo creek was get so high he was had to make sick folks wash off out in the woods.

Please you must tell postmaster I was not want my deed go back to Porter or dead letter office. Maybe so I come soon and get it.

So I write you more news to put in next time.

---

1. Roots of the devil's shoestring plant were pounded in sluggish streams to addle the fish.

2. "Renters" were specifically whites who rented Creek lands.

3. "Due bills" were literally IOU's, redeemable at a later date; the term was sometimes used for warrants, which circulated in lieu of cash and were redeemable from the Creek national treasurer.

4. These "wagons" were streetcars.

5. Though Chitto Harjo was the acknowledged leader of the Snakes, Latah

Micco was the elected principal chief of their opposition government. The Snakes often reported that delegations had been sent to Mexico to locate good hunting lands that might be suitable settlement locations for the disgruntled Creeks.

Letters No.6 and No.7

[*Indian Journal*, December 26, 1902, and January 2, 1903, respectively]

Posey capitalized on the Christmas season to continue his criticism of Chief Pleasant Porter for the delay in delivering Creek allotment deeds. These letters also reflect the growing diversity of the population of the Creek Nation. Those who took an interest in affairs in Indian Territory believed that the completion of the allotment process would most likely result in the opening of lands for sale to non-Indian citizens, as had happened in former allotments of Indian lands. Thus the territory attracted U.S. citizens in greater and greater numbers. Towns such as Muskogee, in the northeastern part of the Creek Nation, became the destination of large numbers of blacks from the South and elsewhere while whites, such as those whom Fus Fixico reports on, generally scattered throughout the countryside, leasing farmland from individual Indians or subleasing from land companies that had obtained leases from Creeks. By 1902, Muskogee had a large black population and a thriving black business district. Fus Fixico's mild case of Negrophobia in Muskogee reflects Posey's racism toward blacks; like the racism among whites in the region, Posey's was sometimes blatant and virulent. Race would be a factor in the election, to be held the following August, for principal chief. Posey broached the subject of the election for the first time in Letter No.7, in which he correctly assumed that Porter would be a candidate for reelection.

✍ [No.6]

Well, so it's put near Christmas times. So I was killed my hogs and was had lots fresh meat to eat, like sausage and ribs and so forth. My wife he was make 'bout three four gallons a good lard, too, that was not smell bad like some stuff what the clerk say was nothing a tall but good hog grease.[1] I was had some more fat bars to knock in the head yet 'bout New Years.[2] Then, maybe so, I was had bacon all the time next summer. But Hotgun and Choela was got left if they was try to borrow it.[3]

So I was to Muskogee last Saturday. Niggers was thick like blackbirds behind a plow. Can't see no white mens hardly, and can't find no Injins neither. But one nigger, with lots a letters in his hand,[4] tell me they was lots white mens and Injins locked up in jail down to the pond. So I was got on the flyer and go back to Checotah before I could find a place to sit down good looks like. Then I was come home in a wagon what I got for Christmas present on my land in Checotah. When I go to Eufaula, maybe so, I was got big fine buggy for Christmas present, too, on my land.

Well, we was going to have big time at Proctor Christmas. Micco Hutka say he was give big dance and Hotgun was play "Sally Gooden" on the fiddle all night.[5] Hotgun was play the fiddle better than any body and make church folks sin like every thing Christmas times. But I reckon so they all get mad and fight 'bout midnight.

White folks at Hillabee[6] was going to have big Christmas, too, like Micco Hutka.

But I stay home Christmas and hang up my socks for Creek deeds maybe.

1. The "clerk" is a storeclerk. The implication is that the stores sold poor-quality goods.

2. "Bars" is a dialect form of barrows, hogs that have been castrated and raised for slaughter.

3. They would be left out or left behind, without results.

4. Posey refers to a postman.

5. Micco Hutka (or Hutke), a Loyal Creek leader from Tallassee Canadian town, was one of the three delegates who had gone to Washington to seek defense against the Confederate Creeks in 1861. See Dean Trickett, "The Civil War in the Indian Territory, 1861," *Chronicles of Oklahoma* 18 (June 1940): 150–52. Micco Hutke served as second chief of the Creek Nation in the late 1860s. Posey probably did not have this historical figure in mind.

6. Hillabee was a Creek tribal town about three and one-half miles east of present-day Hanna, Oklahoma.

✍ [No.7]

Well, so I was had bad luck Christmas times. I was fly out of bed soon about daylight and look in my socks, but I was see nothing in there but big holes. Maybe so, my deed was fall out in the fire, or, maybe so, Old Santa Claus think I was not want any deed, like Chitto Harjo and Hotgun.

So Micco Hutka was give a big dance, like I say last week, and Hotgun he was make music on the fiddle. Long time ago out in the mountain, Old Devil he was show Hotgun how to play on fiddle just like he do himself.[1] So Hotgun was play some good Injin tunes like the devil till Choela's old rooster was crow for daylight before sun-up. They was lots a Injins be at the rag[2] and lots a gals, too, what the preacher was not had chance to marry. Hotgun was pat his foot on the floor all time, like he was want to dance together with them too. One Weogufky Injin[3] was beat on the chair with two sticks like big woodpecker by himself way out in the woods. He say he was do this to make more noise, like hail falling on top of a house while it was raining like everything. One Snake lighthorse[4] was be at the dance and he was steal all the whiskey and run off to Hickory Ground and get drunk two days.[5]

White folks was had a big times at Dogtown, too.[6] They was had more fun than what Micco Hutka was had. One white feller he was try to dance and had his hat on like out doors. Somebody he was tell him he was had to take it off, but he say he won't and so he get shot and the feller what shot him get killed.[7]

Well, so I was had lots to eat Christmas. Maybe so, I was not had that much to eat till Porter was run for chief and give big barbecue. I was had lots visitors too. Hotgun was brought his families and eat. Choela was brought his families and eat. Old Nocose Emarther[8] was brought his families and eat, and lots a others was brought they families and eat. They was all fetch they dogs, too, and they was eat up what they was left. I was tell my wife, maybe so, I was sick and hard up they all go some other place and eat.

1. See Posey's poem "Fus Harjo and Billy Hell," *Indian Journal*, March 22, 1901.

2. "Rag" is slang for dance.

3. The Indian was a Creek from Weogufky tribal town.

4. The "lighthorse" was a policeman of the opposition Snake government, established in 1900.

5. Hickory Ground town was near the North Canadian River south of present-day Henryetta, Oklahoma.

6. Dogtown has not been identified; it might refer to the little hamlet of Senora.

7. The dance was held at the house of Jack Pemberton on Christmas Eve. A man named Christler was dancing with his hat on. When Bill Cheeks asked him to remove it, Christler's brother Leon took offense. He pulled his pistol and started firing, accidentally wounding his brother and then killing Cheeks. *Indian Journal*, January 2, 1903.

8. Nocose Emarther (or Nocus Emarthlar) was a member of the House of Kings in 1874, 1877, and 1881 from Deep Fork (later called Eufaula) District, judge of the district from 1885 to 1887, and member of the House of Warriors in 1899. See Creek National Records 25957, 32528, 32563, 32679, 32847, 33786-B, Record Group 75, National Archives, maintained by Oklahoma Historical Society. Posey probably knew the historical Nocus Emarthlar, since he was a public official in Posey's home district.

The Fus Fixico Letters

Letter No.8

[*Indian Journal*, January 16, 1903]

In the *Indian Journal* on December 26, 1902, Posey wrote a number of editorial comments on the Creek allotment deeds: "Chief Porter, Christmas gift! Make it a fee simple"; "Good deeds are done on Christmas. Chief Porter, please send us ours"; "Behold the Creek citizen awoke and found that Santa Claus Porter had not remembered him"; and "The Creek deeds have arrived but they have not come." The last statement referred to the delivery of nearly one thousand deeds to the office of the Commission to the Five Civilized Tribes, who in turn would deliver them to Porter for distribution to allottees. Posey called delivery of the deeds "the most important piece of news that was ever published in the Creek Nation."

Because it appeared that Creek citizens would soon be receiving their deeds, Posey now turned to other matters. Here, he addresses two issues: statehood and the Snakes' growing disaffection toward the material culture of the Americans. The latter issue appeared as a constant theme, addressed frequently in subsequent letters in later years. The statehood question, though perennial in recent years, was a more immediate political question as a result of a statehood bill then pending in Congress. Believing as he did that separate statehood for Indian Territory would impede its economic, political, and social progress, Posey supported efforts to merge Oklahoma Territory and Indian Territory as a single state. When a single-statehood convention met at Oklahoma City on January 6, 1903, Posey was one of the Eufaula delegates to attend. Among the concerns of such single-staters from Indian Territory was that the territory, although basically Democratic, would be simply merged with Oklahoma, basically Republican, and that its inhabitants would have little influence in writing the state constitution. Another major concern was Prohibition, which Indian Territory supported and Oklahoma did not. Because no bill emerged from Congress during the session, Posey did not deal with the statehood topic for several weeks after this letter.

✍

So I was quit talk about Creek deeds this times. Maybe so Porter was get mad and say he wont issue deeds soon if I was not shut up tight like terrapins. Maybe so he don't give me no office neither, like delegates to Washington and superintendent public instructions.[1] So I was stop bother him about deeds. Hotgun say all I was had to do to get my deed was drink lots sofky and wait till it was come.

Well, so I was hear lots a talk about single statehoods. It was alright, too, and I was like to hear it. The Bible say it is no good to live alone by yourself,[2] and maybe so that's what Injin Territory and Oklahoma say last week when they was had big council. I sure vote for single statehoods quick, too, so next times I was go to Keokuk Fall or Shawnee,[3] I was bought red-eye and don't be 'fraid to go home with it neither, like Christmas times when my old filly was fall down in the night close to John Dutchman's and bust my jug up bad. I think Hotgun and Choela was not go to Mexico quick, like they say, if they was know single statehood good like me and Kid Morgan and them Osage Injins what make big talk in Oklahoma.[4]

So I was to Eufaula last week and stay all night in wagon yard with white folks and Arkansawyers that was come to town to get in debt for sowbelly and tobacco and molasses and things like that.[5] We was walk 'round and see everythings. We was go to depot and look at trains, but we was see nothing but lots a niggers. Maybe so they was fixing to go to Africa, or maybe so Muskogee or Wildcat.[6] Then we was go in one place and eat chili that was put nigh cook my throat. We was go in 'nother place and see big ball play on table that was had sacks to it. But they was not play ball like Injins do, 'cause they didn't had no feathers and tiger tails and paint and lots a fights. And they was not whoop and hee-kee neither.[7] They was just stand round and knock ball with sticks like hoe handle and laugh and cuss maybe. Then we was see some drunk mens going to calaboose with marshal and we thought we better go to bed in wagon yard soon, and left town before daylight.

1. Posey makes fun of the Creek practice of political patronage, which he himself had benefited from: in 1898 he held the office that he mentions last.

2. "And the Lord God said, It is not good that man should be alone; I will make him an help meet for him" (Genesis 2:18).

3. Keokuk Falls and Shawnee were in present-day Pottawatomie County, Oklahoma. The former, located near the western boundary of the Creek Nation, no longer exists; the latter, twenty miles west, is the county seat. In 1903, both were in Oklahoma Territory, where liquor was legal. Posey, who often carried a flask of whiskey with him, was not particularly in favor of Prohibition.

4. Gid (Gideon) Morgan was a well-known Cherokee politician. The Osage Nation representatives in the Indian Territory caucus were T. J. Leahy and John Palmer. Leahy was elected temporary chairman of the convention. See *Daily Oklahoman*, January 7, 1903, for the convention proceedings.

5. Posey particularly disliked Arkansans, considering them more grasping and ignorant that most whites in the Creek Nation. He makes his point here by having Fus Fixico put them in a class separate from other "white folks."

6. Since the 1890s, Indian Territory blacks had discussed plans to emigrate to Africa. Wildcat, eleven miles southeast of Okmulgee, was a black town. Muskogee, a migration point for blacks going to Indian Territory, had a large black population and a thriving black business district in 1903.

7. Posey refers to the regalia of the Creek ball players and the growling sounds (banter) with which they taunted and challenged their opponents.

Letter No.9

[Indian Journal, February 13, 1903]

Commentary on the weather, its sudden changes, and its impact on farming was always of interest to Indian Territory readers, whose livelihood depended for the most part on agriculture and livestock production. During late winter, the weather in Indian Territory could change rapidly, as this letter and the one following indicate. Here, Fus Fixico announces the illness of Choela, one of his main characters. Choela did not recover, as noted in Letter No.13.

✍

Guess so I was had to spit on my hands and plow. But my filly was pretty weak though, like right after sick spell.

Choela say lots wild onions coming up on Shell Creek and was make good eating if you was mix it with hen eggs.

I got one white neighbor that was come over to see me after I was shut up my hogs the other day.

Hotgun was play fiddle more than he was work in his blacksmith shop. I was take him my plow to fix but he was let it stay outside and rust.

Proctor was still like graveyard out in the woods about sundown.

I was to Muskogee before grand jury and they was ask me lots questions, and land buyers want my deed and offer me due bills and things like that.[1] But I shake my head and come home.

Choela was on sick list, but he get off pretty soon, I think. He was lay up and take his own medicine about three weeks maybe. (E-mak-pof-ket).[2]

1. Despite restrictions on the sale of all Creek allotments except those of the deceased, land speculators continued to encumber titles by a system of "leases" that would in effect become bills of sale when a clear title was presented.

2. "Blow in it for him — like making medicine, blowing through a small cane with a hole, into the bucket of medicine." (Translation and explanation by George Bunny.)

Letter No.10

[*Indian Journal*, February 20, 1903]

Although the election of the principal chief would not occur for more than six months, interest in it developed early in 1903 because of its

importance. With allotment in process and statehood apparently imminent, the election would determine who would oversee the dissolution of
the Creek Nation and distribution of its assets. Posey had long been
critical of Chief Pleasant Porter, charging him with dragging his feet on
the delivery of deeds. Here, Fus Fixico criticizes Porter for requiring
Creeks to show identification and to give a receipt on delivery of their
deeds. Posey correctly assumed that Porter would run for reelection and
openly sought an alternative candidate. One potential candidate was
Roley McIntosh, who had served as second chief of the Isparhecher
administration (1895–99). But in an interview for the *Indian Journal* of
January 20, McIntosh had declared that he would not seek public office
again. "I think I can serve my country better by looking after my sofky
patch than running for Chief," he said. Another potential candidate was
Charles Gibson, Posey's longtime friend, whose columns on Creek history, traditional life, culture, and politics appeared in the *Journal* under
the title "Gibson's Rifle Shots."

✍

Well, so I send you some more news to put in Injin Journal.

One Snake Injin he say it was the coldest time he see since he
lay on the ground in the tent when the soldiers was had him
'rested for holding council at Hickory Ground.

Hotgun he say it was get so cold last Sunday night he was had
notion to change his name. I ask him what he call himself then and
he say Blowgun was have more truth to it than Hotgun Sunday
night when the wind was keep on blowing the rags out the cracks
in his cabin.[1] He say he was put near burn all the rails up 'round
his sofky patch and was cover up good with saddle blankets and
wagon sheets and old clothes and things like that and lay right still
'till daylight but was like to freeze to death anyhow and was want
to go to South America all night with Crazy Snake.

Choela's old red rooster was freeze to death on his roost that night, and Choela was stay in bed all day and say it was not day-light yet maybe.

My old filly was had a close call too, but I was had him tied up to south side a hay stack on lots a warm manure and that was save him.

Well, I like to know who we going to had for next chief. I see in Journal Roley say he was tired a running for chief and was going to work.[2] Maybe so he was just say that. Porter was not say nothing yet, but I think he was had his eye on it like buzzard on dead cow in winter time. But I was druther had somebody else for chief. Porter was stay too much in Muskogee and St. Louis and Washington and places like that to make good chief. Injins was not like that. Porter he was send deeds by express like he was not want Injins to had it; or, maybe so, he make you come after it to Muskogee. Injuns was not like that neither. It was cost too much hotel bill to get deeds that way.

I like to know what Charley Gibson say about it next time he was shot his rifle.

1. Posey may have referred to more than simply the blowing wind. Creeks traditionally used blowguns as a hunting instrument.
2. Roley McIntosh.

Letter No.11

[*Indian Journal*, February 27, 1903]

Posey, like many of his fellow Creeks, believed that under the prevailing circumstances, allotment was the best policy for the Creeks. Like others, however, he complained about the bureaucratic policies by which allotment was carried out. Posey made fun of the "rules and regulations" that were steadily issued from the secretary of the interior's office, and he criticized Creek authorities, especially Porter, for cooperating with the secretary. An issue on which most Creeks agreed was that all Creek land should be allotted to Creeks and none reserved for sale to outsiders. On February 20, 1903, Posey's good friend George W. Grayson (Yaha Tustenuggee, or Tustanugga) published a letter in the *Indian Journal*, arguing against the sale of any "surplus" land. Grayson called for strict adherence to the Creek allotment agreement, which reserved no land for sale. Citing what had occurred in the Kiowa and Comanche allotments, he argued that if the Creeks did not allot all lands, "surplus" and mineral lands would be sold to land syndicates. Any "surplus" land should be used, he argued, to equalize the value of allotments.

✍

Well, so that last cold spell was ruin Choela's wild onion crop on Shell Creek bad and make the chickens go out a business laying eggs. So looks like Choela was want a mix onion with eggs too soon and was get left like some Injins at Checotah that was want to go to Muskogee on the flyer after they deeds.[1]

Choela say he think Wacache was try to make it rain in winter time and make a big blizzard out of it. And Hotgun he say maybe so there be lots a drougth [*sic*] next summer 'cause he think Wacache's thunder bullet was freeze up and bust everywhere like firecracker and was no 'count any more for nothing.[2]

Well, I was like to read what Yaha Tustanugga[3] say in Journal last week 'bout surplus land what the white man was had his eye on long time. They is lots a good land like that and Injins ought a grab it theyselves 'stead a letting government sell it cheap for spot cash like storekeeper that think he was going get busted.

So I see Charley Gibson was helping Motey Tiger[4] be chief while Porter was gone to Washington again to get secretary Interior make more laws like he makes all time. Guess so Charley and Motey was had good times bogging up in fine carpet and setting 'round smoking and hearing the typewriter fixing up deeds like some old hen that was find a grub worm.

71

1. To go "on the flyer" was to ride the train.

2. Posey had continued to report the activities of Wacache, who had lately made news because of a beating that he received from one of his followers for alienating the effections of the man's wife. See *Indian Journal*, February 13, 1903. "Medicine men" like Wacache kept thunderbolts, or "thunder bullets," as Posey humorously called them, which they used to make rain. In 1900, Posey had told the story of Chalogee, another well-known "medicine man" whose thunderbolts got out of control. See his "Two Famous Prophets," *Twin Territories* 2 (September 1900): 180–82.

3. This is the Creek name for Wolf Warrior (George W. Grayson), a longtime personal friend of Posey's. For Grayson's life up to the allotment period, see W. David Baird, ed., *A Creek Warrior for the Confederacy: The Autobiography of Chief G. W. Grayson* (Norman: University of Oklahoma Press, 1988).

4. Motey Tiger was the second chief of the Creek Nation and would succeed Porter in 1907. Gibson was free with his political advice and often acted as a translator for Creeks who could not speak English.

Letter No. 12

[Indian Journal, March 6, 1903]

For the first time, Fus Fixico turns his criticism on Tams Bixby, the acting chairman of the Dawes Commission, who had a distinct, unreadable signature. Bixby, a native of Virginia, had grown up in Minnesota and in the mid-1880s had entered the newspaper business at Red Wing. He was active in Republican politics, and by virtue of his connection with the party, he was appointed to the Dawes Commission in 1897 and was soon named its chairman. Fus Fixico's criticism of Bixby became more pointed as time passed.

Posey constantly turned his satire to the plight of the conservative Creeks, especially the Snakes, exemplified in this letter by Hotgun and Wacache, who had difficulty adjusting to the changing status of land tenure in the Creek Nation. Though he understood their desires to be rid of the whites or to escape the white world, Posey believed that there would be no place for these Creeks in the new society if they did not change.

✍

Well, so I was had no paper to write news on it hardly this time but some old slick wrapping paper what the clerk was twist up 'round some things I was buy with due bills in Eufaula last Saturday. Maybe so, that kind of paper was no 'count for nothing but kindling, but I was had no other kind a paper except Creek deeds what Chief Porter and Dawes Commission was scribble up signing they names to it, like they was just learning how to make letters so you could read it. They was one name signed to it that was look like a thousand-leg that was freeze to death in winter time. I was show it to some lawyers in Eufaula and they say, maybe so, Tams Bixby was sign his name that way.

Well, so Hotgun was glad his hair was getting long again like before the white man was put him in jail for making too much medicine at Hickory Ground, while them Snake Injins was hold council and talk about what good times they could had in Mexico, or, maybe so, South America. Hotgun he say they was shaved his head like it was some mule's tail and shut him up with bad men in the bull pen.[1] He say they was too much niggers in there and he was not like it 'cause he not Republican.[2]

So Wacache was great prophet and he was told about big flood, like bible people was had to ford in olden times. Wacache he say his old swimming hole was hide everything so you can't see Bald Hill floating 'round in it.[3] And so he was send Hotgun word he was had to go to work and don't quit till he was make a ark and put all Snake Injins in it. Wacache he say Dawes Commission was had to save other Injins like me and Charley Gibson.[4] When Hotgun was got that word from Wacache he give Choela order to make lots a boards to cover his ark with. But Choela was hardly know where to get board timber that was not filed on.[5]

1. On April 11, 1902, Posey had reported Hotgun's return from jail. Hotgun, claiming innocence of conspiracy, had vowed to sue the United States for false imprisonment and for cutting his long hair. See *Indian Journal*, April 11, 1902.

2. Posey editorially depicted the Republican party as the party of the blacks. On March 13, for instance, he wrote, "The Checotah Times is a Republican paper and has appreciative readers in Africa." As the Creek political campaign heated up the following summer, race would become an important issue for him.

3. Bald Hill was the site of the Posey family home, about eight miles northwest of Eufaula. Wacache's home was about five miles beyond that. The biblical reference is to Noah and the flood. See Genesis, chapter 7.

4. These Indians were Creeks who accepted the changes in Creek affairs.

5. Posey refers to lands unclaimed as allotments and containing trees large enough to be sawed into lumber.

Letter No. 13

[*Indian Journal*, March 20, 1903; *Muskogee Evening Times*, March 20, 1903; *Fort Smith Times*, March 25, 1903]

To Posey, spring 1903 was a critical time for the Creeks. As the territorial period drew near an end, the settlement of Creek national affairs was imminent. Among the unfinished business was the Loyal Creek Claim, which had been a thorny matter in Creek-U.S. relations since 1866. In the treaty that concluded the Civil War, the United States had agreed to pay for property lost during the war by Creeks who had remained loyal. Despite Creek persistence in the matter, the claim had remained unsettled until 1903. The allotment agreement of March 8, 1901, had referred it to the U.S. Senate for determination. The Senate had awarded $1.2 million, but the House cut the award by half. The Creeks needed strong leadership. To Posey, the election of the best man for principal chief was critical. He doubted Porter, accusing him, among other things, of being away from the Creek Nation too often. Posey saw some foreboding signs. The Republican party's preference for blacks over Indians, the hint of graft in the reduction of the Loyal Creek Claim, and declining interest in politics among the Creeks suggested that the interests and concerns of old-time Creeks like Choela, Hotgun, and Fus Fixico would become lost in the bureaucratic shuffle.

In the same issue of the *Indian Journal* in which this letter appeared, Posey published an article titled "Choela Is Dead," in which he gave a brief sketch of the medicine man and colorful figure from Shell Creek. It is significant that he ends the letter with reference to Hotgun, who would in time become the central figure of the Fus Fixico letters.

✍

Well, so Chief Porter and Johnny Goat was go see President Rooster Feather in the White House same as Booker D. Washingtub and talk about Royal Creek claim and statehood and things like that.[1] They was stay long time and wait for dinner, like Booker D. Washingtub, but President Rooster Feather was not say "hombux," like he was rather eat with nigger than full-blood Injins.[2] So Chief Porter and Johnny was had to go to National hotel and drink soup instead a wine. And Johnny Goat he was tell Chief Porter he wish he was back home and eat wild onions what his wife was dig up on Little river.[3] And Chief Porter he was tell Johnny Goat he wish he was in Choska bottom or Cane Creek.[4] They was stay in Washington about a month maybe, but they aint do no good look like but have good time. Congress was cut the Royal Creek claim down to nothing, same as Spain.[5] But the Creek treaty was not read that way. Guess so somebody was make big steal. But maybe so that was all right, 'cause anybody do it anyhow that was had a chance.

Well, so they was not much talk about next chief, and it was look like Creek Injins was lost they grip and they suspenders couldn't hold up they breeches. If Chief Porter was not talk good, maybe so he was had a black filly run over him like at a horse round-up.[6] If I was vote for him next time maybe so he was had to give big barbecue and make me superintendent public destruction like Alice Robertson.[7] Maybe I was make big stride with schools, too, and learn Injin boys how to play base ball.[8]

Well, so I was tell you bad news about my old friend Choela. He was gone to be good Injin, like whiteman say when Injin die. It was look like all old Injins die now and make good Injin that way. Maybe so pretty soon Fus Fixico was make good Injin, too.

Well, so I was write you more news like this next time. I was had to go after my plow what Hotgun was let rust so long in his blacksmith shop.

1. John Goat, the Creek delegate to Washington, was from Wewoka District. A member of Tallassee Little River tribal town, he held a number of public offices in the Creek Nation, including chief justice of the supreme court. Creek National Records 28308, 29061, 29090, 29346, 30269, Record Group 75, National Archives, maintained by Oklahoma Historical Society.

2. On October 16, 1901, Roosevelt had dinner with Booker T. Washington at the White House. The event created a public outcry, especially in the South, where it was seen as an endorsement of social equality for blacks. For years the event was blamed for racial conflict by having sowed seeds of social discontent among blacks. See Willard B. Gatewood, Jr., *Theodore Roosevelt and the Art of Controversy: Episodes of the White House Years* (Baton Rouge: Louisiana State University Press, 1970), 32–61. By having Fus Fixico comment on Roosevelt's failure to issue an invitation to dinner ("hombux") to Porter and Goat, Posey called attention, as he often did, to the relationship between the Republican party and blacks.

3. Little River flows southeast and joins the Canadian River south of present-day Holdenville, Oklahoma, in what was formerly the southwestern corner of the Creek Nation. This was the district where Goat resided.

4. Cane Creek, which heads northeast of Okmulgee, joins the Arkansas River near present-day Taft, Oklahoma. Choska is on the east bank of the Arkansas about five miles above the mouth of Cane Creek. This was the region that Porter called home.

5. This may refer to the U.S. government's payment to Spain of a mere $20 million for the Philippines.

6. That is, Chief Porter might be beaten by a dark horse.

7. Alice Mary Robertson (1854–1931) was a native of the Creek Nation and the daughter of well-known missionaries. From 1873 to 1880, she was a clerk in the Office of Indian Affairs in Washington and then served two years as secretary to Richard H. Pratt, superintendent of the Carlisle Indian School. She taught school in the Creek Nation from 1882 until 1900, when she became superintendent of public instruction for the Creek Nation, a position she held until 1905. She was later the postmaster at Muskogee (1905–13), a dairy farmer and businesswoman (1913–21), and a member of Congress from Oklahoma (1921–23). See *Dictionary of American Biography*, ed. Dumas Malone (New York: Charles Scribner's Sons, 1935), 16:20–21.

8. As opposed to traditional ball play. Baseball was quite popular in Indian Territory. Towns like Vinita, Muskogee, and Tulsa organized baseball clubs and played teams from Missouri, Illinois, and elsewhere. See, e.g., *Vinita Weekly Chieftain*, March 10, April 14 and 21, and October 6, 1904. Posey's *Indian Journal* reported the games of Eufaula's team.

Letter No. 14

[*Indian Journal*, March 27, 1903; *Muskogee Evening Times*, March 28, 1903; *Vinita Weekly Chieftain*, April 2, 1903]

In the wake of the successful meeting at Eufaula in late November 1902, the leaders of the Five Civilized Tribes — except the Chickasaws — continued their efforts to achieve separate statehood for Indian Territory. Leadership fell to Green McCurtain, chief of the Choctaws. He circulated a letter to Porter of the Creeks, T. M. Buffington of the Cherokees, and Hulbutta Micco of the Seminoles, calling for another statehood convention. In the early spring of 1903, Posey still favored single statehood for Oklahoma and Indian Territory. He predicted the failure of the separate-statehood movement, which he believed would hold the Indian back economically and thus thwart economic development in the new state. He believed that the political efforts of Porter and others were in part simply posturing aimed at securing political offices for themselves when statehood was finally achieved. He thought that the rank-and-file Indians would see through their "scheme."

In this letter, Fus Fixico makes the first reference to Secretary of the Interior Ethan Allen Hitchcock as "Secretary Itscocked." That name and his reference to the secretary as "the big man at Washington" would become a hallmark of the Fus Fixico letters.

✍

Well so Choctaw Chief, Make Certain, was had a scheme to put Injin Territory together by itself and make a big statehood out of it, like Rhode Island.[1] So he was had his private secretary get his lead pencil out and fix up long letter about it and send it to Chief Porter and Chief Hullbutta and Chief Puffingtown. Maybe so, that letter was take four cents to send it and was make them chief think they was had a new treaty from Secretary Itscocked.

Chief Make Certain he was say in that letter, "Well, so I was thought about statehood so much I can't sleep good hardly, like I was had toothache, or, maybe so young baby that was had the colic in the night. So, I think, it was good scheme to kill lots a beef steers and hold big council and talk about it long time like Crazy Snake. When we meet that way, I think it was all right to have lots a lighthorsemen, so white man be 'fraid to monkey 'round in the brush where we was holding council."[2]

Guess so, Chief Porter and Chief Hullbutta and Chief Puffingtown was all give big grunt when they was read that letter and say it was all right, like good whiskey.

But, like I say all time, fullblood Injin was not want nothing any more but deeds, but seem like big man at Washington and big man in Creek nation was hold him down so he couldn't get it and he was had to trade it out in due bills.

So, I was not worry about being delegate to statehood council 'cause they was nothing to it no how, like Royal Creek claim. So, I think big man in statehood council was just want office, like governor or, maybe so, send him to Washington and make big promise

78

like old Handy Jackson and lie and everything like a yaller dog and no squirrel in the tree.

So I think big Injin chiefs was just want full-blood to turn grind stone so they could whet they old bone ax on it, like Charley Gibson say when he was shot his rifle off.[3] But Fus Fixico was not much good hand to turn grind stone no how. He was druther had Hotgun turn it.

1. One argument against separate statehood for Oklahoma Territory and Indian Territory was that it would create two small states. Replublican Oklahoma Territory opposed the idea largely because Indian Territory would certainly be Democratic and because Oklahoma might possibly lose some ground to the Democrats.

2. Comparing the proposed statehood conference to one of Chitto Harjo's councils of Snakes reflects Posey's belief that the efforts of one group were as impractical as those of the other.

3. Gibson contributed a regular column, titled "Gibson's Rifle Shots," to Posey's *Indian Journal*. The specific article Fus Fixico has in mind here is uncertain. For an extensive bibliography of Gibson's works, see Daniel F. Littlefield, Jr., and James W. Parins, *A Biobibliography of Native American Writers, 1772–1924* (Metuchen, N.J.: Scarecrow Press, 1981), 60–67.

Letters No.15, No.16, and No.17

[No.15: *Indian Journal*, April 3, 1903; *Muskogee Evening Times*, April 6, 1903; *Fort Smith Times*, April 10, 1903. No.16: *Indian Journal*, April 10, 1903; *Twin Territories* 5 (August 1903): 308–9. No.17: *Indian Journal*, April 27, 1903; *Muskogee Evening Times*, April 20, 1903]

Though he did not drop the statehood issue completely, Fus Fixico set it aside and returned to the topic of the approaching election for principal chief. On March 27, Posey published an announcement of Charles Gibson's candidacy, which he endorsed, having long questioned Porter's leadership. He believed that Porter was politically self-serving and too cozy with federal bureaucrats. Like Gibson's other backers, he believed that Gibson could attract the votes of conservative Creeks (whom he called "fullbloods"), blacks, and Creeks of mixed heritage. He wrote in the *Indian Journal* on April 17 that the Creeks admired Porter "for his ability and for the power he can wield in the councils of the Great White Father at Washington" but that they loved Gibson "for his nearness to them and for his absolute honesty and sound manhood." When Porter's backers met at Okmulgee and failed to agree on a running mate, Posey was encouraged that a candidate like Gibson might have a chance of beating the incumbent.

✍ [No.15]

Well, maybe so when big man that was hold office see this he say Fus Fixico was make to [*sic*] much bad talk, like Crazy Snake when he was hold council at Hickory Ground and get put in the bull pen for it. But I was U. S. citizen, same just like Rob It L. Owing, and was had good right to talk all time till I can't help it.[1] The law say this was free country from soon in the morning before you get up till you was pull off your boots and go to bed too lazy to wash your feet off in the wash pan. You was had lots a liberty all kind and it was make no difference to nobody if you was go to police court or maybe so to big camp meeting at Tuskegee in August.[2]

Well, so I read in Injin Journal Charley Gibson was take exercise to run for Creek chief. Maybe so he was make Porter look like he was stand in the big road same as elm stump so wagon was had to go 'round him. All fullblood Injins on Shell creek say they was vote for Charley Gibson, and lots a niggers on Coon creek say they was support him, too, like blackjack posts under a big brush arbor.[3] Hotgun he say he was big friend to Charley Gibson, like Booker D. Washingtub was to President Rooster Feather. Hotgun he say he think Charley could fix up great message to Creek council with lots a hoss sense and fun it, same like "rifle shots" in

Injin Journal. Maybe so, Hotgun say, if white man was vote for Porter, Charley Gibson was stand no show like William J. Bryan.[4]

Well, so I was read Joe Tiger's letter in Injin Journal and think about it like Chief Make Certain was think about making statehood.[5] Look like Creek Injins was pay lots a money to send they children to school. Maybe so they was pay about $80,000 and get busted in nine months. But it was look like Injin can't get education like white man and was make me think about blackjack tree that was stand on the hill all time and don't make no shade. So I was say Creek Injins was better buy barbed wire with that $80,000 and fence in they allotment with it instead a paying it for teachers and superintendents and things like that. Education was not big thing nohow look like, 'cause they was lots a white folks got corn bread, and maybe so biscuit sometime, that was had no education like John D. Bend A. Stick.[6] Sometime Mr. Injin he stay in boarding school till he could touch the pen and then was go home and was had to let his old filly run outside all winter 'cause he don't know how to raise nubbins to feed it.[7]

1. Robert Latham Owen (1856–1947), an enrolled Cherokee of one-sixteenth blood, had taught school in the Cherokee Nation and served as U.S. agent to the Five Civilized Tribes. He studied law and served various tribes as their legal representative in Washington. He helped draft legislation that passed Congress in 1901, conferring citizenship on the Indians of Indian Territory. Owen held extensive banking and real estate investments. He was often in the news because of his speechmaking on various political issues. Owen was politically ambitious. He was a member of the Democratic National Committee (1892–96) and became a U.S. senator from the new state of Oklahoma (1907–25), distinguishing himself as the author of the Federal Reserve Act. See *Who Was Who in America*, 9 vols. to date (Chicago: Marquis — Who's Who, 1942–), 2:408, and Wyatt W. Belcher, "Political Leadership of Robert L. Owen," *Chronicles of Oklahoma* 31 (Winter 1953–54): 361–71.

2. Tuskegee, the tribal town to which Posey belonged, was located eight miles

west of Eufaula. From 1867 on, the Tuskegee Baptist Church was the center of social life for the community.

3. Coon Creek, west and north of Eufaula, empties into the North Canadian River. It was the location of a large Creek freedman settlement, some of whose members, the Graysons, had been the subject of some of Posey's earlier published sketches. Blackjack is a type of scrub oak that grows prolifically in the sandstone hills surrounding Tuskegee.

4. William Jennings Bryan (1860–1925) was the defeated Democratic candidate for president in 1896 and 1900.

5. Joe Tiger's letter appeared in the *Indian Journal* on March 27. He argued that since the allotment deeds had been delivered, there was no reason to delay division of the tribal assets and settlement of Creek affairs. The next few lines of Fus Fixico's letter imply that the tribal assets were being depleted by the bureaucrats, even those in charge of the schools. The money, Fus Fixico suggests, could be better turned to economic improvement.

6. John Downing Benedict (1854–1946), from Indiana, had been involved in education as a teacher and administrator in Illinois for a number of years. He had also served as chancery judge for four years before President William McKinley appointed him, in 1898, as the first superintendent of forest reserves in New Mexico and Arizona territories. After eleven months at that job, he was appointed superintendent of schools for Indian Territory, whose job it was to oversee the transition in education from Indian national control to federal control. He continued in education after Oklahoma statehood. Muriel H. Wright, "John D. Benedict: First United States Superintendent of Schools in Indian Territory," *Chronicles of Oklahoma* 33 (Winter 1955–56): 472–74.

7. To "touch the pen" was to sign one's name. The implication is that the Indians learned enough to sign their names (i.e., sign away their rights or land) but learned nothing practical to help them survive economically.

✍ [No.16]

Well, so President Rooster Feather was go out west 14000 miles to make big talk about good times to farmers that was not plant they corn yet and was in debt for cornbread. Newspaper say he was hired a train and ride in front on the cowcatcher so he could see good and maybe so scare all the game off with his teeth and spectacles, like when he was made a bad break at Spaniards on his bronco.[1]

He was buy a whole lot a tickets cheap and take his friends with him, but they was had to stay 'way behind in the caboose and keep they hands on the brake like they was going down the hill in Arkansas with a ox wagon full a pine knots. People was get together thick at the depot like chinch bugs in a sofky patch and see him go by before they could get they mouth open. When he was get to Chicago they was lots a fellers meet him at depot and whoop keen and put near had a "stomp" dance. They was tell him they was all vote for him like fullbloods vote for Charley Gibson. This was made him feel big sure 'nough like a rooster that was boss of lots a hens by himself. So he was made them long talk in the Ought To Told Them,[2] like Cowee Harjo in the House of Warriors when they was all asleep or maybe so was trying to rustle some "red eye" out in the woods.[3]

President Rooster Feather he was say, "Well, so this was mighty big country to live in and I was like to be president of it all time till I was lost my grip like Aggy'll Not Do of Fullabeans, or maybe so Lilly Suky Annie of Howareyou. They was put near fifty states in it and lot a Injin land yet. We was had better country than anybody and good laws like More Money doctrine. Maybe so if anyone like Rusher was try to take it 'way from us my Rough Riders was fight them till hell froze plum up and then monkey with them some 'round on the ice!"[4]

When President Rooster Feather was made this talk they was all throw up they hats and yakee (all yelling at once)[5] and so he was had to give it up.

Well, must be Chief Porter was sawing lots a wood and say nothing to nobody. Me and Hotgun was listen good long time, but we was hear nobody running for chief but Charley Gibson.

Well, maybe so Chief Make Certain was just made a flash in the dish pan about statehood and they was nothing to it nohow like railroad talk. Maybe so he was better sneak 'way off and lay down like a yaller dog that was get hit on the head with sofky pestle when he was poke his nose in the crackling.[6]

1. Roosevelt's western tour began on April 2 and lasted until June 6. The comment "on his bronco" refers to Roosevelt's days as the leader of the Rough Riders in the Spanish-American War.

2. "Ought To Told Them" is the auditorium.

3. Cowee Harjo was a member of the House of Warriors (1886, 1891, and 1895) and a member of the House of Kings (1887, 1898). Posey was also a member of the House of Warriors in 1895 and served with Cowee Harjo as a delegate to the International Council at Okmulgee in 1896. See Creek National Records 30868, 32468, 32997, 33188, and 33603, Record Group 75, National Archives, maintained by Oklahoma Historical Society, and *Muskogee Phoenix*, July 2, 1896. "Red eye" is whiskey.

4. Fus Fixico parodies Roosevelt's speech at Chicago on April 3, when the president defended his imperialist foreign policy by invoking the Monroe ("More Money") Doctrine. The references to Aggy'll Not Do, Lilly Suky Annie, and Rusher demonstrate the "big stick" policy. Emilio Aguinaldo (1869–1964), of the Philippines, had rebelled against Spanish rule in 1896 and, believing that he would be made president, worked with the American forces during the Spanish-American War. When he realized that the Philippines would not be given independence, he revolted again, but his revolt was crushed by the U.S. army. In 1893 American planters backed by American money had overthrown Queen Lydia Kamekeha Liliuokalani (1838–1917) of Hawaii. The Republic of Hawaii was proclaimed in 1894, and the United States annexed the territory in 1898. After 1900, U.S.-Russian relations had deteriorated, mainly as a result of both nations' policies regarding China.

5. "Yakee" is a form of the plural *yahkvketv*, to shout or whoop.

6. A sofky pestle was a long wooden handle with a cylindrical head, used to pound corn in a large wooden mortar. Crackling was the solid residue after pieces of hog fat had been cooked and lard rendered from them. Crackling was sometimes eaten like commercially prepared pork rinds are today and was sometimes added to bread dough in preparation for baking.

✍ [No.17]

Well, so it's look like Chief Porter was done had his day in Creek politics and was had to go way off out a sight till he gets over it. His boomers was had a convention at Okmulgee to nominate his partner but they was all come back home like they been in a blizzard up in Klondike.[1] They was nobody there hardly but Johnny Goat and he was done voted 'cause he was had his tail up all time.[2] Chepahny Sopuckhutke and Billy Make Combs[3] was there but they get too lonesome and was glad to get on they 600-pound fillies and light a shuck for Eufaula[4] where Charley Gibson's boom for chief was 96 in the shade and going up higher like a grey squirrel in a water oak tree on Deep Fork late in the evening. They was another fellow there — Albert Gallop — but he was get no vote to be Porter's partner.[5] Maybe so politics was not make a stranger sleep with you.[6]

So it's look like Chief Porter was lose ground bad like coyote when grey hounds was after him on the prairie. Maybe so he was had to drop his wad and give up the ghost. He was too big any way for Creek chief, but maybe so he was make a good senator to Washington like old Matthew Whey[7] when Chief Make Certain was made a big statehood out of Injin Territory.

1. The Klondike River is a tributary of the Yukon in northwest Canada. It was the site of extensive gold mining in the early years of the century.

2. Posey reported on April 17 that only eighteen Creeks gathered at the "convention." The reference to Goat's tail is unclear. A raised tail in animals such as goats and deer usually indicates excitement or alertness.

3. Chepahny (boy or little boy) Sopuckhutke (gray), or "gray boy," may have been an elaborate pun for "gray son," or Posey's friend G. W. Grayson. William McCombs (1844–1929), a well-known Baptist minister from Tuskegee, had held a number of posts in the Creek national government. See "Reverend William McCombs," *Chronicles of Oklahoma* 8 (March 1930): 137–40. His wife's father, Takosar Harjo, was a brother of Posey's grandfather, Pahosa Harjo Phillips.

4. To "light a shuck" is to leave in a hurry.

5. Albert Pike McKellop (1858–1907) had served as clerk of the House of Warriors, tax collector, member of the board of examiners for teachers, delegate to Washington, secretary to Chief Legus C. Perryman, and in other positions in Creek government. He had served briefly as secretary to Chief Porter before becoming attorney for the nation at the Dawes Commission. See D. C. Gideon, *The Indian Territory* (New York: Lewis Publishing Co., 1901), 344–49, and *Muskogee Times-Democrat*, February 2, 1907.

6. The well-known statement "Politics make strange bedfellows" was first used by Charles Dudley Warner in *My Summer in a Garden* (1871).

7. To "drop his wad" means to lose or quickly spend one's money; to "give up the ghost" could mean to die or simply to quit or give up. Hence Posey felt Porter should perhaps give up the race for chief and wait to run for senator from the new state. Saying that he was "too big" for the job may refer not only to his political ambition but also to his size. He was a portly man. Matthew Stanley Quay (1833–1904) was U.S. senator from Pennsylvania.

Letter No.18

[Indian Journal, April 24, 1903]

Having accepted during his teenage years the inevitability of allotment, Posey had embraced the concept of economic, social, and political progress in the sense that Americans understood it at the time. He believed that the Creeks' survival in the twentieth century depended on their ability to join the "march" of progress, and he had made his *Indian Journal* an instrument for boosting Eufaula and the surrounding region. However, not all that came with progress was good. Allotment regulations established by the "Big Man" (Hitchcock) would inevitably lead to graft. Also, the more conservative Creeks, represented by such men as Hotgun and Chitto Harjo (Crazy Snake), were being left behind or pushed aside. Official efforts to force assimilation, represented by such policies as cutting the Indians' hair and changing their names, were not working. Many Creeks had refused to file for allotments, and some found their homesites filed on by more progressive Creeks, whom Posey personified as "half-breeds" or whites who had "rights." In earlier brief editorial statements, Posey had presented the conservatives as impediments to progress or as unfortunate social by-products. In a letter to the *Journal*, his fellow Creek and good friend George W. Grayson (Yaha Tustenuggee, or Wolf Warrior) had criticized the press, and therefore Posey, for lauding allotment and progress and had warned about the potential cost to the Creeks. This Fus Fixico letter was probably in response to Grayson's.

✍

Well, so Big Man at Washington was made another rule like that one about making the Injin cut his hair off short like a prize fighter or saloon keeper.[1] Big Man he was say this time the Injin was had to change his name just like if the marshal was had a writ for him. So, if the Injin's name is Wolf Warrior, he was had to call himself John Smith, or maybe so Bill Jones, so nobody else could get his mail out of the postoffice.[2] Big Man say Injin name like Sitting Bull or Tecumseh was too hard to remember and don't sound civilized like General Cussed Her or old Grand Pa Harry's Son.[3]

Hotgun he say the Big Man's rule was heap worse than allotment, and Crazy Snake he say he was hear white man say all time you could take everything away from a him but you couldn't steal his good name.[4]

Guess so that was all right 'cause they was nothing to a name nohow if you can't borrow some money on it at the bank. Tookpafka Micco he say he was druther had a deed to his land than a big name in the newspaper. When I ask him what he do after he sell his land, he say he don't know, like Bob Ingersoll.[5] Then he say he was let the future take care of its own self like a calf when it was get too old to suck. Guess so Tookpafka Micco was made up his mind to drink sofky and eat sour bread and be glad like a young cat with a ball a yarn before the fire place in the winter time.

Well, so we hear lots a talk about big progress in Creek nation and read about it in the newspaper before breakfast time. They was good news all time about long stride and development and things like that till you can't make a crop and get out of the hole if you was try to hear all of it.[6] Hotgun he say he think he was had to put beeswax in his ears like Few Leases (Ulysses) in olden time.[7]

But look like you don't hear nothing about fullblood Injins 'way back behind the hills that was had they sofky patch and cabin on land that was done filed on by some half-breed or maybe so white man that was had a right. We don't hear nothing about them kind a Injin at all. But we hear all time about some fellow that was find a coal mine with a post auger, or maybe so some other fellow that was strike oil that was shoot up like a squirrel gun soon as he touch it.

Must be the Big Man that was look out for Injin was look out for himself too much. Hotgun he say it was natural for the Big Man to do that way 'cause he was had the chance. Maybe so, Hotgun he say, that was the only law civilized man don't want to break.

---

1. It was common practice for authorities to cut the long hair of Indian prisoners, in part to humiliate them. In 1902 the commissioner of Indian affairs had issued a directive to school officials to cut the long hair of Indian children in federal schools. See "Cutting Indians' Hair," *Harper's Weekly* 46 (March 22, 1902): 357. Posey had witnessed the effects of such policy on the followers of Chitto Harjo, who had been captured and jailed for quite some time in the spring of 1902. Hotgun, according to Posey, had threatened to sue the United States for cutting his hair. *Indian Journal*, March 7 and April 11, 1902.

2. Indian agency officials had been encouraged since 1890 to change Indians' names, which were "incompatible" with the Anglo-American naming system. At the urging of Hamlin Garland and others, Secretary Hitchcock issued a circular

on December 1, 1902, calling for giving each member of a family the same surname. Under this regulation, efforts were made to rename whole tribes. See Daniel F. Littlefield, Jr., and Lonnie E. Underhill, "Renaming the American Indian: 1890–1913," *American Studies* 12 (Fall 1971): 33–45.

3. Sitting Bull (1834?–1890) was a Sioux leader who figured prominently in Custer's defeat in 1876. Tecumseh (1768?–1813) was a Shawnee leader who worked for Indian unity against the whites. George Armstrong Custer (1839–1876), a veteran of several Indian campaigns, led the Seventh U.S. Cavalry into history at the Little Bighorn on June 25, 1876. William Henry Harrison (1773–1841), the ninth president of the United States, became popular as the Indian fighter whose forces defeated the Indians under Tecumseh and Shawnee Prophet at Tippecanoe in 1811. See *Who Was Who in America*, Historical Volume, 200, 306–7.

4. "But he that filches from me my good name / Robs me of that which not enriches him, / And makes me poor indeed" (William Shakespeare, *Othello*, 3:3, 1.155).

5. As a student at Bacone Indian University, Posey had become an admirer of Robert Green Ingersoll (1833–1899), a well-known agnostic writer and lecturer, whose works helped shape Posey's own religious skepticism. Posey's poem "Ingersoll" (ca. 1899), reads, "Words drop from his eloquent lips / Like music from the golden lyre / Swept by Apollo's finger tips / When love and the fireside inspire." See item 4026.8268, Alexander L. Posey Collection, Thomas Gilcrease Institute of American History and Art, Tulsa, Oklahoma.

6. In other words, one could not make a living or get out of debt.

7. In Book 12 of Homer's *Odyssey*, Circe instructs Odysseus to fill his crew's ears with wax and to have his crew tie him to the mast of his ship when they sail near the land of the Sirens, for those who hear the Sirens' song will be enchanted and never return home.

Letters No.19, No.20, and No.21

[No.19: *Indian Journal*, May 1, 1903; *Muskogee Evening Times*, May 2, 1903; excerpted, *Fort Smith Times*, May 7, 1903; excerpted, *South McAlester Capital*, May 21, 1903. No.20: *Indian Journal*, May 8, 1903; *Muskogee Evening Times*, May 9, 1903; *Kansas City Journal*, May 11, 1903; *Fort Smith Times*, May 15, 1903; *Claremore Messenger*, June 5, 1903.

The Fus Fixico Letters

No.21: *Indian Journal*, May 15, 1903; *South McAlester Capital*, May 21, 1903; *Tahlequah Arrow*, May 23, 1903]

Secretary Hitchcock decided to visit Indian Territory in early May 1903, believing that a visit might help accelerate the complex work of winding up tribal affairs. At first, he expected his arrival at Muskogee on May 7 to be accompanied by the usual fanfare. Then he instructed Assistant Secretary Thomas Ryan to request that Tams Bixby keep the reception low-key. To Fus Fixico and his friends, these arrangements reflected the secretary's indecisiveness. The Creeks also found the brevity of his visit typical of federal bureaucrats and legislators who made short visits to Indian Territory and, without taking time to consult the rank-and-file citizens, determined what legislation or policy was "best" for the territory. Chief Pleasant Porter asked Posey and G. W. Grayson to accompany him and Hitchcock in the secretary's private railroad car from Muskogee to Okmulgee. Despite the secretary's protests that he wanted no fanfare, crowds gathered at towns along the track. At Boynton, east of Okmulgee, the people turned out with a brass band, but the train roared through without slowing down, the people not getting so much as a glimpse of Hitchcock. In reporting Hitchcock's visit, Fus Fixico comments also on the growing tensions between Russia and China, the weather, statehood, and potential candidates for Creek chief, the latter two being issues of ongoing concern for his readers.

✍ [No.19]

Well, so Secretary It's Cocked was made up his mind to see what's the matter down here in Injin Territory. So he was had Tom Ryan run to the depot and send a message to Tams Big Pie that was read this way: "Well, so you must had a cab wait for me at the Katy[1] when I was get off of the Pullman in Muskogee. Maybe so I was come there in the night, or after sunup in the morning, or twelve o'clock in the day time. You must had a brass band there, too, and some feller to make big talk, just the same like I was a editor of a newspaper that was printed in the country. Maybe so I was stayed down there twenty-four hours and fixed up everything all right so you think you was had a soft snap."[2]

When I was tell Hotgun about it he say, "Well, so Secretary It's Cocked was had a good time in Muskogee, 'cause Muskogee was does things right and the flyer was stop there all the time."

Then Hotgun he say, "A ticket to Muskogee was like a bird in the hand and was worth two to Denison or Fort Smith."[3]

Tookpafka Micco he was say, "Maybe so the Big Man from Washington was just come down here to see 'cause he was from Missouri."[4]

Well, so Rush Her was had it in for Chiny like the Mad Mule over in Africky was had it in for John Bull.[5]

Rush Her was wrote a note to Chiny and say, "Well, so you was had to go somewhere else and eat rats."

When G. Pan and old John Bull[6] and President Rooster Feather was heard about it they was all get mad like hornets that was had a nest hanging in the woods. So they was send word to Rush Her he was had to left the door open in Chiny so they could get in and help they selves too.

Hotgun he say, "Maybe so Rush Her was act that way 'cause Chiny was get too old to fight."

Well, so I think Charley Gibson was run like a deer in the lane for chief. Everybody was want him for next chief except some that was want to be chief they selves.[7]

Well, so lots a fellers was ask me, "Why don't you talk good English," and was made me think of a story I hear about two Irishmen that was want to do a piece a business at the blacksmith shop in the United States. They couldn't find the blacksmith so they was go to his house and ask his wife, "Is the blacksmith shop in here?" "No," the woman say, "the blacksmith shop was over there." Then the Irishman say, "Well, maybe so we was had to let some body get in front that could talk good English."

1. Tams Big Pie is Tams Bixby; the Katy is the Missouri, Kansas, and Texas (MK&T) Railroad.

2. Posey had made fun of the politicians who made quick tours "to see what's the matter down here in Injin Territory" in "O, Oblivion!" —his first poem to gain much public attention.

3. Denison, a town in Texas, was across the Red River from Durant, Choctaw Nation; Fort Smith, Arkansas, was on the Arkansas River where it crossed the Arkansas–Cherokee Nation boundary. "A bird in the hand is worth two in the bush" (Cervantes, *Don Quixote*, pt. 1, bk. iv, ch. 4).

4. Hitchcock's home was in St. Louis. In subsequent months there were hints, made publicly, that he was connected to St. Louis businessmen who had interests in Indian Territory.

5. In the closing years of the nineteenth century, the United States had become concerned that European powers were carving out "spheres of influence" in China. Afraid of losing its commercial interests and concerned about the division of the Chinese Empire, the United States persuaded Great Britain, France, Italy, Germany, Russia, and Japan to agree to an "Open Door" policy, which stated that no nation could interfere with the commercial interests of other nations operating within its "sphere of influence." After the Boxer Rebellion of 1900 failed to oust the foreigners from China, tensions between powers began to build again, leading to the outbreak of the Russo-Japanese War in 1904. The United States persuaded the two nations to honor the neutrality of China and warned France and Germany not to assist Russia, in which case the United States would join Japan. In his May 8, 1903, *Indian Journal*, Posey predicted the war and anticipated the potential alliance of the United States with Japan: "Russia appears to be hunting for trouble in China, and Japan seems willing to help her find it. It's dollars to doughnuts that the little Jap makes the Big Bear look like thirty cents before the third round is called."

British influence had grown steadily for a number of years in North Africa when Abdul Aziz IV came to the throne in Morocco in 1894. He was friendly with Britain, given to European tastes, and spent lavishly. Meanwhile, the British influence increased. In the winter of 1902–3, a revolt occurred under the leadership of Mulai Ahmed-es-Raisuli, a sharif in the district of Tangier. His revolt was

perhaps less against the British influence than against the taxes levied to re-
plenish the royal treasury, which Abdul Aziz had squandered. See, e.g., *New York
Times*, January 2, 1903, 5:3, January 3, 1903, 9:1, and April 23, 1903, 2:1.

6. Japan and England.

7. According to Posey's *Indian Journal* of May 1, Gibson had strong support
among most classes of Creek society.

🖎 [No.20]

Well, so Hotgun he say he wake up and didn't had no greens to
eat except poke leaves.[1] The frost was left nothing in his sofky
patch but crab grass and his one-horse plow and a set a chain
harness. But Hotgun he say he was glad it wasn't a cyclone.

Well, so I like to know what kind a man Secretary It's Cocked is
anyhow. Look like he didn't had no safety notch and couldn't
stood cocked. He was change his mind every time before he get it
made up good. When he do anything he acts like he was sorry and
take it back after it's too late in the day. So he was had Tom Ryan
change the message he was sent to Tams Big Pie and say, "Well, so
I don't want no monkey business when I get off of the train in
Muskogee. I don't want to hear no brass band playing Dixie or big
talk about statehood and things like that. So you must stay in your
office and work same as a beaver instead hanging up flags and
running down to depot to see if it's train time yet; so when I come
there sure enough the people wont think Ringling Brothers was in
town to give a show."

When I was told Hotgun about it he say, "Well, so I don't see
how Secretary It's Cocked catch on to anything down here if he
don't get out with the boys and had a good time and get acquainted."

Well, so I think Dennis Flynn was smarter man than Rob It
Owing, 'cause he make a stride sometimes and show he wasn't
stood still and study about the same thing all time.[2] Dennis Flynn

93

was change his mind for one statehood, but Rob It Owing was want two statehood like he say ten years ago and was made me think about a poker player that was stood pat on two dueces and nothing to nigger with.

Well, so I see in the newspapers they was lots a candidates for Creek chief 'sides Pleas Porter and Charley Gibson and Legus Perryman and Yaha Tustanuggee.³ But I think it was laid between Yaha and Charley 'cause they get all the Injin votes and was left nothing for Pleas and Legus but niggers to vote for them and maybe so a few half breeds that was hungry for pie.

Hotgun he don't care much for politics like in olden times when he could get on the jury and draw $1.50 a day for three weeks, or maybe so be lighthorse captain and have lots a prisoners to hoe in his sofky patch for nothing and get paid for feeding them on apusky and sour bread.⁴

1. Pokeweed (*Phytolacca americana*) is a wild herb that is cooked and eaten in early spring. In the week before this letter appeared, the Eufaula area had experienced a late heavy frost that devastated the vegetable gardens. *Indian Journal*, May 8, 1903.

2. Dennis Thomas Flynn (1861–1939) was a native of Pennsylvania. After a newspaper career in Iowa and Kansas and service as postmaster and city attorney at Kiowa, Kansas, he was aboard the first train into Oklahoma Territory when it was opened to non-Indian settlement on April 22, 1889. Flynn had previously argued for the admission of Oklahoma Territory as a state and the later addition of Indian Territory to it when the people were ready for statehood. He later advocated admission of both territories simultaneously as a single state, a position Posey had long supported. See *Who Was Who in America*, 1:408; *Muskogee Daily Phoenix*, April 24, 1903; and Victor Murdock, "Dennis T. Flynn," *Chronicles of Oklahoma* 18 (June 1940): 107–13. Only a week before this letter appeared, Posey had made a similar attack on Robert L. Owen's stubbornness in maintaining his stand for separate statehood for Indian Territory. "Robert L. Owen breaks loose in another interview and springs that old chestnut about double statehood, though even Chitto Harjo changed his mind on that proposition long ago." *Indian Journal*, May 1, 1903.

3. Posey wanted a candidate who would give Porter some opposition. He had attacked Porter because of the chief's handling of the allotment deeds and support for the separate-statehood effort. He opposed Legus Perryman, the former chief who had been impeached for corruption in 1895. Fus Fixico's comment about Perryman's and Porter's followers may have been an intentional racial slam, for both had African as well as Creek ancestry.

4. Before the United States assumed control of judicial matters in the Creek Nation, jurors received subsistence pay for their service as jurors. The Creek Nation had no jails; thus the captain of the lighthorse, the nation's law enforcers, kept prisoners under guard while they awaited trial. It was common for the captains to use prisoners as laborers to hoe in the corn (sofky) patches or do other work. Posey's father had been a member of the lighthorse police in the late 1860s and served as captain in Eufaula District in the early 1880s. The elder Posey's descendants claimed that he used prisoners as laborers on his farm. See Jones Gladstone Emery, *Court of the Damned: Being a Factual Story of the Court of Judge Isaac C. Parker and the Life and Times of the Indian Territory and Old Fort Smith* (New York: Comet Press Books, 1959), 183–84. Emery was Alex Posey's nephew.

✍ [No.21]

Well, so Secretary It's Cocked and Chief Porter and Yaha Tustanuggee and Chinnubbie Harjo[1] was ride together to Okmulgee and held a big pow wow in fine private car that was belong to A. Tall Bush who was get rich off of Bud Wiser in St. Louis.[2] "But," Hotgun he say, "maybe so they didn't had nothing to drink but water in the ice tank."

Charley Gibson he was had invitation to get in the swim too, but he couldn't change his jeans before train time and was get left. Then he didn't had no loose change in his pocket except some due bills.

Well, so when Chief Porter was introduce Yaha Tustanuggee and Chinnubbie Harjo, Secretary It's Cocked he say, "Well, so I was mighty glad to shake hands with you Injins. So you must sit down just the same like you was at home and don't be 'fraid of the conductor 'cause you didn't had no ticket to Okmulgee."[3]

When I was told Hotgun about it he say he was druther laid down on the cushion and wallowed on it like a work pony when you was take the harness off of him at dinner time.

Tookpafka Micco he say he don't know how he spit in a fine private car like that and maybe so was had to swallow his tobabco [*sic*] just the same as chewing gum.

While the special train was running like a grey hound after a jack rabbit through the prairie close to Boynton, Secretary It's Cocked he was looked out of the window like he was seed something mighty curious and say, "Well, so what's that out there?" And Yaha Tustanuggee he say, "Well, so that's a frame house with a side room to it. The white man was build it on the lease what he get from the Injin. We got lots a them kind a houses and that show we was made big stride in progress."[4]

Then the Big Man from Washington was put near bit his cigar in two and say, "Well, so it's only a shack. I was druther had a dugout or maybe so a wagon sheet to live in. When I get back to Washington I was made some strong rules and regulations against that kind a thing on Injin land."[5]

But Hotgun he say, "Maybe so Secretary It's Cocked was out a humor 'cause he didn't run onto some wigwams."

Tookpafka Micco he say he was thought all the time a box house with a side room to it was more respectable and civilized than log huts 'cause that's the only kind a house white people was stuck on.

Well, so pretty soon the special train was whistled and Secretary It's Cocked and Chief Porter and Yaha Tustanuggee and Chinnubbie Harjo was looked back and seed a yaller depot and lots a fellers throwing up they hats like they won on a horse race, and the Big Man from Washington he say, "Well, so what's that again?"

And Chief Porter he say, "Must be that's Boynton."[6]

Then the Big man he say, "Well, so it's looked like all the towns down here in Injin Territory was onto me."

When the special was get in sight of Okmulgee the boomers was run 'long side of it till it stop and then they was take the Big Man away from Chief Porter and Yaha Tustanuggee and Chinnubbie Harjo, and they was had to pay they way back to Muskogee in the smoker.[7]

1. The last two were G. W. Grayson and Posey.

2. Adolphus Busch, the beer magnate, was a St. Louis friend of Hitchcock's.

3. Hitchcock was apparently condescending. According to Grayson, he was interested to find in Posey an Indian who was also an editor. He made suggestions to Posey concerning what the editor should try to teach his readers through the paper. See G. W. Grayson, "With Secretary Hitchcock," *Indian Journal*, May 15, 1903.

4. Allotment leases executed for five years required that the lessee improve the property by building a permanent residence on the land. At the expiration of the lease, the improvements became the property of the Indian. The flimsy shacks with siderooms were commonly erected by lessees. According to Grayson, Hitchcock was outraged and said that such structures did not fulfill the contracts.

5. On May 1, Posey had predicted that Hitchcock's visit would result in his issuing more "rules and regulations."

6. Grayson described the train's passage through Boynton, where a large crowd awaited the secretary, as "meteoric"; he caught only "three notes from the horns of the brass band."

7. Grayson and Posey actually spent the day with Hitchcock and accompanied him on his tour of Okmulgee before returning to Muskogee.

Letter No. 22

[*Indian Journal*, May 22, 1903; *Muskogee Evening Times*, May 23, 1903; *Kansas City Journal*, May 25, 1903; *Fort Smith Times*, June 2, 1903; *Claremore Messenger*, June 5, 1903]

In March, the Choctaw chief Green McCurtain had addressed a letter to the executives of the other Civilized Tribes to meet in Eufaula to plan a constitutional convention for Indian Territory. Strong in his support for single statehood for Oklahoma Territory and Indian Territory, Posey had predicted failure for the plan because, he said, it excluded participation by whites, without whom statehood could not be achieved. During the spring, the single-statehood movement flagged, and the double-statehood movement gathered strength. By the time the delegates convened on May 21, Posey had switched sides. Besides McCurtain, the chiefs who attended were Porter of the Creeks, Hulbutta Micco of the Seminoles, Thomas Buffington of the Cherokees, and Palmer Mosely of the Chickasaws. In addition to Porter, the Creeks were represented by Cheesie McIntosh, Lawyer Deere, and Posey, who served as secretary of the convention. Among other points, the delegates called for a constitutional convention of Indians and one of whites and the subsequent appointment of a committee from each group to work out differences in constitutional issues. On May 22, Posey called McCurtain a "wise and far seeing statesman." If his plan succeeded, the Eufaula convention would go down in history as the beginning of a great movement of which McCurtain would be the hero. What swayed Posey was probably the Indian leaders' recognition that any statehood plan must include the white residents of the territory. In the May 22 *Indian Journal*, Posey also wrote, "Our friend Fus Fixico of Shell Creek attended the Indian convention and was a close observer and patient listener."

✍

Well, so Chief Make Certain and Chief Porter and Chief Hulbutta and Chief Puffingtown and Chief Mostly was hold big pow wow in Eufaula this week about double statehood and talk long time like making a horse trade on Sunday. They was fetched lots a delegates 'long to give it a big send off like at a funeral. But I don't know none a them but Cheesie Mac Aint Flush, who was smart enough to fix up everything by hisself 'sides looking after boarding schools in Creek nation and telling the boys they must develop they head in the school room instead they muscle on the base ball ground.[1]

Chief Make Certain he say, "Well, so I was had you all meet here to find out if it was better to stay in the frying pan or maybe so jump out in the fire and get burned up or had the fat all fried out of us so we couldn't make soap grease.[2] Oklahoma was had its mind made up to file on us for a pasture and I think it was time to raise a big kick like a mule that don't want to pull the load up the hill all by itself."

Then Chief Puffingtown he say, "Well, so I was seed where you was had to keep your powder dry."

And Chief Porter he say, "Me too."

And Chief Mostly he say, "Well, so I was made a second to the motion."

And Chief Hulbutta he just give a big grunt like a hog in the middle a the nest in a snow storm.

Then the delegates was all raise they hands and Chief Make Certain he say, "Well, so its carried."

When I was told Hotgun about it he say if they didn't had no saloons in double statehood he was druther be tacked onto Oklahoma so he wouldn't had to drink busthead and get put in the calaboose for being sick on the street.

And Tookpafka Micco he say if they was made a double statehood out of Injin Territory they better had Bud Wiser than Choctaw beer, or maybe so Old Crow than Peruna.[3]

Then Chief Make Certain he go on and say, "Well, so I think it was mighty good idea to hold another big convention and make a strong constitution and send word to our renters to come and join in like at a log rolling.[4] That way I think Injins and white men learn to work together with the double statehood band wagon."

99

Then one Republican delegate he say, "Well, so what we do with the nigger?"

And Chief Make Certain he say, "Well, so I think you was out of order, 'cause no body was had a picnic in double statehood but Democrats."[5]

This was made everybody laugh so it was put near broke up the meeting.

So they powwowed a long time about double statehood and wind up in a dispute about what name to give it. Chief Make Certain he say, "Let's call it Thomas Jefferson," but all the others want some Injin name that was had more poetry in it.[6]

But Hotgun he say he don't care what they call it so they was not name it after somebody that was sign his name like Tams Big Pie.[7]

1. Albert Gallatin (Cheesie) McIntosh (1848–?), son of Daniel N. McIntosh, the well-known leader of the Confederate Creek faction, was educated in Texas. He left Indian Territory in 1874 and lived for many years in Tennessee before returning to the Creek Nation about 1901. See John Bartlett Meserve, "The MacIntoshes," *Chronicles of Oklahoma* 10 (September 1932): 324. McIntosh was serving as superintendent of public instruction for the Creek Nation in 1903. Fus Fixico's play on his name has several implications. In building terms, two pieces of material that do not fit together evenly are not flush. People who have no ready money are not flush. In poker, if a player is drawing to a flush and fails to receive the proper card, his hand is worthless; of course, he may bluff. But not being flush suggests that something is amiss. Perhaps Fus Fixico is referring to McIntosh's having lived in Tennessee under an alias for twenty-five years, in effect having a secret identity.

2. Jumping out of the frying pan and into the fire presents a dilemma. Neither situation is pleasant, but the latter may be more disastrous than the former.

3. That is, it was better to have legal sales of alcoholic beverages than the illegal sale of homemade drinks like Choctaw beer or patent medicines like Peruna, which had a high alcohol content and was dispensed through drugstores. The delegates to the Eufaula convention drafted a strong Prohibitionist article in their resolutions. Unlike the delegates, Hotgun and Tookpafka Micco found

open saloons a point in favor of joint statehood with Oklahoma, where legalized drinking was favored. Perhaps they were simply realists. Alcoholic beverages were illegal in Indian Territory in 1903, but they were easily obtained. Even the opponents of separate statehood granted that the Prohibitionist stand would garner support for the Indian statehood movement. See, e.g., *Indian Journal*, May 29, 1903.

4. This refers to the proposed dual constitutional conventions of Indians and whites.

5. One reason the Republican administrations of McKinley and Roosevelt and Republicans in Congress opposed separate statehood for Indian Territory was that it would, from all indications, be a Democratic state. Fus Fixico, in strong racist overtones, identifies the Republicans with black interests and anticipates the race issue that would be important in the establishment of Oklahoma as a state.

6. In the winter of 1901–2, proposed legislation known as the Moon bill had been introduced in Congress, organizing Indian Territory as the Territory of Jefferson. Posey had argued that the name was not distinctive enough and that it should, instead, be an Indian name. *Indian Journal*, March 7 and 14, 1902. It was reported later that Hampton Tucker, a Choctaw delegate to the Eufaula meeting, had proposed the name Jefferson. *Indian Journal*, May 29, 1903.

7. In Letter No. 12, Fus Fixico had made fun of Bixby's signature, which was distinctive though decidedly illegible.

Letters No. 23, No. 24, and No. 25

[No. 23: *Indian Journal*, May 29, 1903; *Tahlequah Arrow*, June 6, 1903; *Kansas City Journal*, June 8, 1903; *Fort Smith Times*, July 3, 1903. No. 24: *Indian Journal*, June 5, 1903; *Vinita Daily Chieftain*, June 6, 1903; *Tahlequah Arrow*, June 3, 1903; *Cherokee Advocate*, June 13, 1903; excerpt, *Claremore Progress*, June 20, 1903. No. 25: *Indian Journal*, June 12, 1903; *Muskogee Evening Times*, June 12, 1903; *Fort Smith Times*, June 15, 1903; *South McAlester Capital*, June 18, 1903; *Cherokee Advocate*, June 20, 1903]

After Secretary Hitchcock's visit and the successful convention at Eufaula, it appeared to the separate-state proponents that their movement might succeed. By the end of May, Posey was firmly in their camp. The change was evident in his newspaper. On June 5, he quoted a fellow journalist's comment about his new stand on statehood: "Brer Posey of the Indian Journal has about reached the conclusion that — 'Well, maybe so, that's purty good idee, after all.' " Perhaps, like Hotgun, he had first supported single statehood because he had no straw to grasp until Hitchcock and Chief McCurtain made a "raft" to ride on. Whereas Hotgun and Tookpafka Micco had earlier favored joint statehood with Oklahoma because of its legal liquor sales, they now turned against any association with Oklahoma because of what they considered its unappealing weather and topography. Local interest in the statehood question waxed and waned with the debate in Congress. As interest waned in the late spring, the single statehood movement seemed to stall. Although C. E. Castle of Wagoner called for a convention of single-staters to meet at Shawnee, Oklahoma Territory, in late June, Fus Fixico and his friends depicted them as indecisive fence sitters who were waiting to see which statehood movement offered them the best opportunity to gain political office. The meeting that Hotgun and Tookpafka Micco refer to was held at South McAlester to elect delegates to Shawnee. It was so poorly attended, Posey wrote on July 3, that they had to call in a local newspaper editor who supported separate statehood for Indian Territory to act as secretary. As the statehood debate waned, Hotgun turned his attention to other issues: the approaching Creek election, in which not only Pleasant Porter and Charles Gibson but also G. W. Grayson, Legus Perryman, and Chitto Harjo were discussed as candidates; the Loyal Creek payment, which had been a thorny problem in Creek-U.S. relations and Creek politics since the close of the Civil War; and the efforts of Frank C. Hubbard, who was commissioned to raise funds to build the Indian Territory exhibit at the Louisiana Purchase Exposition in St. Louis in 1904.

✒ [No.23]

Well, so Hotgun he say he was for double statehood, 'cause they was too much long-tailed cyclones out in Oklahoma and people was had to live right close to a hole in the ground like prairie dogs to keep out a they way. Hotgun he say he was not used to that kind a living and was get too old to learn to act like a prairie dog. Then he say sometime the people what had a hole in the ground was not out a danger, 'cause the rivers out in Oklahoma had no banks to um and was spread out all over the country when they get up, like maple syrup on a hot flapjack. He say he was druther be where he was had a show for his life.

Then Tookpafka Micco he say Hotgun aint told half of it, 'cause out in Oklahoma they was had a drought in the summer time and hard times in the fall, 'sides blizzards in the winter time and cyclones with long tails in the spring.[1] Tookpafka Micco was mighty bitter and he say he was druther had a sofky patch in Injin Territory than a big county full a debt and chinch bugs in Oklahoma. He say he's glad he wasn't a delegate to the powwow what Chief Make Certain was pulled off in Eufaula[2] 'cause he might got arrested for slander against Oklahoma.

Then Hotgun he say they was no one want to be spliced onto Oklahoma but some thumb papers that was printed out in the country and didn't had no circulation except when they was being printed.[3] He say he was for single statehood long time, 'cause he didn't see no other straw to grab at. But now, Hotgun he say, Secretary It's Cocked and Chief Make Certain was made a good raft to ride on and prospects was bright like a new tin pan for double statehood.

Well, so Creek politics was getting warm like hot tamale and candidates for chief was thick like fleas under a pole cabin in the summer time, or maybe so bed bugs in a dollar day hotel when you blow the light out. Some fellers that was call they selves the Union party was fixing to hold big convention up to Okmulgee putty soon to see how many want to run against Charley Gibson for chief.[4] Charley was fixing to had a convention on Flat Rock, maybe so he could had a good foundation to start on.[5] Chief Porter was had his convention 'bout a year ago, and Hotgun he say maybe so he was trying to fudge.

1. In an editorial statement on June 5, Posey pointed out that Indian Territory was not a semiarid region like Oklahoma and was not subject to blizzards and hot winds. *Indian Journal*, June 5, 1903.

2. The "powwow" was the separate-statehood convention that had met a week earlier.

3. That is, there was no circulation except when the press cylinders were turning.

4. The Union party was formed at Okmulgee on May 20. Eighteen tribal towns were represented at the meeting of citizens, consisting mainly of those who had backed Roly McIntosh and Legus C. Perryman in the election of 1899. They set June 17 as the date for their meeting to nominate candidates for principal and second chief. *Indian Journal*, May 29, 1903.

5. Gibson's followers had designated Flat Rock, west of Eufaula, as the site of their convention on June 3. Posey supported Gibson's candidacy and expected him to garner the votes of the conservative as well as the progressive Creeks. He called the announced convention "the great 'Ne plus ultra' of the Creek nation, which literaly [*sic*] translated means 'Nothing else doing.' " *Indian Journal*, May 29, 1903.

✍ [No.24]

Well, maybe so everything was worked out all right anyhow, 'cause Hotgun he say while the cocklebur was growing tall in his sofky patch his old filly was mending up and getting frisky like a young calf that was had lots a milk to suck. Then he say maybe so while it was too wet to plow he was had a good chance to set out cabbage or maybe so study about the Royal Creek payment.[1]

Tookpafka Micco he say, "Well, maybe so that was good philosophy but I think we was had too much rain and cotton seed was too scarce to find if you didn't had no bank account to offer a big reward for it. Maybe so Hotgun talk that way 'cause he was had it coming to him out of the Royal Creek payment, or maybe so 'cause he was not live down on Canadian where he was had to run for his life up a cottonwood tree that didn't had no limbs to it only at the top when a ten foot rise was come tearing through the woods with shacks from Oklahoma floating 'round on it."

When I was tell Hotgun what Tookpafka say, he was shut his eyes close together and say, "Well, so everybody couldn't see the same thing like it is, and Tookpafka Micco was made me think about these fellers that was all the time sorry they couldn't splice Injin Territory onto Oklahoma so they could get up a big fight in politics and take it all back in a sack a ashes like in olden times."[2]

Well, so Frank See Cupboard was took up a big collection to make Injin Territory show off before the world in St. Louis.[3]

Tookpafka Micco he say, "Well, so how they make her show off?"

And Hotgun he say, "Well, so they was build a big box house up there with a side room to it and fill it up with everything that was raised in the Injin Territory, like coal from South McAlester, and oil from Bootleville, and railroads from Muskogee, and cotton from Eufaula, and natural resources from Fort Gibson, and hot air from Checotah, and prospects from Wagoner, and town lots from Spokogee, and things like that."[4]

---

1. The Creek National Council had just voted to accept the final congressional offer as settlement of the Loyal ("Royal") Creek claim that had existed since Reconstruction. Though Tookpafka Micco anticipated receiving his share, disbursement of funds would not begin for more than a year.

2. This is perhaps a reference to the biblical story of Mordecai, who angered Haman by his refusal to bow in his presence. Haman persuaded King Ahasuerus to issue a decree for the killing of all Jews. Mordecai appeared at the king's gate dressed in sackcloth with ashes, mourning the Jews' fate, and so appealed to

Queen Esther that she interceded in his behalf, causing Haman to be executed and the king to rescind his death decree. See Esther, chapters 3–7.

3. Frank C. Hubbard (1864–1930) had worked for the *Vinita Chieftain* before joining Leo E. Bennett in 1888 in publishing the *Muskogee Phoenix*. In 1903 he was vice president of the First National Bank of Muskogee. Hubbard had been commissioned by the secretary of the interior earlier that year to coordinate Indian Territory's representation at the exposition in 1904. See Grant Foreman, "Frank C. Hubbard," *Chronicles of Oklahoma* 8 (December 1930): 454–56. Hubbard asked towns to raise and contribute funds toward an Indian Territory exhibit. Posey supported the effort, calling Indian Territory the last large tract in the Louisiana Purchase that awaited "material and political development." He wrote in the *Journal* on April 10, "Standing on the threshold of statehood, rich in history and story, with untold natural resources undeveloped, Indian Territory can well afford to give all that is needed to make a great showing at the Exposition." On June 5, Posey thanked Hubbard for his "splendid work."

4. South McAlester was on the MK&T Railroad south of Eufaula in the Choctaw Nation. Bartlesville was in the Cherokee Nation between Tulsa and the Kansas line. Fort Gibson was east of Muskogee and across the Arkansas River in the Cherokee Nation. Checotah was a rival town fifteen miles north of Eufaula in the Creek Nation on the MK&T Railroad. Wagoner was on the same railroad, north of Muskogee. Spokogee was near the site of present-day Dustin, Oklahoma.

🖎 [No.25]

Well, so all the wire-stretchers for single statehood was leaped on the fence but one politician up to Wagoner who was sign his name See A Castle.[1] He was called a big convention over to Shawnee if he could get up a crowd. He was the only one that was still on deck and don't want to give up the ship and swim out alive.

Hotgun he say, "Well, maybe so it was take lots a grit to do that but it don't take no philosophy hardly."

Tookpafka Micco he say, "Well, so I was had lots a doubts about that statehood 'stomp' dance over to Shawnee, 'cause Henry Fur Man down to Ardmore was wrote a letter in the newspapers and say, 'Well, so I don't think it was time to make the wool fly yet. Maybe so the people wasn't with us and we couldn't go to congress from Jefferson.'² So I don't think them single staters was get along well over to Shawnee and maybe so was bust up in a row like the people in olden times that was tried to build a tower too high up."

Hotgun he say, "Well, so I see where Henry Fur Man was a fine politician, like Clarence Dug Last up to Muskogee who was a black cayuse to run again Plenty Soap and Mallet for town king a carpetbagger."³

Then Tookpafka Micco he say, "Well, so its look like this way when the cyclone was switched its tail and made a break for you its time to jump down in the cellar and get religion. So when everybody was solid agin hitching up with Oklahoma the politicians think its time to get on the fence and see what side had the most votes on it."

Then Hotgun he say, "Well, so I think See A Castle was better changed his name to See A Fence."

Well, so the big lawyers was had a powwow down to South Town⁴ and made big speeches like on Fourth of July. Cliff Jack's Son⁵ was rapped on the table and say, "Well, so the meeting must come to order and behave itself while I was made a talk." Then he was get up and looked all 'round like a owl in the daytime and say, "Well, so I was astraddle a the fence, too, 'cause we was had a big fight on hand about statehood. If we don't win out for single statehood maybe so we win out for separate statehood. But I don't care which way we win out so we win out." Then he was ripped Secretary It's Cocked up the backbone for butting in down here. When Cliff Jack's Son was take his seat Judge Stew It was jumped up and say, "Well, so I was made a motion to send Cliff Jack's Son speech to congress."⁶

Hotgun he say the white people in Injin Territory was need

some body to lead them like Chief Make Certain was leading the Injins and maybe so we get statehood like we want it.

Then Tookpafka Micco he say, "Well, so how they get a leader when all the big guns was on the fence and 'fraid a they shadder."

And Hotgun he say, "Well, so that's what's the matter, and maybe so we was all fool along till we had to take what congress give us."

1. C. E. Castle, chairman of the Oklahoma–Indian Territory single-statehood executive committee, issued a call on May 30 for four hundred delegates from each territory to meet at Shawnee on June 24 to decide if a constitutional convention should be called to form a single state. *Muskogee Daily Phoenix*, June 23, 1903.

2. Henry M. Furman (1850–1916), a native of South Carolina, had been county attorney for Bell County, Texas, before going to Indian Territory, where he practiced law. He would be an unsuccessful candidate for the U.S. Senate from Oklahoma in 1907 but would be named one of the first judges of the Criminal Court of Appeals after statehood. *Daily Oklahoman*, April 28, 1907; *Vinita Weekly Chieftain*, September 18, 1908. In his letter, Furman said that he was not in favor of a constitutional convention until Congress had acted on the statehood question because he feared it would not be representative and would be divisive. However, if one was called, he would go along with any plan for single statehood. Hence the accusation that single-staters were fence sitters. The letter appeared in *Muskogee Daily Phoenix*, June 5, 1903.

3. Clarence B. Douglas was the editor of the *Muskogee Phoenix*; Pliny Leland Soper was U.S. attorney for the northern district; and William H. Mellette was U.S. attorney for the western district. The contest for Republican national committeeman was between Soper and Mellette, but some newspapers mentioned Douglas as a good choice. Soper, though implicated in the land-fraud scandal involving federal officials, won. See *Muskogee Daily Phoenix*, June 6, 9, and 23, 1903.

4. "South Town" was South McAlester.

5. Clifford Linden Jackson (1857–1921), a native of Ohio, was educated in Missouri and practiced law at Sedalia. He served as a U.S. district attorney (1893–95) and became attorney for the MK&T Railroad in 1899. Jackson was an

active speech maker on statehood. See Gideon, *Indian Territory*, 213; *Vinita Daily Chieftain*, June 18, 1903; *Vinita Weekly Chieftain*, June 25, 1903.

6. Judge Stew It was C. B. Stuart of South McAlester.

Letter No.26.

[*Indian Journal*, June 26, 1903; *Muskogee Daily Phoenix*, June 25, 1903; *Cherokee Advocate*, July 4, 1903. This letter appeared in the daily *Indian Journal* earlier in the week of June 21.]

The process of electing the last Creek principal chief took an interesting turn in June when a former chief, Legus Perryman, was nominated as the candidate of the Union party over Posey's longtime friend George W. Grayson. Posey's dislike for Perryman dated from 1895, when Perryman had been impeached for corruption. That fall, as a member-elect of the House of Warriors, Posey had served on several committees under appointments from Hotulke Emarthla, the second chief, who completed Perryman's term. To Posey, Perryman's election again to the chieftaincy was unthinkable. In the issue of the *Journal* in which this letter appeared, he wrote: "Perryman for chief? No, not on your life!" and "Whew! What is that? Tut, tut, son, that's the Union ticket you smell." But there was more than political opposition in Posey's attack on Perryman. The racism that had been evident in Posey's editorial statements turned on Perryman because of his part-African heritage. In the same issue of the *Journal*, Posey wrote: "Our command of Creek is fluent and we are more or less familiar with English and Choctaw, to say nothing of our meagre knowledge of stock quotations in Greek and Latin, but language fails us when we attempt to express our disapproval of the choice of the Union party for the next chief of the Creek people. All that we are able to say is that he is a nigger and a bad one at that." Hotgun and his friends reflect this racial bias in their comments about the "sly old coon," making the "wool" fly and sitting at the "first table," and about Perryman's not being "a fullblood Injin." After Perryman's nomination, Porter and even Chitto Harjo, in addition to Gibson, began to look like viable candidates to Fus Fixico and his friends.

✍

Well, so Legus Perryman was a sly old coon and was made Wolf Warrior hide out up to Okmulgee.

Hotgun he say, "Well, so how he do it?"

And Tookpafka Micco he say, "Well, so they was had a big fight over the last bone."

Then Hotgun he say, "Well, so what Chief Porter do when they was get into it?"

And Tookpafka Micco he say, "Well, so he was just set off to one side and watch the wool fly and glad he was not had a hand in it."

Then Hotgun he say, "Well, so what about Charley Gibson?"

And Tookpafka Micco he say, "Well, so he was load his rifle and say nothing."

Then Hotgun he say, "Well, so what kind a bone Legus Perryman and Wolf Warrior was had a fight over?"

And Tookpafka Micco he say, "Well, so they was had a big caucus up to Okmulgee to see who be the last chief. They was get together in the council house and Marcey Harjo was called the roll and say, 'Well, so they was about thirty-one towns had delegates here.'[1]

"This was sound like hombux che (make ready to eat) and Legus Perryman and Wolf Warrior was get ready to help theyselves. Then the chairman he say, 'Well, so who you was want for next chief?' and they was put near all hold up their hands for Legus Perryman, and it was made Wolf Warrior look like white folks that didn't get to the first table. Then the chairman he say, 'Well, so it's carried like a shack on a headrise in Oklahoma.'[2] So this was bust up the powwow and they was all tied they apusky sacks on they pot-bellied fillies and scatter off like poor cows in the spring a the year.'"[3]

Then Hotgun he say, "Well, so I was mighty sorry old Legus got nominated, 'cause he aint a fullblood Injin."

And Tookpafka Micco he say, "Well, so good men like Wolf Warrior don't all time get in office."

Then Hotgun he say, "Well, maybe so that's why it is old Legus was carried off the bone."

And Tookpafka Micco he say, "Well, guess so it was laid between Chief Porter and Charley Gibson to scratch up the bone."

Then Hotgun he say, "Well, maybe so they was had Chitto Harjo to help find it."

1. H. Marcey (or Marsey) Harjo, a Creek attorney, had been superintendent of the Creek boarding schools at Coweta and Wealaka, a member of the House of Warriors, and private secretary to Chief Isparhecher. See Creek National Records 37786-B, 36161, 37182, 38773, and 39367, Record Group 75, National Archives, maintained by Oklahoma Historical Society.

2. That is, it carried like a shack in a flood.

3. Apusky was corn taken at the point of turning hard, shelled, put into a heated pot of clean wood ashes, and stirred until it was parched. It was sifted from the ashes and put into a mortar, where it was pounded to a fine powder. Honey was added and the mixture kneaded until the honey was absorbed. The result was a "cold flour" that was dried and stored and could be added to water and drunk. Apusky was often carried by Creek travelers because the apusky bags could be tied on the saddle. See Jefferson Berryhill (interview), *Indian-Pioneer History*, Archives and Manuscripts Division, Oklahoma Historical Society, 15:18; Charles Gibson, "Ah-pus-kee," *Indian Journal*, May 8, 1908.

Letter No.27

[*Indian Journal*, July 3, 1903; *Muskogee Evening Times*, July 8, 1903; *South McAlester Capital*, July 9, 1903; *Vinita Weekly Chieftain*, July 9, 1903; *Fort Smith Times*, July 10, 1903; *Tahlequah Arrow*, July 18, 1903. This letter may have appeared in the daily *Indian Journal* earlier in the week of June 28.]

The single-statehood convention met at Shawnee, Oklahoma Territory, on June 24. A huge tent had been erected for the meeting, but on the night of the twenty-third, a vicious storm with heavy rain and hail damaged the tent. Nevertheless, delegates from the two territories met as planned and, after much speech making, concluded that calling a constitutional convention at present would be imprudent and that they should appeal to Congress to secure single statehood for the two territories. In short, the convention came to nothing, and Hotgun took the storm as a sign that the Great Spirit was not with the delegates. Posey wrote on June 26, "The most remarkable thing about the single statehood convention at Shawnee yesterday was the terrific wind storm which preceded it."

✍

Well, so Hotgun he say he don't think the Great Spirit was put his name in the pot with See A Castle and Kid Morgan and Ridge Pasture and Henry Be Robbing when they powwowed over to Shawnee.[1]

And Tookpafka Micco he was asked Hotgun, "Well, so what reason was you had for it?"

And Hotgun he say, "Well, so 'cause they didn't had any good weather. A big wind was blowed they arbor down and the rain was drowneded [*sic*] 'em out and the hail didn't had no mercy on 'em."

Then Tookpafka Micco he say, "Well, so the Bible say it was rained on the just like on the unjust."[2]

And Hotgun he say, "Well, so it do; but when it was rained on the unjust by theyselves, like over to Shawnee, it was blow and hail too."

Then Tookpafka Micco he say, "Well, so I hear they was five hundred delegates there from Injin Territory."[3]

And Hotgun he say, "Well, so that's newspaper talk. Muskogee and Wagoner didn't had that many lawyers that could dig up they car fare and settle they hotel bill and blow theyselves for a morning's morning in Shawnee."[4]

Then Tookpafka Micco he say, "Well, maybe so; but they was so many of 'em there they couldn't had order."

And Hotgun he say, "Well, so they was the people that live in Shawnee doing all that milling."

Then Tookpafka Micco he say, "Well, so when the chairman was made a racket with his maul and asked a preacher to say the blessing, they was all bend over the beer kegs except Cliff Jack's Son, and when they was all raised up he was had the floor to make a big talk."[5]

And Hotgun he say, "Well, so that was a big scoop. What sort a oration was he got off?"

Then Tookpafka Micco he say, "Well, so the newspapers say he was talk so fine the band was played ragtime and they was all blister they hands enjoying it like when William Ginning Bran was hoodooed the Democrats in Chicago."[6]

And Hotgun he say, "Well, so who else was get up and recite?"

And Tookpafka Micco he say, "Well, so it was Ridge Pasture."

And Hotgun he say, "Well, so what tribe do he belong to anyhow?"

And Tookpafka Micco he say, "Well, maybe so he was a Cherokee, but I think he was druther be a Republican and had a big apetite [*sic*] for pie. The newspapers say he was had lots a brains he didn't had no use for, but the Keetowahs aint onto it and can't appreciate it like the boomers for single statehood. So when he was say his piece he was throwed 'high life' on the Injins and that was made everybody laugh."[7]

And Hotgun he say, "Well, so no good Injin was do anything like that to a dog."

Then Tookpafka Micco he say, "Well, so when Henry Be Robbing was made his big talk they was something doing. He was had a fine voice with music in it like a mule braying in the meadow, and he was knowed it all like a set a encyclopedia, and maybe so he was seed it all 'cause he was from Missouri. He was worked 'em up like Mark Antony when Ceaser [*sic*] was died with his boots on.[8] He was hold up the map a the United States and showed em how little Rhode Island was and how big Ohio was and say, 'Well, so, my friends, how you like that? Would you druther Injin Territory and Oklahoma was divided up so they was looked like two Rhode Islands or would you druther they was joined together so they was looked like Ohio?' When he say this, See A Castle and Kid Morgan and Cliff Jack's Son was want to lynch Chief Make Certain and Hulbutta Micco and burn they houses down and chop Secretary It's Cocked's head off."[9]

1. C. E. Castle was chairman of the Oklahoma–Indian Territory single-statehood executive committee. Gideon (Gid) Morgan (1851–1937), of Tahlequah, was of Cherokee descent. He migrated from Tennessee to the Cherokee Nation in 1871 and engaged in farming and business. He held several posts in Cherokee government. See H. F. O'Beirne and E. S. O'Beirne, *The Indian Territory: Its Chiefs, Legislators, and Leading Men* (St. Louis: C. B. Woodward Co., 1892), 425–27. Ridge Paschal (1845–1907), grandson of the well-known Cherokee Major Ridge, had been educated in Texas and Virginia. He was first a journalist and then an attorney. He was well-known in legal affairs in the Cherokee Nation. See O'Beirne and O'Beirne, *The Indian Territory*, 420–21. Henry P. Robbins, a journalist from South McAlester, had been elected to the single-statehood executive committee.

2. "That ye may be the children of your Father which is in heaven: for he maketh his sun to rise on the evil and on the good, and sendeth rain on the just and on the unjust" (Matthew 5: 45).

3. The call was for four hundred delegates from each territory. *Muskogee Daily Phoenix*, June 23, 1903.

4. "Morning's morning" is probably a typographical error.

5. Castle was chairman. A footnote attributed to the *South McAlester Capital*

says: "The seats built on beer kegs were popular with the delegates from the Southern district. The kegs were empty."

6. In reality, Jackson made a brief speech in which he nominated H. W. Williams of Pawnee as temporary chairman of the convention. *Daily Oklahoman,* June 25, 1903. At the Democratic national convention in Chicago in 1896, William Jennings Bryan, a delegate from Nebraska, made such a powerful speech in favor of silver coinage that he was nominated for president.

7. One newspaper said of Paschal's speech, "He pooh-poohed the proposition to make two states of the two territories, and used many telling illustrations during the course of his remarks." *Daily Oklahoman,* June 25, 1903. Tookpafka Micco suggests that Paschal is self-serving and ignores the desires of the Keetoowahs, the conservative Cherokees who generally opposed allotment and statehood. The reference to "high life" is not clear. Tookpafka Micco may have in mind something like carbon bisulfide, commonly called "hoky poky," which the vicious-minded liked to put on stray dogs. It was great "fun" to watch the animals writhe in pain and run themselves to death.

8. The reference to Marcus Antonius (ca. 82–30 B.C.) and Gaius Julius Caesar (ca. 100–44 B.C.) is probably based on Mark Antony's speech after Caesar's death in Shakespeare's *Julius Caesar,* act 3, scene 2.

9. One common argument by proponents of single statehood was that admission of the territories separately would result in two small states. Castle, Morgan, and Jackson would be angry at McCurtain of the Choctaws and Hulbutta Micco of the Seminoles for their support of separate statehood for Indian Territory. Secretary Hitchcock, like most Republicans, favored single statehood. The delegates would have been angry at him in general for his land-sale regulations, which they believed were an obstacle to the development of Indian Territory and, therefore, to statehood.

Letter No.28

[*Indian Journal,* July 10, 1903. This letter probably appeared in the daily *Indian Journal* earlier in the week of July 5.]

Critical of Pleasant Porter and disgusted by Legus Perryman's nomination by the Union party, Posey steadily supported Charles Gibson's independent bid for the Creek chieftaincy. On June 26 he wrote, "The war horses of the Independent party are talking about postponing the Gibson convention at Flat Rock next week in order to allow the Creek people time to become thoroughly disgusted with the Union ticket." In reality, Gibson was considering retiring from the race, and a few days later, he did so and endorsed Porter. In this letter, Hotgun and his friends look for a "Moses" among the remaining candidates. They turn to Porter, but more enthusiastically than Posey did. In the same issue of the *Journal* in which the letter appeared, Posey wrote of Gibson's support for Porter, "The Journal has no choice left but to do the same thing — and we might do worse."

✍

Well, so Hotgun he says we was in the same fix as the Jews in Egypt in olden times, and was need a man like Moses to lead us out into the promise land.

And Tookpafka Micco he says, "Well, maybe so Legus Perryman was like to had the job."

Then Hotgun he says, "Well, so he was had it once and warrants wasn't worth 40 cents on a dollar in due bills, and court script was made the jury think it was working for glory. So we was had to turn 'im off and had a lot a trouble with 'im, 'cause he want to keep on signing his name to bogus warrants and leasing big prairies to cowboys from Texas, and doing things like that. He was put near bankrupt us, and then wouldn't give up the stubs in the warrant book so we could see how near busted we was.[1] It's took us put near ten years to get over it and start up in business again. So I don't think a man like that was had a pull enough in a country of good people like this to be chief."

And Tookpafka Micco he was grunt and say, "Well, so how about my old friend Crazy Snake?"[2]

Then Hotgun he say, "Well, so he was a good honest Injin, but he couldn't stop progress by making medicine, and had buffaloes on his allotment instead a renters."

And Tookpafka Micco he say, "Well, so what about Charley Gibson?"

Then Hotgun he says, "Well, so he was good timber like seasoned hickory in his blacksmith shop, but wasn't a applicant for the job. He and Yaha Tustanuggee was fly the track before they get to the homestretch."[3]

And Tookpafka Micco he was grunt again and hang his head between his knees long time, and then he say, "Well, so what kind of Moses was Chief Porter made?"

Then Hotgun he says, "Well, so this time you was hit the nail on the head and drive it home and made me feel like setting 'em up. Show me a Injin that was had a Porter badge on his shirt bosom and I was showed you a Injin that was had a good crop a sofky corn and free transportation on the band wagon. Maybe so Legus Perryman was made a good janitor[4] and Crazy Snake a good leader in the 'stomp' dance, but Pleas Porter was had the brains to be chief. He could trot in the same class with the big men at Washington and hold his own with 'em like a grey hound in a wolf chase. Every time we get in trouble like the Green Peach war, or was had to make peace with the white man, we was always put 'im in the lead and come out of it without a scratch, 'cause he do all the fighting.[5] We was need 'em in the lead now, 'cause we was getting ready to travel a road we aint been over before, and he was already blazed out the way. We was had prosperty [*sic*] while he been chief, and all the stubs was in the warrant book, and warrants was good like a check on the bank. So Porter was my candidate for chief and was your candidate, too, if you aint standing in your own sunshine."[6]

And Tookpafka Micco he listen good and say, "Well, so how many Injins was he had to vote for 'em?"

Then Hotgun he say, "Well, so I was answered you like Uncle

Dick Grayson when I was asked him one time how many children Sam Tobler was had.[7] Uncle Dick he says, 'Well, so, Mistah Hotgun that's a hard proposition in the 'rithmetic and I could give you no answer to it; but I know this much — when Sam's children was got strung out down the lane towards the spring on wash days they was just coming out a the house.' "

1. For an account of Perryman's administration as principal chief, see Angie Debo, *The Road to Disappearance* (Norman: University of Oklahoma Press, 1941), 325–60. Posey was a member of the committee that investigated the fiscal policies of Perryman's administration.

2. Chitto Harjo (Crazy Snake) had steadily opposed social and economic change in the Creek Nation.

3. Gibson and George W. Grayson, much talked about as potential candidates, had been eliminated before summer, the intense campaign season.

4. This is a racial slur against Perryman's part-African heritage.

5. Porter had led the national warriors against Isparhecher's anticonstitutional forces during the Green Peach War in the early 1880s.

6. "Standing in your own sunshine" is obscuring your own view.

7. The Graysons were Creek freedmen who lived on Coon Creek east of the Posey family home at Bald Hill. Uncle Dick was a well-known character who had appeared in Posey's prose pieces "Uncle Dick's Sow," *Twin Territories* 1 (December 1899): 20 and "Mose and Richard," *Twin Territories* 2 (November 1900): 226–28. Sam Tobler was a Creek freedman who lived about four miles south of the Posey family home. Sallie, Tobler's wife of thirty years, had borne fourteen children. See 1910 Census Schedule (Microcopy T624), McIntosh County, Enumeration District 74, p. 137, National Archives Microfilm Publications, Washington, D.C.

Letter No.29

[*Muskogee Daily Phoenix*, July 17, 1903; *Fort Smith Times*, July 22, 1903; *Claremore Messenger*, July 24, 1903. This letter was apparently published in the daily *Indian Journal* before it appeared in the weekly on July 17; no copy of either the daily or the weekly has been found.]

The Fus Fixico Letters

For more than a year, Creeks had made accusations that large land-trust companies were at work in the Creek Nation, acquiring options on large numbers of Creek allotments by fraudulent means. By the summer of 1903, rumors were rife that corruption was widespread among officials of the Justice and Interior departments in Indian Territory. The growing scandal indicated that those officials, including members of the Dawes Commission, were engaged in large-scale land speculation, particularly in the Creek Nation. The process of allotment provided opportunities for the materially ambitious to make money in real estate ventures. Unfortunately, public officials who were charged with overseeing the process found that they were not immune to the prospects, and their integrity failed in many cases. In addition, there were accusations of influence peddling, padding of tribal rolls, conspiring with railroad companies in townsite selection, and holding shares or offices in land companies.

The territorial press called on Secretary Hitchcock to investigate the rumors of fraud. A. P. Murphy, the attorney for the Creek Nation, and Indian Inspector J. George Wright preferred charges against Clarence B. Douglas and J. Blair Shoenfelt. Shoenfelt, the agent to the Five Civilized Tribes, and Douglas, the clerk in charge of land transactions in the agent's office, were accused, among other things, of supplying outsiders with advance information on allotments. Secretary Hitchcock fired Douglas and temporarily stopped all land sales and leases in Indian Territory. Posey had editorially supported an investigation, writing on July 10, "Turn the rascals out — when you find them guilty, Mr. Secretary." Investigation should have occurred long ago, he argued, and it was now proceeding too slowly: "What the gander-leg dudes in Washington, who presume to run our affairs, need is hickory poles instead of twine string for backbones." Like most editors, he believed that Douglas was only a minor figure in the scandal. In this letter, Hotgun and his friends comment on Douglas's firing and speculate on the possibility that the investigation will be expanded to "smoke out" larger game.

Well, so, Hotgun he say they was lots a smoke keep b'iling up from Muskogee like when a Arkansawyer was burning brush on a lease in the spring a the year.[1]

And Tookpafka Micco he say, "Well, so must be they was had a fire up there and the chief of the fire couldn't put it out. How the newspapers say it was started?"

Then Hotgun he say, "Well, so I was think it was Secretary It's Cocked started that fire when he was smoked Clarence Dug Last out a hole after J. Gouge Right and See My Fee was run him into it."[2]

And Tookpafka Micco he say, "Well, so I was thought all the time Secretary It's Cocked and Clarence Dug Last was stick close together and was lonesome for one another, like David and Jonathan in olden time. The newspapers say Secretary It's Cocked was had a tintype taken of himself and was send it to Clarence Dug Last, with a note that was said, 'Well, so, Clarence, old boy, when you see this, remember me.'"[3]

Then Hotgun he say, "Well, so, that what hatched all the trouble, so nobody could see the end of it with a spy glass from the top of a Chimley mountain.[4] It like I say all the time, friendship was a good thing to fall out over and was soon fade, like a red muskeeter bar.[5] I druther had a sofky jug full a gold at the end a rainbow than a big friend in politics. So I think Clarence Dug Last was better throw Secretary It's Cocked's picture in the alley among the tin cans and let the chickens scratch dirt over it."

And Tookpafka Micco he say, "Well, so the newspapers say half of it aint been said yet and they was lots a stink that aint got scattered."

Then Hotgun he say, "Well, so, how's that?"

And Tookpafka Micco he say, "Well, so the newspapers say

Secretary It's Cocked was raking up more leaves to smoke out some more old stayers like J. Bear Sho'-am-fat and Tams Big Pie."[6]

Then Hotgun he say, "Well, so I hope Secretary It's Cocked was singed they hair so the people could smell it. Maybe so that was made 'em quit running up good hands for theyselves instead a giving the Injun a chance to shuffle the deck after 'em."[7]

And Tookpafka Micco he say, "Well, so, how they do that?"

Then Hotgun he say, "Well, so they was do it all the time, like putting 1,800 [18,000] Creek Injins on the roll when they was aint that many, counting the Seminoles too.[8] 'Sides that they was get together and form big trust companies so they could get a corner on good times and drink Bud Wiser in they summer homes on the Grand River."[9]

And Tookpafka Micco he say, "Well, so, it's looked like Secretary It's Cocked didn't smoke out nothing but a rabbit when he smoked out Clarence Dug Last."

Then Hotgun he say, "Well, maybe so this time he was smoked out the fox."

1. Muskogee, the seat of the federal bureaucracy in Indian Territory, had more federal officials than any other town outside Washington, D.C.

2. Clarence B. Douglas (1864–?), of Missouri, practiced law at Ardmore, Chickasaw Nation, before going to Muskogee, where he began publishing the *Muskogee Phoenix* in 1902. He published the newspaper and worked in the agent's office as well. See *Who Was Who in America*, 5:192. J. George Wright (1860–1941), of Illinois, had entered Indian service in 1883 at the Rosebud agency and was in charge of that agency from 1886 to 1896. In 1898 he was appointed Indian inspector for Indian Territory and continued in that office until it was consolidated with that of the commissioner to the Five Civilized Tribes in 1907, which office he assumed. He continued there until 1914, when the office was abolished. In 1915 he transferred to the Osage agency and retired in 1931. See Grant Foreman, "J. George Wright," *Chronicles of Oklahoma* 20 (June 1942): 120–23.

Arthur Phillips Murphy (1870–1914), of Missouri, was attorney for the St. Louis and San Francisco Railroad (1889–1905) and attorney for the Creek Nation (1903–5). He was later elected to Congress from Missouri (1905–7, 1909–11). See *Who Was Who in America*, 1:882.

3. "And it came to pass, when he had made an end of speaking unto Saul, that the soul of Jonathan was knit with the soul of David, and Jonathan loved him as his own soul" (I Samuel 18:1). Hitchcock had sent Douglas a photograph of himself as a token of appreciation for the courtesies Douglas had shown him while he was in Muskogee in May. *Muskogee Daily Phoenix*, June 9, 1903.

4. Chimney Mountain is about eight miles south of Muskogee, near the community of Summit.

5. Mosquito netting ("bar") came in a variety of colors, including red.

6. J. Blair Shoenfelt, the agent to the Five Civilized Tribes, had apparently survived the charges that resulted in Douglas's firing. Tams Bixby was the chairman of the Dawes Commission. A common way of chasing game out of hollow logs or trees was to build a fire in one end or at the bottom and wait for the smoke to drive the animals out. Leaves, in the early stages of burning, create an especially acrid smoke.

7. That is, federal officials who had inside information on the best lands were like the dishonest card dealer who refused to let the other players shuffle the deck and dealt himself a good hand.

8. Reports had circulated that the Dawes Commission had enrolled over eighteen thousand Creeks. On July 3, Posey had published "The Creek Roll" by Charles Gibson, who challenged the figure and alleged that fraud was involved. Charles Gibson, "The Creek Roll," *Indian Journal*, July 3, 1903.

9. The Town and Country Club had been established in 1903, with Tams Bixby as president. Bixby purchased some of the property that was formerly Fort Gibson, east of the Grand River, and the club members refurbished one of the large buildings for a clubhouse. See *Muskogee Democrat*, December 29, 1904. The membership list included many federal bureaucrats.

Letter No. 30

[*South McAlester Capital*, August 6, 1903; *Cherokee Advocate*, August 15, 1903. This letter had appeared earlier in the *Indian Journal*, probably in the daily edition early in the week of August 2 and in the weekly on August 7; no copies of those editions have been found.]

By August, the prospects of an early investigation into the allegations of fraud were fading. Posey had written in late July: "Hitchcock has a hide on him like a rhinoceros and a quart of 'high' couldn't phase [*sic*] him. He cares no more for editorial grape shot than a dry land terrapin does for hail stones." Hitchcock had left the capital to spend the summer at his vacation home. Assistant Secretary Thomas Ryan had denied rumors that the Interior Department would not investigate but insisted that none of the complaints that had reached the secretary indicated criminal misconduct by department officials. The secretary, he said, had limited powers to investigate, and he hoped that a grand jury would be convened in Indian Territory. William Mellette, the U.S. attorney for the Western District of Indian Territory, who had jurisdiction in the Creek Nation, said that press reports of a pending investigation had been exaggerated and that he would convene no special grand jury but would wait for the regular grand jury to convene two months later, unless something "urgent" arose.

Without doubt, the complexity of legal requirements governing the sale and lease of Indian land invited fraud. Under the Creek agreements, town lots and the allotments of deceased allottees could be sold, with the remaining allotments restricted from sale. Rules issued by the Interior Department regulated the leasing of allotments. Many people, including government officials and Indians, argued that the rules and restrictions discouraged investment by corporate interests, entry into the market by honest real estate dealers, and ultimately, economic development in the territory. Thus in the summer of 1903, organizers of a movement calling for the removal of restrictions on land sales called for a convention at Checotah in early August to plan strategy. Meanwhile, the campaign for principal chief entered its last month. It was rumored that Chief Porter was discouraging an investigation because it would hurt his chances for reelection. He, of course, denied the charge. Posey remained steadfast in his support for Porter and hammered away at Perryman's African background, writing on July 24: "Legus Perryman will address the negro citizens of Eufaula in the near future. Legus sticks to his own people."

✍

Well, so Hotgun he say they was something doing all the time and the newspapers was had lots a things to talk about.

And Tookpafka Micco he say, "Well, so what kind a frauds been plowed up this time?"

And Hotgun he say, "Well, so Clarence Dug Last was chunked down a hornet's nest on Secretary It's Cocked and made 'im tear out through the woods with the swarm under his shirt tail so Tom Ryan was had to put a stray notice in the Phoenix. Chief Porter he say maybe so Secretary It's Cocked was out in the hills in New Hampshire picking the briars out a his foot and waiting for the swelling to go down."[1]

Then Tookpafka Micco he say: "Well, maybe so if that been Bill Mellette he couldn't get a move on 'im like that, 'cause it was too hot."[2]

And Hotgun he go on and say: "Well, so they was fixing to had a big war dance at Checotah putty soon to make the Big Man at Washington sic the land grabber on the Injin like when the Romans was sic the lions on the prisoner in olden times."[3]

Then Tookpafka Micco he say: "Well, maybe so they was nobody mixed up in it but white people, 'cause no good Injin was help do anything like that."

And Hotgun he say, "Well, so that's where you ain't on to it, 'cause Henry Clay Fisher was made his mark to the call and was a delegate to it and couldn't hardly wait for his badge."[4]

Then Tookpafka Micco he say, "Well, so then that's all right, 'cause the Big Man at Washington was knowed his business better than Henry and was not let Henry run through with his land like his daddy's store over to Fishertown."

And Hotgun he say, "Well, so I think you was had it down right, and maybe so that war dance was all whoops and no scalps and was a picnic for nobody but the soda pop man and the bed bugs in the hotel."

Then Tookpafka Micco he say: "Well, so what the newspapers say about the next chief?"

And Hotgun he say: "Well, so they was had a hot time in Creek politics and old Legus Perryman was sweating like a nigger at a 'lection. Chief Porter he was sweat, too,[5] and was had a big barbecue up to Wetumka, and made a stump talk to about two thousand Injuns and was pinned badges on they hickory shirts and took 'em to one side and tell 'em to vote it straight.[6] Chitto Harjo was cutting up pretty considerable, too, and couldn't hardly stay in the chute. He say if he was had hold a the reins he was soon had buffaloes eating grass 'round Spokogee instead a carpetbaggers hunting leases and sofky and sour bread at Muskogee instead a Bud Wiser and pie."[7]

Then Tookpafka Micco he say: "Well, so who you think was got there?"

And Hotgun he say, "Well, so I think Chief Porter was made old Legus Perryman and Chitto Harjo feel like sofky dogs after a jack rabbit."[8]

1. Clarence B. Douglas, the editor of the *Muskogee Phoenix*, had waged an editorial war against the injustice of his being fired as clerk in charge of land transactions. He demanded that Hitchcock show cause and vowed to take his case to the president if he did not get satisfaction. See *Indian Journal*, July 10 and 24, 1903, and *Claremore Messenger*, July 24, 1903. Hitchcock's summer home was in New Hampshire. A "stray notice" was an announcement placed in the local newspaper, describing livestock that had strayed or was stolen.

2. Mellette was reported to have said that it was too hot to call a grand jury. Whether he referred to the weather or the politics of the controversy, Posey saw the humor:

The Fus Fixico Letters

He hates to sweat
Does Bill Mellette.
He'll wait till frost, no doubt;
It's too hot yet
For Bill Mellette
To turn the rascals out.
(*Indian Journal*, August 14, 1903)

3. The Checotah convention was called by the Checotah Commercial Club to draft a petition to Congress asking for the removal of restrictions on land sales and the placement of Indians on the same footing as U.S. citizens. As indicated, Creeks were involved. However, a group led by Cheesie McIntosh and George W. Stidham bolted, called their own convention, drafted resolutions condemning the Checotah Commercial Club's convention, and called on the secretary of the interior to keep regulations regarding land transactions intact. See *Indian Journal*, August 14, 1903.

4. Henry Clay Fisher was born at Fishertown, east of present-day Eufaula, in 1862. He graduated from Drury College in 1881 and entered the mercantile business with his father at Fishertown. In 1892 he moved to Checotah. Fisher held a number of offices in Creek government, including membership in the House of Warriors, to which he was elected in 1895, the year Posey was elected. See Carolyn Thomas Foreman, "Fishertown," *Chronicles of Oklahoma* 31 (Autumn 1953): 247–54.

5. This may be a reference to Porter's part-African ancestry.

6. The meeting at Wetumka was reported as the "annual picnic of full-bloods," which was attended by over twelve hundred people. Speakers included Porter, J. W. McCombs, and Moty Tiger. The crowd was reported to be enthusiastic for Porter's candidacy. See *Muskogee Daily Phoenix*, August 1, 1903. Hickory shirts were made from cotton cloth, usually with a checked or striped design.

7. Chitto Harjo's activities are described in rodeo terms. Bucking horses or bulls often "cut up" in the chutes before being released into the arena. Spokogee, near present-day Dustin, Oklahoma, was a center of Snake activities. The implication is that Chitto Harjo's election would be a step backward for the progress that Posey favored. Sofky and sour bread were favorite Creek foods. "Pie" was Hotgun's word for graft. Though alcoholic beverages were illegal in Indian

Territory, it was popularly believed that they were kept and served at the Town and Country Club, frequented by federal officials at Muskogee.

8. Sofky dogs were curs or mutts.

Letter No.31

[*Indian Journal*, August 28, 1903; *Fort Smith Times*, August 26, 1903; *Vinita Daily Chieftain*, August 27, 1903. The letter had appeared an additional time: clipped copy, undated, source unknown, in Posey Collection, Thomas Gilcrease Institute of American History and Art. The letter had appeared earlier in the week of August 23 in the daily *Indian Journal*; no copy has been found.]

By the middle of August, possible evidence of fraud and corruption was too widespread to be ignored. Unwilling to wait for Secretary Hitchcock or the Justice Department to act, S. M. Brosius of the Indian Rights Association had conducted his own investigation. His published report was far-reaching, naming public officials — both prominent and little known, the high-ranking and the flunky — and accusing them of being a part of trust companies, which appeared to have "systematic" monopolies in land transactions, especially in the Creek Nation. Among other things, he accused company officials of leasing land from allottees at twenty-five to seventy-five cents per acre and subleasing to farmers for a dollar or two, of using the Indian's lease money to pay for improvements, which were supposed to have been paid for by the renter, and of making the lease in effect a contract for sale, with the Indian receiving no additional money at the end of the lease. Prominent among the officials Brosius singled out were Pliny Soper, the U.S. attorney for the Northern District of Indian Territory, and all members of the Dawes Commission except W. E. Stanley, who was later also found to have connections to the trust companies.

Brosius's report pointed out how these officials were connected to the land companies. Soper, for instance, was vice president and a substantial stockholder in the Tribal Development Company of Tishomingo; Guy

P. Cobb, a former internal revenue inspector for the territory, was the largest stockholder. Soper was also a stockholder in, and attorney for, the Cherokee Oil and Gas Company. Tams Bixby was vice president and a large stockholder in the Muskogee Title and Trust Company; J. George Wright, the Indian inspector, was one of its directors. Bixby was also president of, and a stockholder in, the Canadian Valley Trust Company of Muskogee. Dawes Commissioner Thomas B. Needles was vice president and a director of the International Banking Trust Company at Vinita. A director in the company was Charles A. Davidson, clerk of the U.S. court at Vinita; the attorney for the company was James H. Huckleberry, assistant U.S. attorney for the Northern District of Indian Territory. And Commissioner C. R. Breckenridge was a stockholder in the Eufaula Trust Company.

Brosius's accusations could not be ignored. On August 20, Secretary Hitchcock reported that he was looking for a suitable man, someone who was not in government service, to conduct an investigation. Posey wrote on August 28 that Hitchcock had "emerged from his hiding" and was "incensed at Brosius for flushing his game'" in Indian Territory.

✍

Well, so Hotgun he say Secretary It's Cocked was trimmed the wick in his lantern and stuck a match to it, like old Diogenes, and was set out to see if he could find a man that didn't had his breadhooks hung up under his coat tail for boodle.[1]

And Tookpafka Micco he say, "Well, so must be honest men was put near all left the range if It's Cocked was had to fire hunt for 'em like deer."[2]

Then Hotgun he say, "Well, so I was had to 'gree with you. They was put near all extinct in politics, and they was hardly 'nough left in the Republican party for seed."[3]

And Tookpafka Micco he say, "Well, so how about in the Democratic party?"

Then Hotgun he say, "Well, maybe so they was some good seed in it, but it was take it too long to come up."

And Tookpafka Micco he say, "Well, maybe so it was need some good manure on it."

Then Hotgun he say, "Well, so that's not what's the matter — it was had too much hot air."

And Tookpafka Micco he say, "Well, so they'll be lots a time to talk politics some other time. So I want to know what Secretary It's Cocked was up to anyhow with his lantern?"

Then Hotgun he say, "Well, so it was like this way: President Rooster Feather was ordered Secretary It's Cocked to go see what Brosius was had treed in Injin Territory, but It's Cocked was too busy in the office fixing up rules and sitting down on skin games to climb up in the tree and see what's up there. So he was go out and tried to find a honest man that could made a good investigation. But maybe so he was had bad luck same like Diogenes in olden times."

And Tookpafka Micco he say, "Well, so what do you guess Brosius was barking at?"

Then Hotgun he say, "Well, so I think it was lots a coons he was chased out a the Injin's sofky patch.[4] The newspapers say they was some old raccoons, like Tams Big Pie and Jay Gouge Right and Tom Needs It and Plenty So Far, laying up the tree."[5]

And Tookpafka Micco he say, "Well, so reckon he was had 'em all treed?"

Then Hotgun he say, "Well, so I don't think it, 'cause they was lots a young coons mixed in with the big ones, like little Charlie Divide Some and little Cry For The Cobb and little Jimmy Eats Huckleberries, that is hugging the limbs way up close to the top so you couldn't see nothing but the rings 'round they tails."[6]

And Tookpafka Micco he say, "Well, so what Secretary It's Cocked do with 'em when he was shaked 'em out?"

Then Hotgun he say, "Well, maybe so he was put 'em in the zoo so everybody could take a look at 'em."

1. Diogenes of Sinope (ca. 400–ca. 325 B.C.), the Greek founder of the Cynic sect, allegedly went around with a lighted lamp in broad daylight, looking for an honest man. See *The Oxford Classical Dictionary*, ed. M. Cary et al. (Oxford: Clarendon Press, 1949), 285, and Catharine B. Avery, *The New Century Classical Handbook* (New York: Appleton-Century-Crofts, 1962), 395.

2. In fire hunting, the woods or prairies were set afire to drive the game toward the hunter.

3. Posey was fiercely Democratic and strongly anti-Republican in party politics.

4. The Indian's sofky, or corn, patch was symbolic of Indian land. Raccoons could be very destructive, pulling green corn ears from the stalks just before the kernels reached maturity.

5. Tams Bixby (1855–1922), born in Virginia and reared at Red Wing, Minnesota, was a newspaperman and Republican politician. He served as private secretary to three governors (1889–97) before becoming acting chairman of the Dawes Commission. He became the sole commissioner to the Five Civilized Tribes in 1905 and served until 1907. He became owner of the *Muskogee Phoenix* in 1906. See *Who Was Who in America*, 1:99. Thomas B. Needles (1835–?), an Illinois merchant and banker, served in a minor political office until 1876, when he became auditor of the state. He then served eight years in the state legislature. In 1889 he was appointed U.S. marshal for Indian Territory. See O'Beirne and O'Beirne, *The Indian Territory*, 166–68. In 1903, Needles was also a member of the Dawes Commission. Pliny Leland Soper (1861–?) was U.S. attorney for Kansas (1899–94); attorney for the Atchison, Topeka and Santa Fe Railroad (1894–97); delegate-at-large from Indian Territory to the Republican national convention (1896, 1900); solicitor in Indian Territory for the St. Louis and San Francisco Railroad from 1894; and U.S. attorney for the Northern District of Indian Territory from 1897. See *Who Was Who in America*, 4:885.

6. Charles A. Davidson was clerk of the U.S. court for the northern district at Vinita. Guy Pulford Cobb (1866–?) of Wisconsin, was the revenue inspector for Indian Territory. After leaving government service, he openly admitted that he held leases, and he brazenly challenged the government to do something about it. It was also alleged that he trafficked in whiskey. Cobb lived at Ardmore, where

he later engaged in oil, livestock, and farming enterprises. See Statement of Guy Pulford Cobb, *Indian-Pioneer History*, Archives and Manuscripts Division, Oklahoma Historical Society, 77:453, and *Vinita Weekly Chieftain*, October 20, 1904. James H. Huckleberry (1840–1904), of Indiana, was a graduate of Columbia Law School and went to Arkansas in 1868, where he served as attorney for the Western District of Arkansas and as a member of the Arkansas state legislature. He then moved to the Cherokee Nation and in 1903 was assistant attorney for the Northern District of Indian Territory. See D. C. Gideon, *The Indian Territory* (New York: Lewis Publishing Co., 1901), 729–31, and *Vinita Weekly Chieftain*, October 13, 1904.

Letter No.32

[*Indian Journal*, September 11, 1903; *Fort Smith Times*, September 10, 1903; excerpt, *South McAlester Capital*, September 17, 1903. The letter appeared in the daily *Indian Journal* earlier in the week of September 6.]

In the last weeks of the campaign for chief, Posey had been relentless in his attacks on Legus Perryman. On August 14 he reminded his readers that Perryman had been impeached eight years earlier and said, "He hasn't changed a bit — he has the same kind of pigment under his skin that doesn't fade." He also reported that at the Porter barbecue at Flat Rock, there would be "a nigger doll rack for the benefit of those that desire to throw it into Legus" and that Perryman was not really running for chief but had "invented a potient to take the kinks out of wool" and was "only seeking a little free advertising." Even after Porter's victory, Posey called attention to Perryman's sizable majority in all three of the black tribal towns. Hotgun continues the racial theme in the opening statement of this letter.

Meanwhile, as Secretary Hitchcock looked for an honest man to investigate allegations of graft, Posey argued that the regulatory changes following Douglas's firing were not sufficient to protect the Indians. He also cast doubt on the results of an investigation. "After the investigation, then what? Why whitewash, to be sure." Hitchcock's delay gave federal bureaucrats time to distance themselves from land speculation. Tams Bixby denied that he or the companies he belonged to had bought any land. Pliny Soper and U.S. Marshal Benjamin Colbert left the Tribal Development Company. Joseph McCoy, who allegedly worked as an attorney for leasing in Bixby's Canadian Valley Trust Company, resigned his federal post as assistant district attorney for the western district. The Dawes commissioners stonewalled. They called for an investigation to clear the air of allegations by "fanatical reports and questionable journalism." Bixby stood firm. He admitted his connection to the trusts but asked his critics what they could do about it and insisted on his right to engage in "private business." In response, Posey argued that Bixby's position in the allotment process gave him too much of an advantage over the "legitimate" land investor. Despite this, as Hotgun and Tookpafka Micco note, Bixby had his defenders.

✍

Well, so Hotgun he say maybe so Legus Perryman could do the cake walk but he couldn't scorch fast enough to be chief.[1]

And Tookpafka Micco he say, "Well, maybe so old Legus better go way back and sit down."

Then Hotgun he say, "Well, so Pleas Porter was kicked up a big cloud a dust and went out a sight in it like the flyer when it was give Checotah the go by and old Legus and Jim Gregory and Chitto Harjo couldn't keep up no more than a hand car with some Irishman pumping it up grade against the wind."[2]

And Tookpafka Micco he say, "Well, so it's looked like a race between a thoroughbred and two scrub ponies that aint bridle wised yet and a old breachy hoss mule that had to hump up before it could strike a trot."[3]

Then Hotgun he say, "Well, so the country was saved."

And Tookpafka Micco he say, "Well, maybe so if we could had that investigation and put Dam Big Pie and Jay Gouge Right and

Break in Rich and Plenty So Far and Tom Needs It and grafters like that out a business."

Then Hotgun he say, "Well, so I think the fuse was put near burn the powder 'cause they was lots a dry wood popping in the tall timber."[4]

And Tookpafka Micco he say, "Well, maybe so the grafters was flushing so Secretary It's Cocked couldn't get a pot shot."[5]

Then Hotgun he say, "Well, so it's looked that way to the Injin in the sofky patch."

And Tookpafka Micco he say, "Well, so who was take to the wilds first?"

Then Hotgun he say, "Well, reckon so it was Charley McCoy, 'cause he was shy in the jack pot."

And Tookpafka Micco he say, "Well, maybe so he was called it a misdeal and jumped the game."[6]

Then Hotgun he say, "Well, so Ben Called Burt and Plenty So Far was cashed in they stack too and slide down the back way, but they was a good game going on yet and they was lots a reds on the green cloth to be gobbled up."[7]

And Tookpafka Micco he say, "Well, so who you think was sewed up the game?"

Then Hotgun he say, "Well, so Dam Big Pie was a stayer and had lots a nerve and aint afraid to set in the whole gob."

And Tookpafka Micco he say, "Well, so the Muskogee Phoenix say Dam Big Pie was a hero and could tell the police judge, 'Well, so what you do about it?' "

Then Hotgun he say, "Well, maybe so he was learned to talk that way from Boss Tweed a New York."[8]

And Tookpafka Micco he say, "Well, so the Muskogee Phoenix was go on and say Dam Big Pie ought to had a monument, 'cause he could 'fess up like George Washington and set a good example to young America."

Then Hotgun he say, "Well, so the Muskogee Phoenix might say Charley Barrett ought to been turned loose 'cause he said he killed the old section hand over to Calvin for his roll."[9]

And Tookpafka Micco he say, "Well, maybe so confession was good for the soul."

Then Hotgun he say, "Well, maybe so it was saved the soul from destruction but it don't keep a feller's name out a the newspapers or his body out a the bull pen."[10]

1. A cakewalk was an entertainment, popular among American blacks, featuring competition in fancy stepping or walking. The winner received a cake as a prize. In vaudeville, a cakewalk was a dance associated with minstrelsy or other productions in blackface. To "scorch" is to move at great speed.

2. James Roane Gregory (1842–?), a Yuchi, was a successful farmer and cattleman who had a long career in Creek politics. He sat in the National Council in 1869, was judge of Coweta District (1873–76), and served as superintendent of public instruction. Gregory had been Chitto Harjo's running mate on the Snake ticket but was dropped when it was learned that he had become a U.S. citizen some years earlier. Chitto Harjo then ran with Concharty Micco. Their platform had been essentially that the Treaty of 1832 was sufficient to protect Creek lands, money, and people. See Gideon, *Indian Territory*, 543–44, and *Indian Journal*, August 28, 1903. A handcar was a small platform on wheels, propelled along railroad tracks by the rider's pumping a handle. Many railroad workers were Irish, hence the stereotype.

3. Until a horse becomes "bridle wised," it fights the bit in its mouth and is hard to control and therefore keep in the race. A mule is the hybrid offspring of a horse and an ass. Though broke ("breachy") to ride, it may be given to stubbornness or balking. This is probably a reference to Perryman as a "hybrid" of two races.

4. To run to tall timber means to attempt an escape. The sound of dry twigs or limbs popping indicates that the "game" is attempting its escape.

5. In quail shooting, the sporting hunter flushes the covey and aims at individual birds in flight, but the pot-shooter fires into the covey while the birds are bunched together on the ground. Thus the grafters scatter so that Hitchcock will

not be able to "shoot" at many of their numbers and will be less likely to "hit" any of them.

6. One news report claimed that the Justice Department refused Joseph ("Charley") McCoy's resignation until an investigation could be held and, instead, gave him ten days' leave. McCoy denied that his connection to the Muskogee trust company had anything to do with his resignation, which he attributed to bad health. See *Indian Journal*, September 4, 1903. With McCoy, Hotgun and Tookpafka Micco begin a series of references to poker, drawing an analogy between the card game and grafting. The jackpot is the amount of money the players ante and bet in a hand. If the "pot" is "shy," it does not have the correct amount in it; the only conclusion that can be drawn is that one or more of the players did not put as much money on the table as they were supposed to. Wrongly dealt or misdealt cards nullify the game.

7. The red chips on the green cloth of the gambling table suggest more money to be made in the "game" of grafting.

8. Bixby, like the cool poker player who stays in the game, asked his critics what they could do about his connection to the trust companies. The *Muskogee Phoenix*, a strong Republican paper, always supported Bixby. Of his challenge to his critics, the *Phoenix* said: "This country honors Bixby for his integrity, his ability, his individuality and his manhood. No subterfuges has he sought — no apologies has he made. This work is a monument to his genius and time will erect to his memory the largest shaft in this Territory. Bixby, the brave, will be his epitaph, and that will endure when the apologetic sycophant has become a nauseous memory." *Muskogee Phoenix*, September 17, 1903. The Tweed Ring, begun in 1869, robbed New York City of thirty to sixty million dollars in the thirty months ending July 31, 1871, through fraudulent bond issues, franchise sales, tax reductions, and other means. Its members controlled the police, the courts, and most newspapers. When they were brought to justice, most got off, but "Boss" William Tweed, president of the board of supervisors, was sent to jail, where he died in 1878. See Wayne Andrews, ed., *Concise Dictionary of American History* (New York: Charles Scribner's Sons, 1967), 969–70.

9. The details of Charlie Barrett's crime are not known. Barrett was convicted of murder and sent to federal prison at Leavenworth, Kansas, for five years. *Muskogee Phoenix*, November 26, 1903. Calvin, where the killing occurred, is west of McAlester, Oklahoma.

10. A "bullpen" is a jail.

The Fus Fixico Letters

Letter No. 33

[*Fort Smith Times*, October 25, 1903]

Secretary Hitchcock finally ended his search for an honest man and in mid-September appointed Charles J. Bonaparte, apparently with instructions to conduct a limited investigation. Posey wrote, "Give us a bona fide investigation, Mr. Bonaparte." Though his arrival was anticipated and the investigation long delayed, he remained in Washington, conducting his preliminary inquiries through correspondence. In Indian Territory, Tams Bixby still defied his critics, other officials kept low profiles, and attention focused on lesser officials, like Dwight Tuttle of the Choctaw Townsite Commission. Meanwhile, Posey had sold the *Indian Journal* and briefly continued the Fus Fixico letters in the *Fort Smith Times* at Fort Smith, Arkansas, which had been reprinting the letters for several months. Believing that *Times* readers might not be familiar with his characters, he appended the following note to his letter of October 25:

Hotgun and Tookpafka Micco are real Indian characters of the Snake persuasion. Hotgun is the most unique of the two. He is a jack of all trades and pretty good at all. He is a medicine man, blacksmith, carpenter, fiddler, orator and a sofky farmer all in one. Tookpafka Micco is an easy going philosophical sort of noble red man. "Dam Big Pie" means Tams Bixby, chairman of the Dawes commission; "Plenty So Far," Pliny Soper, prosecuting attorney for the Northern district of Indian territory; "Tight Tuttle," Dwight Tuttle, chairman of the Choctaw townsite commission (formerly of the Creek townsite commission) against whom grave charges were made a few weeks ago by the Russell American, "Rustling American."

✍

"Well, maybe so," Hotgun he say, "when Charley Bonaparte was land here from Washington and saw how it is, he was looked grand, gloomy and curious, like he was smelt something dead a long time and no buzzards flying 'round."[1]

And Tookpafka Micco he say, "Well, so he was not deceived his looks if he was got wind a Muskogee, where the grafters was skinning the Injins and burying the hides. But, maybe so, he was looked that way anyhow, 'cause he was a chip off a the old block."

Then Hotgun he say, "Well, so it looks like if he was a chip off a the old block he could fly off any direction and hit a grafter in the eye."

And Tookpafka Micco he say, "Well, so I think when Bonaparte was loomed up on the horizon Dam Big Pie was looked like a cold batter cake and Plenty So Far was looked like a soda check when you was thirsty for Peruna."

Then Hotgun he say, "Well, so but Dam Big Pie he say he was stood pat."

And Tookpafka Micco he say, "Well, maybe so, if Bonaparte was called his hand he didn't had anything but a three-carder and no joker to nigger with."

Then Hotgun he say, "Well, so I was stood pat too on a three-flush if I was had Uncle Sam to stake me."[2]

And Tookpafka Micco he was smoked a long time and say, "Well, so the transgressor was had a hard time of it, and Dam Big Pie ain't the only one."

Then Hotgun he say, "Well, so you was talked like the Rustling American when it was got behind my old friend Tight Tuttle with his cap-and-ball and tried to smoke him off a the range."[3]

And Tookpafka Micco he say, "Well, so must be the Rustling American was a cowboy that was tried to run amuck in the town-site."

Then Hotgun he say, "Well, so I see you was not kept up with the times, 'cause the Rustling American was a country newspaper printed east a Checotah. It was fell out with my old friend Tight Tuttle, like I say, and maybe so they was further developments.

Tight Tuttle he say they was a law agin talking bad language through the mail, and maybe so the Rustling American was found it out in the bull pen."

And Tookpafka Micco he say, "Well, so what was start the rucus?"

Then Hotgun he say, "Well, so I couldn't swear how it was, but looks like they was a woman to the bottom of it."

And Tookpafka Micco he say, "Well, guess so that was a mistake, 'cause your old friend Tight Tuttle was a big church member 'way back yonder where he come from and was kept the amen corner warm all the time till he had to come out here to straighten up this townsite business. And 'sides that he was too feeble to cut up much and go the gaits."[4]

Then Hotgun he say, "Well, so how about my old friend Tom Platt? The bible say his time was done already up, but he was still sowing lots a wild oats and was not kept his promise with the gals."[5]

And Tookpafka Micco he smoked again a long time and say, "Well, maybe so it was all come out in the whitewash."

1. Charles Joseph Bonaparte (1851–1921), of Maryland, was a graduate of Harvard Law School and a founder of the National Civil Service Reform League. He had known Roosevelt when the latter was civil service commissioner. In 1905 he would become Roosevelt's secretary of the navy and in 1906 his attorney general. See *Dictionary of American Biography*, ed. Dumas Malone (New York: Charles Scribner's Sons, 1929), 2:427–28. The comment relating Bonaparte's grand and gloomy looks to his ancestry probably refers to his kinship to Napoleon Bonaparte.

2. In poker, to stand "pat" is to refuse a card from the dealer, an indication that the player will bet on the cards already dealt. Bixby may have chosen to stand pat because he had a good hand or because he was bluffing. When the hand is called, the players must show their cards. The implication is that Bixby may be bluffing and holding only three cards of the same suit but can play the hand because the government backs him. The joker, or wild card, would give him an

edge (something "to nigger with"), creating four cards of the same suit, but still not a good hand.

3. Dwight Tuttle, formerly a member of the Connecticut legislature, was appointed by Hitchcock in 1899 as chairman of the Creek Townsite Commission and then to the Choctaw commission. He had not been chairman of the Choctaw commission long, having been appointed in early September to replace Dr. John A. Sterrett, who had been removed for neglect of duty and absence from office. *Indian Journal*, January 17, 1902, and September 25, 1903; *Vinita Daily Chieftain*, September 12, 1903; Creek National Records 39035, Record Group 75, National Archives, maintained by Oklahoma Historical Society; *New York Times*, September 12, 1903, 2:3. The charges against Tuttle made by the *Russell American* have not been found.

4. The reference to Tuttle's religion is probably to his having entered the Episcopal ministry. See *Indian Journal*, January 17, 1902. Horses are trained to "go the gaits," that is, perform certain foot movements, or gaits, such as amble, pace, canter, or single-foot.

5. Senator Thomas Platt, of Connecticut, who was advanced in years, made national news when, on the eve of his wedding in New York, a young typist from Washington arrived and accused him of breach of promise. Platt was instrumental in securing Tuttle's appointment. See *New York Times*, September 12, 1903, 2:3; October 14, 1903, 3:2, and October 16, 1903, 5:3.

Letters No.34, No.35, and No.36

[No.34: *Fort Smith Times*, November 1, 1903; *Cherokee Advocate*, November 7, 1903; *Vinita Weekly Chieftain*, November 12, 1903; this letter was reprinted elsewhere, date and source uncertain, clipping, in Posey Collection, Thomas Gilcrease Institute of American History and Art. No.35: *Muskogee Evening Times*, late November 1903, date uncertain, clipping, in Posey Collection; *Fort Smith Times*, November 29, 1903; *Vinita Weekly Chieftain*, December 3, 1903. No.36: *Muskogee Evening Times*, December 1903, date uncertain, clipping, in Posey Collection; *South McAlester Capital*, December 17, 1903]

With the fraud investigation on hold, Posey turned his attention to matters of speculation generated by the approaching session of Congress. Foremost among these was the statehood question. Letter No. 34 deals with a convention held at South McAlester on October 26. Ostensibly the purpose was to petition Congress to authorize a regular delegate to Congress from Indian Territory, but single-state adherents sought a resolution in favor of statehood. They attempted to get a statehood article inserted into their resolutions, but separate-staters managed to keep it out of the final draft. Because this letter, like his last, appeared in the *Fort Smith Times*, Posey attached the following note: "See A. Castle, C. E. Castle, the Wagoner lawyer and single statehood champion; Clarence Dug Last, Clarence Douglas, editor of the Muskogee Phoenix, who acted as temporary chairman of the delegate convention; Rustle, U. S. Russell, editor of the South McAlester Capital and champion of the cause of separate statehood for Indian Territory."

By the time the next letter appeared, Posey was city editor of the *Muskogee Evening Times*. In this letter, Hotgun speculates on whether the conservative Creeks, personified in Chitto Harjo, will ultimately bow to the inevitable or continue to oppose the allotment process.

In October, Charles Curtis, a member of Congress from Kansas, made a quick trip to Muskogee. His visit was followed by a short visit by the newspaperman and congressman William Randolph Hearst, whose party aboard his private train included other members of Congress. Ostensibly they were to "assess" conditions in Indian Territory and recommend legislation. Such short visits had been common. Each resulted in recommendations, but Congress dragged its feet on the statehood question. These issues are the substance of Letter No. 36.

✍ [No. 34]

"Well, so," Hotgun he say, "they was a fine opportunity for some lawyer to pay his board bill and saw off his practice in the police court."

And Tookpafka Micco, he say, "Well, so you was had to sight me."[1]

Then Hotgun he say, "Well, so I think they was a good chance for some lawyer that didn't had anything but bright prospects and the Arkansaw Digest[2] to start something 'sides powwows to make resolutions and delegates to congress, 'cause the people was burned out on old chestnuts like that and they appetite was craved for green things."

And Tookpafka Micco he say, "Well, maybe so my old friend See A Castle up to Wagoner could conjure up something new under the sun."[3]

Then Hotgun he say, "Well, so See A Castle was done lost lots a practice trying, but his medicine looks like was had something the matter with it and the people was had no faith in it any more."

"Well, maybe so," Tookpafka Micco, he say, "my old friend See A Castle was not kept good time with his foot when he was sung and blowed in the medicine."[4]

Then Hotgun he say, "Well, so they was more than that the matter — he was sung the same song too many times and left out the variations."

And Tookpafka Micco he say, "Well, so I think Clarence Dug Last a the Muskogee Phoenix was tried to ring in the changes for him down to South Town, when the coming senators and congressmen and county judges and sheriffs and justices a the peace and school trustees and single state house janitors and dog pelters was asked the Great White Father in Washington for a handout from the pie counter."

Then Hotgun he say, "Well so what kind a variations was Clarence Dug Last introduced?"

And Tookpafka Micco he say, "Well, so you see he was the big man in the powwow and when the committee on how to resolute was submitted its report he was knocked for order and say, 'Well, so the report was unanimously adopted. What other business was they before the meeting?' When Clarence Dug Last was made this bad break they was a big Rustle in the convention, like a cyclone busy up in Kansas."[5]

"Well, so," Hotgun he say, "how you mean by a big Rustle in the convention?"

And Tookpafka Micco he explain, "Well, so I mean the editor a the South McAlester Capital was start an objection agin that kind a despotism and fond recollections a Tom Reed, and was throwed more pine knots in the fire when he was p'inted out a bad verse in the prayer to the Great White Father in Washington."[6]

Then Hotgun he say, "Well, so you p'int it out to me."

And Tookpafka Micco he say, "Well, so you see Secretary Lamb a the convention on how to resolute was got lost from the subject and took refuge in a refrain on single statehood."[7]

Then Hotgun he say, "Well, maybe so a fox could get a fit in the sheep's tailor shop same as a wolf."

1. Sights on rifles could be adjusted up or down and to the right or left to ensure the accuracy of fire. To sight a rifle was to adjust the sights until the gun could be aimed accurately. Tookpafka Micco does not understand Hotgun's allusion and wants to be clued in so that he might focus on the topic.

2. *Arkansas Digest* was a compendium of cases decided in the courts of Arkansas. The laws of Arkansas would be extended to Indian Territory in 1904.

3. C. E. Castle had been prominent in the single-state convention at Shawnee the preceding summer. The implication is that his is an old routine.

4. One traditional Creek medicine ritual included blowing through a hollow reed into the medicine pot. Castle's "medicine" is no longer working.

5. Douglas, a single-state proponent, had used a heavy hand with the gavel, and the resolution containing a statement on statehood had passed. U. S. Russell challenged Douglas's actions as chairman and argued that the purpose of the convention was to elect a delegate, not to pass resolutions on statehood. Another vote was taken, and the language about statehood was removed. *Muskogee Phoenix*, October 29, 1903. The convention adjourned until November 5, when it reconvened and elected C. E. Foley of Eufaula as the Indian Territory delegate to Congress. *Muskogee Phoenix*, November 12, 1903.

6. Thomas Bracket Reed (1839–1902), known for his speaking ability, was a U.S. representative from Maine. In 1889 he became Speaker of the House and revolutionized House rules. What became known as "Reed Rules" substituted a "counted" quorum for a "voting" quorum. See *Dictionary of American Biography*, ed. Malone (1935), 15:457–59. The "prayer" refers to the resolution to be sent to President Roosevelt and to Congress. The "bad verse" was the language regarding statehood.

7. F. F. Lamb of Okmulgee was chairman of the committee on resolutions. *Muskogee Phoenix*, October 29, 1903.

✍ [No.35]

Well, so Kono Harjo's wife was made some good sour bread and a big dish of sakonipkee and a wash pot full a sofky, and Kono Harjo was invited Hotgun and Wolf Warrior and Tookpafka Micco they was welcome to had a feast with 'im and be thankful, like the Yankee, for prosperity.

And Hotgun and Wolf Warrior and Tookpafka Micco was sent word back to Kono Harjo, "Well, so you could count on it we sure be to your house Thanksgiving, 'cause they was a good crop a pecans and acorns and hickory-nuts and persimmons and a fancy price for cotton on account a the boll weevil."[1]

So Kono Harjo and Hotgun and Wolf Warrior and Tookpafka Micco was all celebrated Thanksgiving together, and Hotgun was made 'em a speech after dinner.

"Well, so," he say, "when Crazy Snake was called the fullbloods together 'round the council fire last Thanksgiving, up to Hickory Ground, he say, 'Well, so if they was any Injin here that was thankful, let 'im hold up his hand, so the lighthorse could take 'im out and give 'im fifty lashes next to the skin for lying like a dog and then lop off his left ear, so everybody could see he was not a good Injin.' " (Wolf Warrior he made a big grunt.)

"But," Hotgun he go on and say, "they was nobody raised his

hand to receive the punishment, and then Crazy Snake he say, 'Well, so that was a good sign; maybe so we better had a big stomp dance.' "[2] (Wolf Warrior he was grunt agin and Kono Harjo and Tookpafka Micco they was listened close.)

"So," Hotgun he go on and say, "Crazy Snake he was whooped right keen and took the lead in the stomp dance and start lots a trouble for the Big Man at Washington. But, maybe so, I could n't blame 'im 'cause the Injin could n't dig up the cost in the police court for patronizing home industry and was had nothing to be thankful for."[3] (Wolf Warrior and Kono Harjo and Tookpafka Micco they was all grunt this time like it was getting interesting.)

"But," Hotgun he go on and say, "maybe so, it was had to be that way anyhow like boodling; and, maybe so when Crazy Snake was got used to it, he was druther lived on his allotment in a box shack[4] with a side room to it than lounge round on a buffalo hide in the corner a the wigwam and nothing to do but make his toilet and had a good time on the reservation. Then again, maybe so when Crazy Snake was got civilized good, like Carrie Nation waving her hatchet and butting into things at Washington,[5] and William J. Brian wearing a bee gum 'stead of a hat in London,[6] he wouldn't give it up for a circus with three rings in it and the band playing 'Hiawatha' and the ticket man hollering, 'Well, so you was had to hurry if you see Bosco eat the copperhead alive!' "[7]

1. The boll weevil had been especially devastating to the cotton crop in the South during 1903. See, e.g., *Muskogee Phoenix*, September 24, 1903.

2. The original read "storm dance."

3. "Patronizing home industry" means getting drunk on homemade whiskey.

4. The original read "sack."

5. Carry Amelia Moore Nation (1846–1911), of Kentucky, lived in Missouri and Texas before settling in Medicine Lodge, Kansas, in 1889. The next year she became involved in a campaign to defeat liquor by destroying saloons. After 1900 she was widely known as a hatchet-wielding fanatic who believed that the ends

justified violent means. On November 19, 1903, she disrupted the U.S. Senate by creating a disturbance in the gallery. She was arrested and fined. See *Dictionary of American Biography*, ed. Dumas Malone (New York: Charles Scribner's Sons, 1934), 14:394–95, and *New York Times*, November 20, 1903, 3:2.

6. William Jennings Bryan was in London in late November. A stovepipe hat was sometimes called a bee gum. The reference to the beehive (or bee gum) for a hat, however, may be a way of saying that Bryan had "bees in his bonnet," perhaps because Bryan had offered the name of his friend and Ohio millionaire John W. Bookwalter as a possible candidate for president in 1904. *New York Times*, November 26, 1903, 7:1, and November 27, 1903, 1:2.

7. "Hiawatha" was a popular tune written by Neil Moret and James O'Dea and published in 1901. "Bosco" was Posey's name for a geek. Esau was a geek well-known to Indian Territory audiences for his feat of eating live snakes. See *Cherokee Advocate*, September 3, 1904.

📖 [No.36]

"Well, so," Hotgun he say, "looks like it was a big fad in congress to be a Injin philanthropist and do about in a private car and had a nigger porter to pour out the snake pizen and tell what town the special train was passed through without blowing the whistle."

And Tookpafka Micco he say, "Well, so I was 'fraid good statesmanship was decline like Rome in olden times."

Then Wolf Warrior he put in, "Well, so I think it was take a smart statesman to go through the Injin Territory and grasp the situation like it is without getting off a the right-a-way, like Charley Curtis and William R. Hearst.[1] Old Cicero and Patrick Henry couldn't go the gaits like that,[2] 'cause maybe so when they was poked they heads out a the window to see the Injins swallowed up by the land sharks and white children in the cotton patch that didn't had no advantages except in the reform school,[3] they was forget and break they skull again the bridge and make lots a litigation for the railroad."

"Well, so" Hotgun he say, "the Injin was in bad luck, 'cause he didn't had no statesmen to look out for his interest same as Cicero and Patrick Henry."

And Tookpafka Micco he say, "Well, guess so it was my time to set up the bottle a Peruna and be abreast a the times."

Hotgun he was drunk first and tell Wolf Warrior and Took-pafka Micco, "Well, so you all could kill it."[4]

Then Hotgun he was clear his throat and go on and say, "Well so it was like I say all the time and you could take it for what it was worth and had patience like old Job when he was ailing with the boils,[5] 'cause congress and Secretary Hitchcock was had to make up they mind. The Bible say it was no use to butt out your brains 'cause you was up again it. Maybe so after while it was come to show down in congress and we could all be glad of it like the greasers down to Panama when President Rooster Feather was gloried in they spunk."[6]

Then Wolf Warrior he say, "Well, so if the greasers that was druther roll cigarettes and wait for the moon to change so they could plant the flag of rebellion could get recognized in congress, the dyed-in-the-wool United States citizens in the Injin Territory could had a smell in Washington too and no stink raised about it in the Old Country."[7]

1. Charles Curtis (1860–1936), of Kansas, was admitted to the bar in 1881 and practiced law until he was elected to the House of Representatives in 1892. He would serve until 1907, when he was elected to the Senate, where he remained, with one interruption, until 1929. He was elected vice president on the ticket with Herbert Hoover in 1929. See *Dictionary of American Biography*, ed. Harris E. Starr (New York: Charles Scribner's Sons, 1958), 22:136. William Randolph Hearst (1863–1951), after failing to graduate from Harvard, worked for Joseph Pulitzer's *New York World*. In 1887 he became publisher of his father's *San Francisco Examiner* and launched a successful newspaper career. He engaged in the journalistic practices associated with "yellow journalism" and earned a reputation for ruthlessness. In 1900 he became active in politics and in 1902 was

elected to Congress from New York. See *Dictionary of American Biography*, ed. John A. Garraty (New York: Charles Scribner's Sons, 1977), Suppl. 5:283–88. Curtis, slated to become chairman of the House Committee on Indian Affairs, was in Muskogee on October 12–14, when he visited the Union agency and talked with local dignitaries, many of them advocates of single statehood. Hearst's party scheduled only a two-and-one-half-hour stop at Ardmore on October 20. See *Muskogee Phoenix*, October 15, 1903.

2. Marcus Tullius Cicero (106–43 B.C.), of Arpinum, was well-known for his oratory before the Roman bar. Patrick Henry (1736–1799), the American revolutionary orator, made himself famous for his statement "Give me liberty, or give me death."

3. One of the common arguments for statehood was the claim that the children of U.S. citizens living in Indian Territory received inadequate education.

4. That is, they could drink what was left in the Peruna bottle.

5. In the second chapter of Job in the Bible, Job is stricken with boils as the second test of his faith. Despite his misery, his faith abides and he is ultimately restored.

6. The original read "Rooster Father." In 1903 the United States signed the Hay-Herrán Treaty with Colombia, giving the United States a ninety-nine-year lease on a zone ten miles wide across Panama Province in order to build a canal. After the Colombian senate failed to ratify the treaty, the Panamanians revolted in the summer of 1903 and the United States immediately recognized the Republic of Panama. The result was a grant to use the ten-mile zone in perpetuity.

7. That is, they could gain statehood with little opposition, just as Panama had acquired nationhood with little opposition from Colombia ("the Old Country").

Letters No.37 and No.38

[No.37: *Muskogee Evening Times*, December 1903, date uncertain, clipping, in Posey Collection, Thomas Gilcrease Institute of American History and Art. No.38: *Muskogee Evening Times*, late December 1903, date uncertain, clipping, in Posey Collection; *Vinita Weekly Chieftain*, December 31, 1903; *Claremore Progress*, January 2, 1904; *Tahlequah Arrow* January 9, 1904]

The promised investigation of graft finally got under way in late November. Charles Bonaparte had worked on the case in Washington, but he was also investigating graft in the U.S. postal service. Thus in late October, Clinton Rogers Woodruff, a Philadelphia attorney, was hired as Bonaparte's assistant and sent to Indian Territory. From the start, Posey had predicted a whitewash, and the two investigators' activities seemed to support his belief. Woodruff arrived in Muskogee in late November and set up headquarters. He traveled to Okmulgee, Tishomingo, Atoka, Tahlequah, and South McAlester but spent most of his time in Muskogee. After only ten days, he returned to Washington to report to Bonaparte. Woodruff returned with Bonaparte on December 13, and the two held inquiries in the office of J. Blair Shoenfelt, the Indian agent, in the Katy Hotel. Muskogee citizens called the investigation the "star-chamber plan" because it was conducted behind closed doors. The investigators did not carry their inquiry outside the agency office, and in less than a week the investigation was completed. Bonaparte and Woodruff returned to Washington to analyze their findings and draft a report. Few people had much belief that anything would come of it.

✍ [No.37]

"Well, so," Hotgun he say, "Charley Bony Parts was drinking sofky locked up by himself in the Katy hotel and didn't want to be familiar with anybody but Clarence Bee Dug Last."[1]

And Tookpafka Micco he say, "Well, so when was he slipped in from Washington?"

And Hotgun he say, "Well, so all the newspapers was guessed different."

Then Tookpafka Micco he say, "Well, so what kind of a looking duck was this Bony Parts, anyhow?"

And Hotgun he say, "Well, so he was a fine looking Dutchman and was put me in mind of a big nubbin."[2]

Then Tookpafka Micco he say, "Well, maybe so the side show was start up now pretty soon with variations and the people was had a chance to say it was a fake and want they money back."

"Well, so," Hotgun he say, "the people was done begin to murmur already and they was good prospects for lots a righteous condemnation, 'cause Bony Parts was act like the mogul a China and was had two big Injin policemen to guard the dead line with Winchesters against the tale bearers."[3]

Then Tookpafka Micco he say, "Well, so that was star chamber doings."

And Hotgun he say, "Well, so I think it was the biggest republican whitewash that was ever come down the pike."

1. Bonaparte began his questioning on the afternoon of his arrival in Muskogee. Clarence B. Douglas was the first person questioned. *Tahlequah Arrow*, December 19, 1903.

2. Bonaparte was of French, not Dutch, descent, belonging to the family of one of Napoleon's brothers. A "nubbin" is an ear of corn in which some of the kernels fail to mature; it is therefore often small and is poor quality.

3. Bonaparte used Indian policemen as bailiffs. *Tahlequah Arrow*, December 19, 1903. A "deadline" is a boundary drawn around a military prison; prisoners who cross the line can be shot.

✍ [No.38]

Well, so Hotgun and Tookpafka Micco and Wolf Warrior and Kono Harjo was all happened to meet up together last Sunday at the Weogufky stomp ground and was weighed Bony Parts in the balance and found him whitewashing.[1]

"Well, so," Hotgun he say, "I think Bony Parts could made a good organizer a secret societies, 'cause it come natural for him to do that kind of business. When he was to Muskogee he was bolted the doors and plugged the key holes and pulled down the blinds so nobody could catch on how he was initiated the grafters in the mysteries a the calcimine."[2]

And Tookpafka Micco he say, "Well, so how many was took advantage a the opportunity and got in as charter members?"

And Hotgun he say, "Well, so maybe Bony Parts was organized a big lodge, but the applicants didn't all get in, 'cause Clarence Dug Last and Robit Owing was got in first and blackballed them all except Gay Blair Shoenfelt and Dam Big Pie and Break-in-rich and Plenty So Far and household names like that."[3]

(Wolf Warrior and Kono Harjo they was paid close attention and didn't butt in.)

"Well, so," Hotgun he say, "it was Jay Gouge Right and Attorney See-my-fee. They was something happen last summer that was made Clarence Dug Last had it in for them. So when Bony Parts was passed the ballot box around he was put in a black ball and winked at Robit Owing to follow suit and a hint to the wise was sufficient."[4]

Then Tookpafka Micco he say, "Well, so what kind a questions was Bony Parts was put to Clarence Dug Last?"

"Well, so," Hotgun he say, "Bony Parts was made inquires [*sic*] to see if Clarence Dug Last was fit to be a member and didn't find any objection except one."

And Tookpafka Micco he say, "Well, so what was that?"

"Well, so," Hotgun he say, "Clarence Dug Last was tried to claim all the credit for the president's message."[5]

(Wolf Warrior and Kono Harjo they was grunt and keep on listening close.)

Then Hotgun he go on and say, "Well, so when the lodge was organized Bony Parts he was made them a talk and say, 'Well, so you all must stick close together like a leech in time of trouble. Our order was teach that. When a brother was getting the worst of it in the dark he must holler, "blow the cap off!" 'cause that was the grand signal a distress.'"[6]

Then Tookpafka Micco he say, "Well, maybe so he could holler 'whitewash' too."

Then Hotgun he say, "Well, so when Bony Parts was got back to Washington he was promised to send a charter to the lodge."[7]

1. Weogufky tribal town was on Shell Creek near the site of present-day Hanna, Oklahoma. See Mrs. Willie Blair (interview), Indian-Pioneer History Papers, Archives and Manuscripts Division, Oklahoma Historical Society, 104:83. "Let me be weighed in an even balance, that God may know mine integrity" (Job 31:6).

2. Calcimine is whitewash for plaster.

3. Clarence Douglas and Robert L. Owen were the first two people Bonaparte interviewed. See *Tahlequah Arrow*, December 19, 1903. The implication is that they defended the likes of Shoenfelt, Bixby, Breckenridge, and Soper.

4. Douglas told Bonaparte that he had been fired the previous summer because J. George Wright made misrepresentations of his actions to Secretary Hitchcock. Wright and A. P. Murphy, the attorney for the Creek Nation, had also made charges against Shoenfelt because of his handling of a lease case. Owen had been attorney for the defendant in the same case and defended Shoenfelt's actions. See *Tahlequah Arrow*, December 19, 1903.

5. Douglas reported in the *Muskogee Phoenix* that he had called on President Roosevelt on November 23 to discuss conditions in Indian Territory and to stress the need for public schools there. Roosevelt allegedly told him that any suggestion he made would be included in the president's annual message to Congress. Douglas wrote a recommendation calling for the establishment of a public school system in Indian Territory. See *Muskogee Phoenix*, November 26, 1903.

6. In muzzle-loaded firearms, "blowing a cap" meant that the percussion cap exploded without igniting the powder in the barrel. Here, it is a signal for the grafters to close ranks and protect one another.

7. The "charter" is the report, which would whitewash the affair.

Letters No. 39 and No. 40

[No. 39: *Muskogee Evening Times*, early January 1904, date uncertain, clipping, in Posey Collection, Thomas Gilcrease Institute of American History and Art; *Eufaula Tribune*, January 8, 1904. No. 40: *Muskogee Evening Times*, January 1904, date uncertain, clipping, in Posey Collection; *Eufaula Tribune*, January 15, 1904; *Tahlequah Arrow*, January 23, 1904]

With the fraud investigation at an end and Bonaparte and Woodruff back in Washington, the public interest in the scandal waned once more while the investigators wrote their report. Convinced that the investigation would come to nothing, Posey dropped the subject. The advent of a new year, 1904, was an opportunity for Hotgun and his friends to assess the condition of the conservative Creeks in the face of social and economic change in Indian Territory. Like Posey, they nostalgically looked back to the Creek Nation of twenty-five years earlier; present-day realities indicated that economic well-being depended on the removal of restrictions from the sale of allotments and that the efforts of Snakes like Chitto Harjo to have the old treaties reaffirmed and old lifeways maintained were detriments to progress.

✍ [No.39]

Well, so Kono Harjo's wife was made some more sour bread and some more suck-ko-nip-kee and some more blue dumpling and some more good hickory nut sofky, and old time Indian dishes like that, for New Year;[1] and Kono Harjo was sent word to Hotgun and Wolf Warrior and Tookpafka Micco to come over and help eat it up so he could throw the scraps out to his squirrel dogs.

"Well, so," Hotgun he tell Wolf Warrior and Tookpafka Micco, "Well, so better be on hand, 'cause maybe so if the restrictions aint removed it's the only chance we was had to get a belly full in Nineteen Hundred and Four."[2]

And Wolf Warrior and Tookpafka Micco they was coincided with him and didn't take no exceptions. So they was all on hand in time to had a good chat before Kono Harjo's wife was holler, "hombux che."[3]

Hotgun he was put a live coal in his pipe and say, "Well, so the New Year was made me lonesome for olden times put near twenty-five years ago, when you could go up to Muskogee and hear the cayotes [*sic*] howling in the back ground and yanking up the shoats where they was now talking about putting up a opera house large enough for fifteen hundred people to all get killed in."[4]

And Tookpafka Micco he say, "Well, so they was lots a changes been made up to Muskogee and you couldn't hardly locate yourself if you didn't had a policeman."

(Wolf Warrior and Kono Harjo they was nod their heads and put fresh coals in they pipes.)

Then Hotgun he say, "Well, so then you could go in the shack restaurant and eat and didn't had to have a string band to whet your appetite."

And Tookpafka Micco he say, "Well, so them days the store keeper and hod carrier didn't eat dinner at supper time and jackasses didn't try to be elks."

1. Blue dumplings were made by adding finely beaten parched hickory nutshells, bean hulls, corncobs, or corn shucks to finely beaten corn, shaping the dough into five- or six-inch rolls, wrapping the rolls in corn shucks, and boiling them until they were done. See "Sarah Scott Phillips," *Indian-Pioneer History*, Archives and Manuscripts Division, Oklahoma Historical Society, 40:7–9, and Jackson Lewis (informant), "Creek Ethnologic and Vocabulary Notes, October, 1910," file 1806 Creek, National Anthropological Archives, Smithsonian Institution, Washington, D.C. Sofky, the most favored Creek food, was sometimes made tastier by adding hickory nutmeat.

2. There had been much discussion of restrictions on sales of allotments during the summer of 1903. See, e.g., *Muskogee Daily Phoenix*, July 22, 25, and 26, August 7, 11, and 12, 1903. Debate continued as special-interest groups agitated for a change in regulations. Among them was the Muskogee Chamber of Commerce, to which Posey belonged. In the early days of 1904, the chamber created a commission to tour the territory and find out how the people felt about restrictions. Posey was one of the first to make a statement, saying that the Indians were competent and did not need the protection of sales restrictions and that a failure to remove the restrictions would retard economic progress. U.S. Congress, Senate, 59th Cong., 2d sess., S. Rep. 5013, pt. 2:1908–9.

3. This was an invitation to eat.

4. The reference is probably to a fire at the Iroquois Theatre in Chicago in late December 1903. Nearly six hundred people were killed. The story of the tragedy was carried in Indian Territory newspapers. See *New York Times*, December 31, 1903, 1:1, and *Vinita Weekly Chieftain*, January 7, 1904. Muskogee had come into existence in 1872 with the construction of the MK&T Railroad. By 1904, it was the largest town in Indian Territory, containing a population of about ten thousand, served by seven railroads. See *Muskogee Daily Phoenix*, June 30 and July 25, 1903. Thus Muskogee was not only the political but also the economic hub of Indian Territory.

✍ [No.40]

"Well, so," Hotgun he say, "when Connie Foley and Crazy Snake was run onto each other in Washington they didn't had to take refuge in the back alley to kill the busthead in a hurry, like in Eufaula.[1] Soon as they was met up round the capitol soon of a morning and feeling sort a dry and brown taste in the mouth, all they was had to do was push and the barkeeper was there with the goods and ice water on the side."

"Well, maybe so," Tookpafka Micco he say, "they was had better than busthead and white mule, like the druggists get rich on and bootleggers was go to the pen for in the Territory."

And Hotgun he say, "Well, so they was had heap better stuff than that. They was had Bourbon and Monongahela, older than the Dawes Commission; and booze like that was put a man in congress instead a the calaboose."[2]

(Tookpafka Micco and Wolf Warrior and Kono Harjo they was listened close like it was getting interesting.)

And Hotgun he go on and say, "Well, so Connie Foley he was take a small one, but Crazy Snake he don't care for style and was make a hog a himself."

"Well, so," Wolf Warrior he put in, "I couldn't blame Crazy Snake for improving his opportunity."

Then Hotgun he was pardon the interruption and go on and say, "Well, so it's natural when the other fellow was say, 'It's on me,' and Crazy Snake was only human."

(Tookpafka Micco and Kono Harjo they was nodded.)

And Hotgun he go on and say, "Well, so when Connie was settled the bill, Crazy Snake he want to know where was hung out at and Connie he say, 'Well, so to the National Hotel;[3] pay me visit sometime.' So when it was about dinner time Crazy Snake he was shown up with Effa Ematha and Nocos Yahola[4] and other Snake lobbyists like that and they was all go and had something more on Connie and tell him he was good white man and paid him nice compliments like that. And that was made congressmen and senators think Connie Foley was had the Snake endorsement too."[5]

Then Tookpafka Micco he say, "Well so what government was foot the bills Connie Foley and Crazy Snake was running up in Washington?"

And Hotgun he say, "Well, so they was foot they own bills except Crazy Snake. He was strapped and maybe so was had to hire out to a patent medicine show to get back to Hickory Ground. But Connie was had a good bank account and his check was good for several figures on sight."[6]

Then Tookpafka Micco he say, "Well, so what authority was they had in Washington anyhow?"

And Hotgun he say, "Well, so Connie Foley was a delegate from the South McAlester convention, and was had good prospects to be senator from Injin Territory. But Crazy Snake he go there to help Secretary It's Cocked to nip the progress in Injin Territory in the bud so the country could lay out and grow up in sprouts."

1. "To kill the busthead in a hurry" was to drink up the illegal whiskey to avoid being caught with it. Cornelius "Connie" E. Foley (1857–?), a native of

Iowa, had gone to Indian Territory in 1881. He was a merchant and banker at Eufaula. See C. E. Foley (interview), *Indian-Pioneer History*, Archives and Manuscripts Division, Oklahoma Historical Society, 24:378–79, and Rex Harlow, comp., *Makers of Government in Oklahoma* (Oklahoma City: Harlow Publishing Co., 1930), 406. Foley was attempting to get himself recognized as the Indian Territory delegate to Congress and was busily engaged in lobbying congressional members.

2. Monongahela was rye whiskey, originally made in the Monongahela River region of Pennsylvania. If it was older than the Dawes Commission, it would be considered "aged."

3. The National Hotel in Washington, D.C., had been a stopping place for Creek as well as other Indian delegates for many years.

4. Effa Ematha (or Efi Emarthla) had been a judge of the Creek Supreme Court in 1873, prosecuting attorney for Deep Fork (renamed Eufaula) District in 1877 and 1878, judge of the district in 1879, Creek delegate to Washington in 1885, and a member of the House of Warriors from Arbeka town in 1887. See Creek National Records, 25911, 25913, 28699, 29936, 32562, 32594, and 32933, Record Group 75, National Archives, maintained by Oklahoma Historical Society. Nocos Yahola (also known as Taylor) served in the House of Warriors in 1868 and as second chief in 1882. See Creek National Records, 32468 and 35736, ibid. It is uncertain whether Posey was referring to these historical figures.

5. Connie Foley and Chitto Harjo had two different agendas. Foley was a single-state advocate, though he claimed his first priority was to establish his position as delegate. Chitto Harjo, who had led the Snakes in their refusal to enroll for allotments, had persuaded many Snakes not to prove their rights to a share of the Loyal Creek payment, which had been reduced to half of its original $1.2-million settlement. He went to Washington in late 1903 allegedly to see the president about restitution of the original amount. *Muskogee Phoenix*, December 3, 1903. Posey's humor turns on making these two unlikely compatriots drinking buddies in Washington.

6. It was common for delegations of Indians, especially the poorer classes, to become stranded in Washington and to appeal to federal officials for means to return home to Indian Territory. Foley not only had the backing of the people who had elected him at the McAlester convention in early November 1903 but also owned a mercantile establishment in Eufaula. The suggestion that Chitto

Harjo might have to join a traveling "Indian medicine" show is subtle but devastating criticism.

Letter No.41

[*Vinita Weekly Chieftain*, January 28, 1904; this letter was reprinted from *Muskogee Evening Times*, but no copy of the original has been found.]

Because 1904 was a presidential election year, political party activities began early. In addition to the national elections, the prospect of statehood added political interest in Indian Territory. Prevailing sentiment leaned heavily to the Democrats; thus the Republicans started early in attempting to organize on the local level. Posey was an ardent Democrat, and as a journalist, he attacked the Republicans without mercy. A theme that ran through his commentary was the Republican party as the party of the blacks. In his commentary on a convention of the Muskogee Republicans gathered on January 25, Hotgun reflects Posey's bias against both Republicans and blacks.

✍

Well, so when Tookpafka Micco and Wolf Warrior and Kono Harjo was come to visit Hotgun he was chucked up the fire and say, "Well, so I didn't had much style to put on like the Wauhillau club,[1] but maybe so I could lay some hickory sticks in the fire place and had the old woman put on a pot a sofky, so my friends could sit down to something that was had more substance to it than a cup a weak tea and a cracker with salt on it."

Tookpafka Micco and Wolf Warrior and Kono Harjo they was smoked their pipes and spit in the ashes and make theyselves comfortable, like they was at home with lots a corn in the cribs and brown middlings[2] hanging up in the smokehouse and a big padlock on the door and several mean, sofky dogs coiled up in the chimney corner.[3]

157

Then Tookpafka Micco he say, "Well, so what's in the atmosphere this time?"

And Hotgun he say, "Well, so they was so much you could smell it if the wind was blowing from Muskogee."

And Tookpafka Micco he say, "Well, must be the Lily Whites and the Dam Blacks was stirred up harmony up that way."

And Hotgun he say, "Well, so that's what's the matter. They was had a convention and gobs a peace and good will big as pawnbrokers signs was float round in the air in the Grab-a-gun opera house.[4] They was niggers there from Cane creek and Wybark and Wildcat and Crapshoot and Chickenroost and Cakewalk and Ragtime and all the Katy waiting rooms.[5] And then they was Shoamfat from Wyoming and Tom Needsit from Illinois and Clarence Duglast from It and Nute Brewery from the Sunflower state.[6]

"But these mugwumps was looked like missionaries up near the head a the Nile in Africa, and the manager a the Grab-a-gun opera house was had to turn on more electric lights so the scribe from Uganda could see how to write the minutes.[7] About this time Clarence Duglast was butt in anyhow and blowed the cap off and make Nute Brewery chairman all the time. Then the niggers was take charge a the meeting and made theyselves all second chiefs and first secretaries a the blowout and then tacked the Creek nation and Oklahoma together and nominated Plenty Sofar to congress to get postoffices for his constituents and a pass on the Frisco for Sango and Twine."[8]

Tookpafka Micco and Wolf Warrior and Kono Harjo they was listened close and was visibly affected.

Then Hotgun he go on and say: "Well, so the darkest time was just before daylight."[9]

1. The Wauhillau Club was an organization that began with ten acres on Barron Fork Creek in the Cherokee Nation. It soon expanded to more than fifty

acres and contained a large log clubhouse on a bluff overlooking the creek. The number of members was limited to fifty, which included many public officials and well-known personages such as Clarence B. Douglas, William H. Mellette, and J. Fentress Wisdom. Indian Agent J. Blair Shoenfelt was its first president. The general public believed it to be "open"; that is, intoxicants flowed freely in the private club. See *Muskogee Daily Phoenix*, January 22, 1904; *Vinita Weekly Chieftain*, January 28, 1904; and *Muskogee Democrat*, May 12 and July 27, 1905. This passage reflects Posey's disdain for what he called the "high life."

2. "Middlings" were sidemeat, or the middle portion of a hog carcass, turned brown by smoke curing.

3. The original read "softy dogs."

4. Gavagan Opera House in Muskogee.

5. Cane Creek, which headed between Muskogee and Okmulgee, was the location of a large settlement of Creek freedmen. Wybark was a black town on the MK&T Railroad north and across the Arkansas River from Muskogee. Wildcat, renamed Grayson, was a black town in the northwestern corner of present-day McIntosh County, Oklahoma. Crapshoot, Chickenroost, Cakewalk, and Ragtime were not places but are terms of social and cultural stereotyping. The reference to the waiting rooms at the Katy depot suggests the Democrats' stand on segregation of blacks. In the campaign leading to Oklahoma statehood, support for Jim Crow legislation would become a major plank in the democratic platforms.

6. J. Blair Shoenfelt, the Indian agent, had come to Indian Territory from South Dakota by way of Wyoming; in South Dakota he had worked for statehood, had served as a member of its constitutional convention, and had been a county judge. Thomas B. Needles, an Illinois merchant, businessman, state auditor, and state legislator, was appointed U.S. marshal for Indian Territory in 1889. See O'Beirne and O'Beirne, *The Indian Territory*, 166–68. Clarence B. Douglas, of It (Indian Territory), was the editor of the *Muskogee Phoenix*. Isaac Newton (Newt) Ury, of Kansas, was formerly an appraiser of lands for the Dawes Commission. He was an official of the U.S. Loans Trust Company and a member of the Muskogee city council. See *Kingfisher Free Press*, September 20, 1900, and *Twin Territories* 4 (July 1902): 213.

7. The mugwumps were Republican reformers who gave their support to the Democrats and helped elect Grover Cleveland as president in 1884. The identity of "the Scribe from Uganda" is undetermined.

8. The suggestion that the Creek and Seminole nations should be annexed to

Oklahoma first, to be followed by the rest of Indian Territory, had been made years before. As recently as early 1903, the idea had been offered as a compromise in a statehood bill before Congress. *Vinita Weekly Chieftain*, January 29, 1903. Both Lewis Sango and A.G.W. Sango were present. The reference is probably to the latter, who was quite visible in Republican political affairs in Muskogee. W. H. Twine was an attorney and the editor of the *Muskogee Cimeter*, the longest-running black newspaper in Muskogee's history. See *Muskogee Daily Phoenix*, January 26, 1904.

9. This common saying — "It is always darkest just before the day dawneth" — appeared in Thomas Fuller, *Pisgah Sight* (1650), bk. 3, ch. 11.

Letter No.42

[*Muskogee Daily Phoenix*, April 10, 1904; *Eufaula Tribune*, April 15, 1904]

The Congress of 1903–4 seemed less likely than several before it to produce statehood legislation. Late in the session, the House committee on Indian affairs reported a bill that called for the admission of Oklahoma and Indian Territory as one state and New Mexico and Arizona as another. Introduced by the committee chairman, Edward L. Hamilton of Michigan, the bill passed the House, but the Senate delayed the bill until the next session of Congress, which would convene in December 1904. Inaction, as in Congresses past, resulted from partisan political maneuvering. Hotgun, however, blamed it on too many statehood plans.

🖎

Well, so Hotgun he shut his eyes right close together and look in the fire a long time, maybe so like federal judge trying to figure how many ounces a Izzard county Arkansaw statutes and how many Injin laws that was lost they strength it was take to hand down a decision to suit the grafter.[1]

Then Hotgun he spit in the ashes and go on and tell Tookpafka Micco and Wolf Warrior and Kono Harjo, "Well, so they could be to [*sic*] many other kind a people get together 'sides cooks and spoil the sofky."[2]

And Tookpafka Micco he say, "Well, so look like the more, the merrier."

And Hotgun he say, "Well, so that was all right to a stomp dance, but it was different in congress — too many congressmen was get a bald scald on statehood.[3]

"Old Quay he say he was part Injin and raised on sofky in Pennsylvania, and so he want his way. Charley Curtis he say he was proud a his Injin blood and wigwam in Kansas, and he want to had his way. Old Foster he say he was a Yankee Crazy Snake, and he want to had his way. Then old Robinson he say he was smoked the pipe with Connie Foley, and he want to had his way."[4]

Then Hotgun he light his pipe and go on and say, "Well, so there you was, and maybe so the wild onions was come up again on the creeks several times and old Brosius was caused consternation at the pie counter, like Daniel in olden times, before Injin Territory and Oklahoma could had statehood."[5]

(Tookpafka Micco and Wolf Warrior and Kono Harjo, they was kind a hold the smoke in their mouth and pay close attention and grunt some time.)

Then Tookpafka Micco he tell Hotgun, "Well, so you was talked like you was favored going in with Oklahoma."

And Hotgun he say, "Well, so you was bad mistaken. Maybe so Oklahoma was had lots a good clay for brick and some good sand for plaster and plenty mean whisky, but it was had no water to mix 'em with. So I was druther lived in a pole pen in Injin Territory than a sod house dug out in Oklahoma,[6] where I was had to pick up cow chips on the prairie or waste coal on the railroad right-of-way to start a fire in the kitchen for the old woman to get breakfast."

Then Tookpafka Micco he say, "Well, so then what was made the newspapers say all the time they was lots a prosperity in Oklahoma?"

And Hotgun he say, "Well, so that was very easy to explain. Oklahoma was had lots a attractions to sell. So when a drummer down to South Town or maybe so a store clerk up to Sapulpa, or maybe so a single statehood delegate down to Ardmore,[7] or grafter up to Muskogee was want to trot the gaits and spludge, he buy a round trip ticket to Oklahoma City and take his roll along to blow in.[8] That was how Oklahoma was had prosperity like rolling off a log."

Then Tookpafka Micco he say, "Well, so them fellers didn't get they money's worth, 'cause they come home and was had to go away again to Hot Springs, Arkansaw, for they health."[9]

(Wolf Warrior and Kono Harjo they was grunt big and spit in the ashes again.)

1. Arkansas statutes replaced tribal laws in Indian Territory in March, adding to the complexity of legal matters and increasing the possibilities for grafters to do their work. Izard County is in the Ozark Mountain region of north-central Arkansas. To Posey, ignorant poor whites who came out of the Ozarks typified the squatters and white renters in Indian Territory. He often equated squatters, renters, and "Arkansawyers."

2. The old adage "Too many cooks spoil the broth" dated from at least the seventeenth century and was probably drawn from one known in the previous century: "The more cooks, the worse the pottage."

3. "Bald scald" is probably a mistyping of "bad scald." In hog butchering, the carcass was dipped in boiling water and then scraped to remove the hair. If the scald was good, the bristles were easily scraped away; if the scald was bad, the scraping was hard, and it became difficult to prepare the pork for curing.

4. Matthew Quay, a Democratic senator from Pennsylvania, had persistently offered a bill admitting Oklahoma and Indian Territory as one state and New Mexico and Arizona as another. Bill S3625 differed from others, however — and was therefore popular among some Indian Territory residents — because it pro-

posed to remove restrictions on the sale of all but homestead allotments. *Vinita Weekly Chieftain*, April 7, 1904. Quay claimed one-twentieth Delaware blood. See *Red Man and Helper*, May 27, 1904. Charles N. Curtis exploited his claim to one-sixteenth Kanza (Kaw) and one-sixteenth Osage blood. Representative David Johnson Foster, of Vermont, allegedly proposed to restore to the Cherokee Nation everything guaranteed it in the treaties of 1828 and 1835. The conservative Cherokee Nighthawks refused to sign up for allotments in part because they believed such legislation would be passed. *Cherokee Advocate*, December 17, 1904. Representative James M. Robinson, of Indiana, had introduced a lengthy bill for the admission of Oklahoma and Indian Territory as a single state, detailing at length how the new state should be organized. *Cherokee Advocate*, January 23, 1904. Connie E. Foley, the unofficial delegate to Congress from Indian Territory, spent time in Washington lobbying for statehood. See C. E. Foley (interview), *Indian-Pioneer History*, Archives and Manuscripts Division, Oklahoma Historical Society, 24:378–79, and Harlow, *Makers of Government*, 406.

5. In March, rumors circulated that S. M. Brosius, of the Indian Rights Association, was abroad in Indian Territory once more and was preferring new charges against members of the Dawes Commission. *Vinita Weekly Chieftain*, March 24, 1904. Hotgun is apparently comparing Brosius's revelations about federal officials to the revelations made by the biblical Daniel in his interpretations of dreams.

6. A "pole pen" was a fence made by peeled saplings laid horizontally between posts. Because of a lack of timber for building, settlers in Oklahoma often dug rectangular pits, cut sod and stacked it around the pits to form low walls, built a roof structure, and covered the roof with sod. Such structures were called dugouts.

7. "South Town" was South McAlester, in the Choctaw Nation; Sapulpa was in the Creek Nation west of Tulsa, and Ardmore was in the Chickasaw Nation.

8. "To trot the gaits" was to make a show. Some gaits or steps that horses are taught, such as the amble, canter, and single-foot, are rather showy. "Spludge" was probably meant to be "splurge." A "roll" was a roll of bills to spend.

9. Hot Springs was a well-known health resort where the ailing bathed in the hot springwater. The implication is that Oklahoma is so unhealthful that visitors have to go to a spa to recuperate.

The Fus Fixico Letters

Letters No.43, No.44, No.45, No.46, and No.47

[No.43: *Muskogee Daily Phoenix*, April 17, 1904; *Vinita Weekly Chieftain*, April 21, 1904; *Eufaula Tribune*, April 22, 1904; *Cherokee Advocate*, April 23, 1904. No.44: *Eufaula Tribune*, April 29, 1904; the letter had probably appeared earlier in the *Muskogee Daily Phoenix*. No.45: *Muskogee Daily Phoenix*, May 1, 1904; *Eufaula Tribune*, May 6, 1904; *Cherokee Advocate*, May 7, 1904. No.46: *Muskogee Daily Phoenix*, May 8, 1904; *Eufaula Tribune*, May 13, 1904. No.47: *Eufaula Tribune*, May 27, 1904; *Cherokee Advocate*, May 28, 1904; the letter had probably appeared earlier in the *Muskogee Daily Phoenix*.]

With the statehood question set aside and the political campaign season not yet under way, Hotgun and his friends use the lull in the news to take stock of the prospects for conservative Indians like themselves and Chitto Harjo. They conclude that the Indians must learn to live with grafters, who are there to stay. Two recent events lead them to that conclusion. First, in an Indian appropriations bill, Congress removed restrictions from the sale of surplus allotments of adult non-Indians, thus making available for sale thousands of acres of land allotted to freedmen and to adopted or intermarried whites. Restrictions on Indians' land might be removed by application to, and approval by, the secretary of the interior. Second, Bonaparte and Woodruff filed a report of their investigation into graft by federal officials in Indian Territory. Although it gave credence to most of Brosius's charges, the report rejected other allegations of wrongdoing, except in the case of the Dawes commissioners, whose positions it recommended the government abolish. Overall, the report was simply a mild indictment of the way government business had been conducted in the territory. For land speculators, it meant little change. Hotgun and his friends weigh the merits of political aspirants of both parties and find them all to be "spoil hunters." The conservative Creeks, philosophically at odds with the materialism of the new society, are pushed farther from the political and economic mainstream.

✍ [No.43]

"Well, so," Hotgun he say, "the Injin he sell land and sell land, and the white man he give whiskey and give whiskey and put his arm around the Injin's neck and they was good friends like two Elks out for a time."

"Well, maybe so," Tookpafka Micco he say, "the white man was cut it out when the Injun was all in."

Then Hotgun he make the smoke b'il out a his pipe good and answer Tookpafka Micco, "Well, so the Injin was had to go up against it to learn and, maybe so, after while he catch on, same like the white man and go to Mexico and bunco the greaser."

Then Hotgun he take another puff and go on and say, "Well, so like I start to say history was repeat itself. The Injin he sell his land in the old country (Alabama) and he sell his land in Injin Territory and was had a good time out here like back there in olden times. But back in old country he was live different, 'cause he was sit on a long chair like a fence rail — but he was no mugwump.[1] Now the Injin was sit on a chair that was had fore legs and hind legs too, like a oxen, and also a cusion [*sic*] soft like moss. He was got civilized and called the old chair a bench. He wear a white shirt now and black clothes and shoes that was look like a ripe musk melon.[2] Then he was buy bon bons for his papoose and drop-stitch stockings for his squaw[3] and part his name in the middle, J. Little Bear.

"Then the white man he tell the Injin, 'Well so your wagon was out of date and you better buy you a fine buggy; or, maybe so, a fine surrey.' The Injin he grunt and say, 'Well, so let's see um.' Then the white man he say, 'Well, so I sell it cheap like stealing it — sell it to Injun the fine buggy and harness and all for hundred and fifty dollars. That was cheap, 'cause Injun he was sell land and got it lots a money and was out of date riding on two horse wagon.' Then the Injin he look at fine buggy a long time and make good judgment and buy um. His little pony mare team look mighty weak and woolly and got colt, but they was pulled the fine buggy home all right. Then when the Injin was got home he was put the fine buggy under a tree to look at like fine painting."

(Tookpafka Micco and Wolf Warrior and Kono Harjo they was look in the fire and spit in the ashes and pay close attention like they was interested.)

Then Hotgun he go on and say, "Well, maybe so about three years from now the starch was go out a the Injin's white shirt and make it limber like a dish rag, and his black suit was fade like the last rose a summer and his breeches was get slack like a gunny sack,[4] and his big toe was stick through his tan shoes like a snag in Deep Fork,[5] and his fine buggy was tied together with bailing [*sic*] wire[6] and his old fillies was made good crow bait pulling the fine buggy to stomp dances." Then, Hotgun he go on and say, "maybe so the Injin was awakened up to his sense a duty and earn his bread by the sweat a his brow like a good republican or maybe so a democrat."[7]

And Tookpafka Micco he say, "Well, maybe so he be a middle of a the roader."

Then Hotgun he say, "Well, so they was only two sides to a clapboard and it's the same way in politics. The Injin couldn't cut any ice or raise any sofky sitting on top a the rail looking at the crabgrass."[8]

(Then Tookpafka Micco and Wolf Warrior and Kono Harjo they was grunt and spit in the ashes again and say, "Well, so we vote it straight.")

1. Hotgun's comparison of the traditional Creek split-log bench to a rail fence suggests that the mugwumps were engaged in political fence-sitting, which he urges his friends to avoid.

2. Tan shoes were in fashion.

3. These were machine-knitted stockings in which patterns were created by dropping stitches at intervals.

4. A gunnysack was made of coarse jute. See "The Last Rose of Summer," a poem by Thomas Moore (1779–1852).

5. That is, the toe looked like a tree stump or limb visible above the surface of the water in the Deep Fork River, a tributary of the North Fork of the Canadian River.

6. Baling wire was used to tie bales of hay produced by mechanical balers.

7. "It is not necessary that a man should earn his living by the sweat of his brow unless he sweats easier than I do" (Henry David Thoreau, "Economy," *Walden* [1854]).

8. Crabgrass (*Digitaria sanguinalis*) was particularly bothersome to farmers.

✍ [No.44]

"Well, so," Hotgun he say, "the white man was graft hard all week and, maybe so, think a heap a Jesus on Sunday."

"Well, so," Tookpafka Micco he say, "must be you mean the white man was worked hard instead a graft hard, cause they was no one graft but the fruit tree man."[1]

And Hotgun he say, "Well, so the fruit tree man didn't had a monopoly on the business; but, same time, maybe so work hard was do well as graft hard, 'cause both words was mean the same thing — like Creek freedmen and nigger.

"If I was had you put up your land for sale and bid it in cheap and then borrow the money, that was grafting; or, maybe so, if I was sold you a block a stock in a big oil company and made you vice-president and squared off with you, that was working you."

(Tookpafka Micco he grunt like he was heard something new and Wolf Warrior and Kono Harjo they was cleared they throats and spit in the back a the fire place.)

Then Hotgun he was scooped up a big coal in his pipe and go on and say, "Well, so the grafter he been here a long time and was a pioneer, like the Dawes Commission. He was first come and sell the Injin lightning rod for dollar foot and run it all over the cabin and maybe so stick it in the ground two three times for good measure.

"Then the grafter come and sell the Injin steel range cook stoves too big to get in the cabin and burn up too much wood. So the Injin was had to build a brush harbor [*sic*] over it out in the yard and let it rust.

"Then the grafter he come 'long again with a big clock that was keep time like a almanac and didn't had to be wound up till it run down.

"Then the grafter he go through the country and sell Gale harrows too heavy for four mules to pull to Injins that didn't had nothin to plant but a pint of sofky corn and a hill a sweet potatoes.

"Then the buggy grafter come 'long and done business with the Injin.

"So everywhere you go now you find lightning rod for clothes line and steel range cook stoves for the children's play house, and calender [*sic*] clocks for ornament over the fire place and Gale harrows for scrap iron and old buggies for curiosities.

"Now," Hotgun he go on and say, "we was had the land grafter and lots more coming from Kansas and the Injins was still good picking and ready to bite like a bass when you was used grasshopper for bait."

(Tookpafka Micco and Wolf Warrior and Kono Harjo, they was listen like when they was heard a good sermon and grunt and spit in the back a the fire place again and kind a look at each other.)

Then Tookpafka Micco he tell Hotgun, "Well, so you was talked lots a horse sense and, maybe so, when I was sold my land I was took good care a the bucks and fight shy a the walled-up streets in Muskogee."

And Kono Harjo he tell Hotgun, "Well, so come see me and,

maybe so, I was took you out to drive in my new buggy and leave colt at home."

1. The pun implies agricultural grafting: inserting a scion into another plant and forming a compatible union, as in fruit growing.

✍ [No.45]

"Well, so," Hotgun he say, "It was time to go barefooted and quote poetry and spark some widow woman that was had a good family history on the Loyal Creek roll, 'cause every evening after sun down the frogs was give a concert, like the Muskogee Merchants Band,[1] and the old plow filly was picking up on the green grass and scattering lots a dead hair where she wallows."

(Tookpafka Micco and Wolf Warrior and Kono Harjo they was grunt and look way off towards the creek like they want to go fishing.)

Then Hotgun he smoke slow and look at red ants on the ground, go on and say, "Well, so I dont know what the newspapers was had to fill up on, 'cause Crazy Snake was made a assignment and gone out of business and retired to cabin to fix up the fence around his sofky patch and clean out his old spring and start over again."

"Well, so," Tookpafka Micco he say, "the newspapers could find lots a stuff to fill up on, like the removal a the restrictions so the niggers could squander they land for a blue suit of clothes and rubber-tired buggy and make room for progress, while the Injin he look on and learn a good object lesson."[2]

Then Wolf Warrior he join in and say, "Well, so the newspapers was had lots other news 'sides that to fill up on, like when Chief Porter go to St. Louis and get married and Secretary Its Cocked was approved the matrimony;[3] or maybe so, when Muskogee was had the state capital and all the railroads and street car lines, and all the senators and congressmen and members a the legislature and judges and road overseers and coroners, notary publics and things like that."[4]

Hotgun he look at the red ants and smoke a long time and say, "Well, so all that kind a thing was looked good in print, but it was not made spicy reading like bad news from Hickory Ground, where the Snakes was uprising and throwing tomahawks at the pale face prisoner for practice."[5]

"But," Hotgun he go on and say, "like I start to say, Crazy Snake he was called his people together and made a motion to give it up.

"He says, 'Well, so I was want to advise you they was no hope — and no provisions neither. So we better give up and be reconciled, like the Chinese.[6] The United States was break treaty and break treaty, and the white man he has come from Arkansas and come from Arkansas and stay and write back to kinfolks and say this was the garden spot a the earth and you better come out here before it's all gone. So that way the country was settled up and settled up, and they was no game left but swamp rabbits. We couldn't had any fish fry and stomp dance like in olden time. The white man he was make town and make town and build railroad and build railroad and appoint federal judge and appoint federal judge to say it was all right and we couldn't help it. So if we was had a council to talk it over, the marshal and soldiers was arrest us for trying to kill the president and put us in jail to catch consumption and maybe so lice. So I was make a motion to give it up and see what become of us anyhow.' Everybody was give a big grunt and the motion was carried."

(Tookpafka Micco and Wolf Warrior and Kono Harjo they was look mighty sorry.)

"Well, so," Hotgun he go on and say, "that was made me think about the old chief that was want to die long time ago, because he knew too much. The old chief he think he learn everything and maybe so he better lay down and die. So he was called his warriors around his buffalo hide and made 'em long talk about how to run the government when he die. Then he called for his pipe so he could die in peace, and was ask a little boy to get him a coal of fire. The little boy he go to the fire and bring the coal on some ashes in his hand instead of a chip or maybe so bark. The old chief he was watch him do it and jumped up and say, 'Well, so I was a damn fool and was had lots of sense to learn, maybe so from a little boy.' "7

1. The Loyal Creeks in convention and the Creek National Council had voted in the spring of 1903 to accept the congressional appropriation of six-hundred thousand dollars to settle the claim of the Loyal Creeks for losses sustained during the Civil War. It appeared, a year later, that the payment was about to be made. Few of the original claimants were still living; thus the payment would be made to their descendants. A widow whose family was on the Loyal Creek roll would have prospects of receiving a small sum in cash. See *Muskogee Daily Phoenix*, May 23, 1903, and *Vinita Weekly Chieftain*, June 30, 1904. The Muskogee Merchants Band was a group of local musicians who played for special occasions. See *Muskogee Democrat*, January 3 and May 31, 1905.

2. When restrictions were removed from the freedmen's allotments, many of them quickly lost their land. See Angie Debo, *And Still the Waters Run: The Betrayal of the Five Civilized Tribes* (Princeton, N.J.: Princeton University Press, 1972), 114.

3. A week earlier, Porter had announced his engagement to a woman from St. Louis, whose name he refused to divulge until her family made the announcement. *Cherokee Advocate*, April 30, 1904. Secretary Hitchcock was from St. Louis, where he and Porter had friends in common.

4. It was generally conceded that Muskogee would become the state capital if Indian Territory succeeded in becoming a separate state.

5. Though the Snakes still met occasionally at Hickory Ground and other places, there had been no public perception of a threat to the peace since early 1902. Chitto Harjo kept a low profile during the next five years, but subsequent

events would demonstrate that the Snake leader—contrary to Hotgun's indication in this letter—had not accepted the new order.

6. This is perhaps a reference to the carving up of China into "spheres of influence" by European powers. The Snakes might be loosely compared to the Boxers, who tried to resist the so-called Open Door Policy.

7. Posey had published a version of this story as a poem in *Muskogee Phoenix*, November 2, 1899, end of the century edition.

✎ [No.46]

Well, so Hotgun and Tookpafka Micco they was talked politics and Wolf Warrior and Kono Harjo they was paid close attention and grunt.

"Well, so," Hotgun he say, "they was lots a good political timber decaying 'cause we didn't had statehood, and maybe so some of it was rotten enough to make fox fire and lead Bony Parts a long chase for nothing."[1]

(Tookpafka Micco and Wolf Warrior and Kono Harjo they was grunt soft and study about it, while Hotgun was filled his pipe so he could warm up to the occasion.)

"But, maybe so," Hotgun he go on and say, "we could afford to let the timber go to waste, 'cause they was plenty more where that was come from 'sides the improved variety that was shipped down here from the states on fifty years trial."

And Tookpafka Micco he say, "Well so who was the most prominent before the people anyhow and was stirred up the most feeling?"

And Hotgun he say, "Well, so I think they was most prominent among themselves and the people didn't had nothing to do with it and was innocent. It was like this way: These politicians was get together like wolves when they was get hungry and want to forage—and the wolf in front was Plenty So Far. He was sit 'round on the knolls a Cooweescoowee prairie looking for signs till he was had big callouses on his hips. When congress was get in session and was busy with statehood bills and didn't had no time to look after the Injun, then Plenty So Far he was sit down on top of a knoll and look 'way off and howl lonesome.[2] Pretty soon Judge My Fee hear him 'way down on Kendall Heights and howl back and pretty soon come to him with lots a black wolves from Cane Creek.[3] Then maybe so the constable 'way down about Eufaula come and join with lots a cayotes [*sic*]. Then maybe so directly the postmaster down to Okmulgee come trotting up with a big following.[4] So that way they was come to him from Wildcat and Twine till Plenty So Far could look back over his shoulder and see a big pack behind so hungry they couldn't hardly stay together."[5]

(Tookpafka Micco and Wolf Warrior and Kono Harjo they was listen so close they pipes was go out and they didn't know it.)

Then Hotgun he go on and say, "Well, so it was the same way among the Democrats too and it was about a stand off. They was two, three down to Choctaw nation and Chickasaw nation howling with they packs. But I think maybe so Old Hailey was prowling 'round in the hills close to South McAlester with the biggest pack, while Bob Willing was sneaking 'round on the Blue with a few cayotes and Mayor Dick was sent up a lonesome howl from down about Ardmore.[6] So these was the Democrat wolves, but the trouble with them is they was too hungry to stay together and much disturbance among the sheep. The Republican wolves was better organized and had better hunting ground."

(Then Tookpafka Micco he was passed 'round the "home-made,"[7] and Hotgun and Wolf Warrior and Kono Harjo they was pinched off some for a fresh smoke.)

Then Tookpafka Micco he ask Hotgun, "Well, so who all want to be large delegates and little delegates to the big convention in the states to nominate a new president?"[8]

And Hotgun he say, "Well, so the Republicans was already picked out Plenty So Far from the Seminole nation and Cherokee nation and Quapaw agency to lead the delegates from the rest a the Territory. He was had a Choctaw Injun in the bunch that was not old enough to vote and was had to had a white man go with him to show him how to cast his ballot and make excuse for him."[9]

"Then," Hotgun he go on and say, "The Democrats was had lots aspirants to be large delegates and little delegates to trot out nominee for president. The most prominent ones was Cliff Jack's son and Jim's Living and Lick's Broke and Sam Rather Ford and C. B. Stew It."[10]

"But," Hotgun he go on and say, "like I first start to say, the people was busy putting in more land and building shacks and say nothing. Maybe so when the time was ripe they was take a hand in politics and make these spoil hunters look like an order on the store for merchandise during the Loyal Creek payment."

1. "Fox fire" is the glow of decaying wood caused by luminous fungi and is often mistaken for a light. Hence Bonaparte was misled in his investigation of fraud by federal officials in Indian Territory.

2. Soper, the U.S. attorney for the northern district and Republican national committeeman in Indian Territory, lived at Vinita, in Cooweescoowee District, Cherokee Nation.

3. Murphy, attorney for the Creek Nation, lived in Kendall Heights, a fashionable residential area west and south of downtown Muskogee. Cane Creek, west of Muskogee, was the site of a large settlement of Creek freedmen. "Black wolves" were black voters and politicians who generally supported the Republican party.

4. The constable at Eufaula and the postmaster at Okmulgee have not been identified.

5. That is, blacks were rallying behind Soper. Wildcat, in the northwestern corner of present-day McIntosh County, and Twine, presently called Taft, in Muskogee County, were both black towns.

6. Dr. D. M. Hailey (1841–1919), of Louisiana, had been a teacher in Indian Territory before establishing himself as a physician and a businessman at South McAlester. In 1876, he had been copublisher of the newspaper *Star-Vindicator*. In

later years he was involved in developing the coal resources in the Choctaw Nation. See W. E. Hailey (interview), *Indian-Pioneer History*, Archives and Manuscripts Division, Oklahoma Historical Society, 106:3–8. Robert Lee Williams (1868–1948), a native of Alabama, was an attorney who went to the Choctaw Nation in 1896. He was destined to make a name for himself in politics: member of the Oklahoma Constitutional Convention (1906–7); chief justice of the Oklahoma Supreme Court (1907–15); governor of Oklahoma (1915–19); U.S. judge for the Eastern District of Oklahoma (1919–37); U.S. circuit judge, Tenth District (1937–39). See Charles Evans, "The Robert Lee Williams Memorial Dedication," *Chronicles of Oklahoma* 31 (Winter 1953–54): 375–77, and Baxter Taylor, "Robert Lee Williams as I Knew Him," *Chronicles of Oklahoma* 31 (Winter 1953–54): 378–80. The "Blue" is Blue River, which joins the Red River southeast of Durant, Williams's home. Robert W. Dick, of Ardmore, was a native of Arkansas who had migrated to Oklahoma by way of Texas in 1889 and later moved to the Choctaw Nation. He served two terms as mayor of Ardmore, a position he held in 1904. After statehood, he served as warden of the Oklahoma State Penitentiary (1908–16). *Daily Oklahoman*, May 21, 1904, March 12, 1907, and July 23, 1916.

7. "Home-made" was home-grown and home-cured tobacco.

8. Tookpafka Micco refers to delegates and alternates to the national presidential nominating conventions.

9. The delegates were Soper, representing the Seminole Nation; E. E. Morris, the Chickasaw Nation; C. W. Raymond, the Creek Nation; W. H. Darrough, the Cherokee Nation; G. W. Bingham, the Quapaw agency; and Victor E. Locke, the Choctaw Nation. Locke was the only Choctaw in the delegation. *Muskogee Daily Phoenix*, March 18, 1904.

10. Clifford L. Jackson; James M. Givens, an attorney with the Zeveley and Givens firm in Muskogee, represented eastern capitalists with interests in Indian Territory oil and gas production. See *Muskogee Daily Phoenix*, June 14, 1903. Eck E. Brook was the former city attorney of Muskogee; Samuel M. Rutherford was the mayor of Muskogee; and C. B. Stuart was an attorney from South McAlester.

✍ [No.47]

Well, so, while the young warriors was played Injun ball and gobbled at one another,[1] like in olden times, last Sunday, at the Weogufky square ground, Hotgun and Tookpafka Micco and

Wolf Warrior and Kono Harjo they was go off to theyselves under the brush arbor where it was cool and no flies buzzing 'round and talked over they pipes and made lots a strong smoke rise up.

"Well, so," Hotgun he say, "this neighborhood wasn't incorporated and they was no policeman standing on the corner with a big six-shooter to throw down on you for being absent from Sunday school."

(Tookpafka Micco and Wolf Warrior and Kono Harjo put on a dry grin and chew the pipe stem and listen right close, like they was like to hear it.)

"Well, so," Hotgun he go on and say, "we was had something yet to be thankful for to the federal judge. We could turn the old work filley [*sic*] out on the grass Sunday morning and, maybe so, shoulder the rusty grubbing hoe and go off down toward the creek and enjoy the sunshine and scenery, while the line was slack in the water. That beat holding down a bench with a straight back to it and no dash board to rest your feet on in the amen corner, where the last Sunday air was musty and the people remember the Lord once a week to be in style."

"The best place," Hotgun he go on and say, "to be sorry for grafting and to get close to the Great Spirit was out in the woods, where you couldn't had any temptation except to feel like swearing when something was stole your bait, or maybe so when a seed tick try to strike up acquaintance with you. That way you can catch mudcat and bass, or maybe so pluck a bouquet, and live and enjoy life."

"Well, so all the same," Hotgun he say, "the butcher was had to kill the frying chicken fo 'em and the family horse was had to stand up in the stable and eat dry hay so he could take the Christians sight seeing."

"Well, so," Tookpafka Micco he say, "that sound like good philosophy, but maybe so it was not good policy."

22. Theodore Roosevelt, president of the United States
(1901–9). Photograph by Baker Art Gallery, courtesy of
the Oklahoma Historical Society, No.20510.

23. Alice Mary Robertson, postmaster at Muskogee
(1905–13), later congresswoman (1921–23). Coffey
Collection, courtesy of the Oklahoma Historical
Society, No.5310.

24. William H. Murray, constitutional planner and first
speaker of the Oklahoma legislature. Courtesy of the
Oklahoma Historical Society, No.19762.

25. Charles N. Haskell, constitutional planner and first governor of Oklahoma. Courtesy of the Oklahoma Historical Society, No. 2063.

J. WENTDRESSED WITHEM,

26. J. Fentress Wisdom, Indian agency clerk
(1892–1905). Caricature by Charles H. Sawyer, from
Muskogee Phoenix, clipping in Alexander L. Posey
Collection, Thomas Gilcrease Museum of
American History and Art.

(Wolf Warrior and Kono Harjo was paid close attention.)

Then Hotgun he tell Tookpafka Micco, "Well, so, that's what's the matter with the country now — they was too much policy used. So if a man was talked common horse sense and tried to rake some facts out a the dark so the sun could shine on it you was lost lots a trade by it. So if you was a store keeper, or maybe so a politician, or maybe so a deacon in the church, you was compelled to had a good stock a policy to stay at business. You couldn't let your light so shine, or maybe so show your hand, 'cause policy was the key to prosperity."

"But," Hotgun he go on and say, "philosophy was like the treasure laid up in heaven, and rain couldn't rust it and the flies couldn't corrupt it and was all you could be remembered by.[2] If you was laid up a big roll a greenback in the bank, or maybe so a fine dress suit in the clothes press, you needn't need 'em in your business when you was dead and your tombstone leaning to one side."

(Wolf Warrior and Kono Harjo they was grunt big and approved it.)

1. The gobbling was part of the banter, challenging, and taunting of opponents during ball games.

2. "Lay not up for yourselves treasures upon earth, where moth and rust doth corrupt, and where thieves break through and steal: But lay up for yourselves treasures in heaven, where neither moth nor rust doth corrupt, and where thieves do not break through nor steal: For where your treasure is, there will your heart be also" (Matthew 6:19–21).

Letter No.48

[*Muskogee Daily Phoenix*, May 29, 1904; *Eufaula Tribune*, June 3, 1904; *Cherokee Advocate*, June 4, 1904]

In April 1904 Posey left journalism and went to work for the Interior Department as an interpreter in the Indian agency and as a fieldworker for the Creek enrolling division of the Dawes Commission. As Hotgun and his friends consider their options in the new order of things, they perhaps reflect some of Posey's thoughts as they balance the life of a country editor against that of a minor bureaucrat or political flunky. This letter was apparently a response to the annual meeting of the Indian Territory Press Association, to which Posey belonged. In addition to the business meeting, the programs of the association included presentations on special issues or problems faced by editors and publishers. In 1904, after the business meeting in South McAlester, the members traveled to St. Louis to attend the World's Press Parliament held at the Louisiana Purchase Exposition. The presentations were given aboard the train en route to St. Louis.

✍

"Well, so," Hotgun he say, "if I was had the nerve and the old hand press and no family to support, maybe so I like to be a country editor, with five thousand readers in some town that was had a good future and put near two hundred souls in it. The country editor was a big man in the community and was received lots a compliments. The prominent farmer was lugged big pumpkins into his sanctum for remembrance, and the women a the ladies' aid society was left fresh bouquets on his desk for advertising the ice cream festible [*sic*], and the candidate for office was dropped in and paid up his back subscription for his support, and the business men was cut down they space in his weekly so he could had more room to boost the town and blow they horn."[1]

(Tookpafka Micco and Wolf Warrior and Kono Harjo they was looked kind a mystified, like Hotgun was getting too far 'way from the sofky pots and they didn't know what he was driving at. But they was smoked slow and watched the red ants and paid close attention and wait for chance to grunt.)

"Well, so," Hotgun he go on and say, "sides that maybe so I

could be toastmaster for the press association and called on Editor Holden, a the Post, for a story about Fort Gibson the time old Heroditus [*sic*] was come there to write up the town.[2] Or maybe so I was called on Colonel Clarence Dug Last, a the Phoenix, for a sonnet on Secretary Its Cocked.[3] Or maybe so I called on Sidney Suggs, a the Ardmoreite, for a talk on how to graft in the newspaper business.[4] Or maybe so I was called on Editor Rustle, a the Capital, on how to fill up the front page on a tip or grapevine special.[5] Or maybe so I was called on Kirt Whitmore, a the Enquirer, to tell why he run a thumb sheet daily in his town instead of a monthly.[6] Or maybe so I was called on Bert Greer, a the Times, for a set speech on how to be afraid a your shadder in politics and gobble up the patronage after the election.[7] Or maybe so I was called on the Durant News man and Wagoner Record man to explain how to swipe stuff without credit."[8]

(Tookpafka Micco and Wolf Warrior and Kono Harjo they was looked like they was more interested in the red ants.)

And Hotgun he go on and say, "Well, so if I was a country editor[9] I could had lots a mileage sticking in my vest pocket that wasn't good on the Katy Flyer nor in Texas neither."

Then Tookpafka Micco he say, "Well so I was druther had a pass to ride on, like a flunkey a the federal court, or maybe so a roustabout for the Dawes Commission or Injin agent. So, when the conductor was come 'round and holler, 'tickets?' all I had to do was flash the paste board[10] and keep my eye on the landscape like I was had a deed to it."

Then Hotgun he say, "Well, so, anyhow I was druther had my name to the head a the column and lots a snap shots hanging under it than a pass on the railroad and privilege to bog up when I want to in the palace car carpet and no votes to make me sanitary policeman."

1. This description is a composite of Posey's experiences as editor of the *Indian Journal*, which he used in 1902 and 1903 to boost Eufaula. The following parody of the press association program reflects the good rapport Posey had with most Indian Territory editors.

2. J. S. Holden (1843–1920), a native of Ireland, grew up in Detroit, where he learned the printing trade. He established and edited a number of papers in Michigan before going to Muldrow, Cherokee Nation, in 1890 and establishing the *Muldrow Register*. In 1897 he moved to Fort Gibson, where he edited the *Post* for many years. A friend of Posey's, he had a literary bent. He wrote poetry and was an avid reader of Leo Tolstoy. He took a special interest in the history of Fort Gibson and used his paper to promote it. In 1904 he was historian for the press association. See Gideon, *Indian Territory*, 760–62; *Daily Oklahoman*, February 10, 1920; and *Vinita Weekly Chieftain*, May 19, 1904. Herodotus was a Greek historian of the fifth century B.C.

3. Clarence Douglas, the editor of the *Muskogee Phoenix*, dabbled in verse. Though Douglas generally supported Republican policies, he had been fired by Hitchcock in 1903 and had subsequently been critical of Hitchcock's policies concerning allotted Indian land.

4. Sidney Suggs, a native of Mississippi, had migrated to the Chickasaw Nation in 1895 by way of Texas and engaged in a number of enterprises before becoming owner of the *Ardmoreite* in 1897. He was particularly interested in the development of effective transportation systems, working especially to bring the Rock Island Railroad to Ardmore and to develop good roads. After statehood, he became a member of the Oklahoma Highway Commission. See Gideon, *Indian Territory*, 328–31; *Daily Oklahoman*, October 8, 1922; *Times-Record* (Oklahoma City), June 15, 1911.

5. U. S. Russell (1879–?), of Missouri, had gone to Norman, Oklahoma, in 1898 and the next year to South McAlester, Choctaw Nation, where he edited the *South McAlester Capital*. After statehood, he edited the *Shawnee Herald* and, finally, *Harlow's Weekly* at Oklahoma City. See Harlow, *Makers of Government*, 575.

6. Kirt Whitmore, the editor of the *Checotah Enquirer*, had edited the *Indian Journal*, which Posey later owned, from 1898 to 1900. In 1904 he was secretary of the Indian Territory Press Association. *Vinita Weekly Chieftain*, May 19, 1904. A thumb paper was a folded sheet used by schoolchildren to prevent soiling the pages of books. A "thumb sheet" suggests a newspaper that is small, perhaps with smudged type.

7. Bert Greer edited the *Muskogee Times*.

8. The *Durant News* was edited by Lewis Paullin, a member of the executive committee of the press association. Posey's reference to the *Wagoner Record* is uncertain. It was owned and edited in 1904 by R. K. Jacks and M. Phillippi. Indian Territory editors frequently charged their rivals with plagiarism.

9. The original read "century editor." "Mileage" here refers to a pass, or lack of one.

10. The "paste board" refers to a pass or free ride given to bureaucrats and politicians.

Letter No.49

[*Muskogee Daily Phoenix*, June 1904, date uncertain, clipping, in Posey Collection, Thomas Gilcrease Institute of American History and Art; *Vinita Weekly Chieftain*, June 23, 1904; *Eufaula Tribune*, June 24, 1904; *South McAlester Capital*, June 30, 1904]

Though a staunch Democrat, Posey had little faith that the Democrats could unseat the Republicans in the presidential election of 1904. As his letters during the spring indicate, he was particularly disenchanted with territorial politics, fertile ground for political opportunists. The territorial Democratic convention was held at Durant, Choctaw Nation, on June 16. Members chose Robert Lee Williams of Durant as Democratic national committeeman and elected delegates and alternates to the Democratic national convention to be held in St. Louis. The territorial Democratic convention was less troubled than the Republican convention had been, but it was marked by political infighting and wrangling. Nevertheless, the territorial Democratic press reported the convention as harmonious.

✍

"Well, so," Hotgun he say, "the Democrat stomp dance down to Durant was tame doings and no box cars jarred off a the main line with enthusiasm. So the Republicans was surprised and couldn't understand how come they was no quick witted Irishman present, like Mike Conlan, with sticks a dynamite for firecrackers to make it more interesting."[1]

Tookpafka Micco he listen close and tell Hotgun, "Well, so you was talked in parables."

And Hotgun he look wise and explain, "Well, so, you see the Republicans was had a big cat fight down to South Town last winter and all the newspapers was served it while hot.

"The fun was commence down to Atoka, where Mike Conlan, the bloody Irishman, was head a mob agin another mob from Coalgate, and tried to stir up harmony in the old Elephant party with a bundle a dynamite. He teched it off and throwed a string a box cars off a the right a way and pied all the roasts set up and ready for press in the print shop a Sister Smiser.[2] So that's the way the Republicans was start they powwow."

Then Tookpafka Micco he say, "Well, so, now you could go on and tell about the big Democrat stomp dance down to Durant."

(Wolf Warrior and Kono Harjo they was propped theyselves on they elbows and look on the ground and pay close attention.)

And Hotgun he go on and say: "Well, so when Cliff Jack's son was mauled on the table for order they was lots a familiar faces looked up, like Judge Stew It, and Russell Steal Well, and Mansfield, Make Merry and Corner It, and J. B. Stump Some, and Same Rather Ford, and Colonel Tom Bark Some, and Jim Misgivings and W. W. Has Stings, and Ben Lay For It, and Colonel Clarence Dug Last, and old stayers like that."[3]

Then Tookpafka Micco he say, "Well, so but Colonel Clarence Dug Last was a big Republican."

And Hotgun he say, "Well, so he is; but he was like to butt in."

(Wolf Warrior and Kono Harjo they was moved further in the shade under the catapa[4] tree and still pay close attention.)

Then Hotgun he go on and say, "Well, so, the Democrats was

got down to stomp dancing right good like a green corn busk and made Ben Lay For It ring leader, while Cliff Jack's [son] was beat on the tum-tum and Judge Stew It was made strong medicine and Mansfield, Make Merry and Corner It was gobbled right keen and throw they hair back on they shoulder.

"They was three candidates running for chief and maybe so you couldn't count all that want to be large delegates to the big stomp dance at St. Louis,[5] and also drivers on the band wagon.

"The ring leader he say, 'Well, so all who was friends to Mayor Sick could hold up they hands for the secretary to count.'[6]

"But they was no one hold up his paw but a feller that was looked like the picture a Christ called Lead Better.[7]

"Then the ring leader he say, 'Well, so, who want to vote for old Hailey anyhow?'[8]

"And Judge Stew It and Us Rustle was showed they hands.

"Then the ring leader he say, 'Well, so, let's see who vote for Bob Willing.'[9]

"And Cliff Jack's Son and Sam Rather Ford and Tommy Owing was bolted they instructions for old Hailey and flopped over like a eel out a water and the band was played Dixie.[10] (See A Loon and Fred Barde[11] they was sit back under the arbor under the premium crayon pictures a Lee and Jackson and Jefferson and forefathers a democracy like that and kept score for the powwow.)

"Then they was all vote to see who be large delegates to the big stomp dance to St. Louis, and lots a yokels was elected that never had they names in the neighborhood notes a they home paper. Maybe so they was easy game for the bunco man and the police-man in the park.[12]

"Then the powwow passed lots a time honored resolutions agin the Philippines and George the Third and federal pie counter and Injin Territory Volunteer Militia.[13]

"Then Lead Better was submitted a resolution to take out the partition between Oklahoma and Injin Territory, but he was ruled out a the ring by the medicine man."[14]

And Tookpafka Micco he say, "Well, so, who they follow for next president?"

And Hotgun he say, "Well, maybe so they was followed the Hearse."[15]

1. Mike Conlan (1859–1942), of Black River Falls, Wisconsin, had engaged in the lumber business before moving to Fort Smith, Arkansas, in 1883. In 1887 he went to Atoka, Choctaw Nation, and became a farmer, rancher, and banker. In 1903 he was elected mayor of Atoka. He moved to Oklahoma City in 1910. *Daily Oklahoman*, September 24, 1942. The reference to explosives indicates the Republican fighting at the convention a few months earlier.

2. Conlan was chairman of the executive committee of the Republican party for the Choctaw Nation. At the Atoka district convention in March, the Coalgate delegation, who wanted to seat some blacks, challenged the chair, and a fight ensued. *Indian Citizen*, March 3, 1904. The references to dynamite are not documented. Norma Standley Smiser, of Choctaw descent, was the owner and editor, with her husband, of the *Indian Citizen* at Atoka. See Carolyn Thomas Foreman, *Oklahoma Imprints, 1835–1907* (Norman: University of Oklahoma Press, 1936), 140–41. "Pie," in printing, is to mix up type. To pie the "roasts" suggests, perhaps, the mixing up of critical editorials already set for press.

3. Clifford L. Jackson, of Muskogee, was the presiding officer during the election of temporary officials for the convention. See *Muskogee Democrat*, June 17, 1904. A "maul," used here to refer to a gavel, is a heavy hammer used for driving wedges. C. B. Stuart, the South McAlester attorney, gave the response to the welcoming statement. Stillwell H. Russell was an attorney from Ardmore, Chickasaw Nation. George Alfred Mansfield (1865–1929) was a former justice of the Arkansas Supreme Court, a legal scholar, and a resident at McAlester since 1899; his firm represented the Choctaws and Chickasaws. J. F. McMurray, a former schoolteacher and lawyer from Gainesville, Texas, had been a resident of McAlester since 1899 and was a law partner with Mansfield. Melvin Cornish, a former clerk for the Dawes Commission, was a member of the McAlester firm of Mansfield, McMurray, and Cornish. J. B. Thompson was from Pauls Valley. Samuel Morton Rutherford was the mayor of Muskogee. Thomas Marcum and

James M. Givens were attorneys from Muskogee. William Wirt Hastings, of Tahlequah, Cherokee Nation, was the secretary of the executive committee. Ben F. Lafayette was from Checotah. And Clarence B. Douglas was the editor of the *Muskogee Phoenix*. See "George Alfred Mansfield," *Chronicles of Oklahoma* 7 (December 1929): 491–92.

4. Catalpa.

5. That is, the candidates were running for national committeeman ("chief") and delegates ("large" — as opposed to "small delegates," or alternates). The three candidates for committeeman were Robert Lee Williams, Robert W. Dick, and D. M. Hailey.

6. Robert W. Dick, the mayor of Ardmore, went to the convention with 44 of the 253 delegates committed to him for national committeeman. See *Muskogee Democrat*, June 17, 1904.

7. Walter A. Ledbetter (1863–1934), a native of Texas, had practiced law there before going to Ardmore, Chickasaw Nation, in 1890. He later served in the Oklahoma Constitutional Convention as chairman of the judiciary committee. See *Who Was Who in America*, 1:714.

8. D. M. Hailey had seventy-five delegates committed to him. See *Muskogee Democrat*, June 17, 1904.

9. Robert Lee Williams had only fifty-one delegates committed to him. See *Muskogee Democrat*, June 17, 1904.

10. Not only Jackson, Rutherford, and Tom Owen but others as well bolted and voted for Williams. Owen delivered a speech seconding Williams's nomination. See *Muskogee Democrat*, June 17, 1904. The reference to "Dixie" relates to Williams's Alabama roots, his name (Robert Lee), and "Little Dixie," a designation for the Red River valley, where Durant is located.

11. Charles A. Looney was the editor of the *Muskogee Democrat*. Frederick Barde, of Guthrie, Oklahoma Territory, was a correspondent for the *Kansas City Star*.

12. The list included a number of delegates and alternates who were little known in territorial politics: L. M. Poe of Tulsa and H. J. Stanley of Prucell, delegates at large; Ed M. McConkey of Peoria and S. M. Rutherford of Muskogee, alternates at large; C. A. Skeen of Wapanuka and Tom Ainsworth of McAlester, delegate and alternate from the central district; T. L. Wade of Marlow and J. T. Blanton of Pauls Valley, delegate and alternate from the southern district; W. C. Rogers of Pryor Creek and Thomas J. Watts of Wagoner, dele-

gate and alternate from the northern district; Robert Reed of Holdenville and James M. Givens of Muskogee, delegate and alternate from the western district. In the election of Reed over Givens, Rutherford — whom Posey accused of bolting in favor of Williams — carried the contest to the convention floor. His critics charged that he had manipulated not only this vote but the entire convention in favor of Williams. *Muskogee Democrat*, June 18, 1904.

13. Among the resolutions reported by the resolutions committee was one denouncing "carpetbaggers" and "political vultures," charging the Republican party with responsibility for graft ("federal pie counter"), and demanding home rule. *Muskogee Democrat*, June 18, 1904.

14. According to news reports, sentiment among the delegates ran two-to-one in favor of single statehood, but the statehood resolution was tabled for the sake of party harmony. *Muskogee Democrat*, June 17, 1904.

15. This was a pun on the name of William Randolph Hearst, who made a bid for the presidency in 1904. He had two hundred delegates pledged to him at the St. Louis convention, which nominated Alton B. Parker. See *Dictionary of American Biography*, ed. Garraty, Supp. 5:283–88. As Hotgun predicted, the Democratic candidate was "buried" by a landslide.

Letter No.50

[Muskogee Daily Phoenix, July 3, 1904]

E. L. Berry, the city recorder of Muskogee, died on June 20, 1904, and three days later the city council met to take steps to replace him. Mayor Samuel Morton Rutherford, a Democrat, disagreed with the councilmen, all Republicans, on how this should be done. Councilman Morgan Caraway moved for an immediate election by the council, believing that he and his six fellow councilmen had the power to replace Berry. Rutherford refused to call for the question on the motion and did the same when Caraway tried to appeal; Rutherford argued that election by council was illegal and that Berry's successor should be elected by the voters. With the council at an impasse, the question was debated in the press until Rutherford called another meeting. He appointed an interim recorder, and City Attorney W. F. Rampendahl issued an opinion that election by voters was the legal means of replacing Berry. A number of councilmen walked out of the meeting in protest. An election was finally set for July 12.

✍

Well, so, the wind was from the south and Hotgun and Took- pafka Micco and Wolf Warrior and Kono Harjo they was light they pipes and get in the shade a the catapa [*sic*] tree, and talk on politics, while the women folks was go out and pick up some dead wood and start a fire under the sofky pot and make the smoke bile out a the chimley [*sic*] like it was put near dinner time. The old squirrel dog he was come out a the fence corner and get in the way 'round kitchen door and keep order 'mong the chickens and choates.[1]

"Well, maybe so," Hotgun he say, "the boll weevil was ruin the cotton and the chintz bug[2] was get in his work on the corn and the Big Man at Washington was put a few more kinks in the red tape a the Loyal Creek payment, but all the same the Japs was still doing a Rushing business and they was lots a good prospects in the Flowery kingdom."[3]

(Tookpafka Micco and Wolf Warrior and Kono Harjo they was grunt and listen close and kind a keep one eye on the kitchen.)

"Well, so," Hotgun he go on and say, "the Japs was fine scrap- pers, like Mayor Rather Ford a Muskogee, and I was gloried in they spunk. They was fight to win and they efforts was crowned with success."

"Well, so," Tookpafka Micco he say, "how come you was think Mayor Rather Ford was like the Japs, anyhow?"

"Well, so," Hotgun he say, " 'cause they was both about the same size and they was both get the right sow by the ear."

(The old squirrel dog he wag his tail and peep in the kitchen and the bees grumble in the flowers and the south wind was blow over the hills from Kialegee and make it cool under the catapa tree.)[4]

And Hotgun he go on and explain why Mayor Rather Ford was like the Japs.

"Well, so," he say, "when Mayor Rather Ford was called the city forefathers together to elect a city finer, he say, 'Well, so, we better left this thing with the Democrats and Republicans, and let 'em fight it out at the polls. The people know who they druther had to jolt 'em with the cost and trimmings, or assignment on the rock pile.[5] If they was made bad judgment and put in some feller that didn't had any milk a human kindness in his brisket and give 'em the limit, they couldn't laid it on us and get even with us next election.' "[6]

"But," Hotgun he go on and say, "this kind a hoss sense didn't set well on some a the city forefathers, like Tear Away and his pikers.[7] So Tear Away he rise up high as he could and say, 'Well, so, they was 'nough Republicans here to let the people be damned. The ring that was had the votes was had the right to the pie with short crust.[8] 'Sides that we forefathers was had to dig up all the taxes and stand the price a the million dollar state house and things like that.[9] So I was made a motion to escort some good pie eater to the counter.'

"And Mayor Rather Ford he say, 'Well, so, you was out a order and maybe so you better sit down, 'cause I was refused to put the motion.'

"Then Tear Away he was made a motion to left it to the house, but Mayor Rather Ford he was used his authority and stand pat, like he was had four of a kind and playing the joker cut and slash.[10] So the meeting was bust up in bad odor, and the Phoenix and the Democrat was put a scare head over it and tell all about, but the Times was take a hammerlock on its pull and look 'way off somewhere else and lay for the announcements."[11]

"Pooty soon," Hotgun he go on and say, "Mayor Rather Ford was call another meeting to bury the hatchet, but Tear Away and his pikers was bolt the meeting, like the Marcum Democrats down to Ardmore.[12]

"Then pooty soon agin Mayor Rather Ford was send a telegram to City Lawyer Ram-it-in-all, who was up to the World's Fair drinking red lemonade and bucking the knife rack and trying his strength on the striking machine instead of mauling rails, and called another meeting in the fire engine house.[13]

"Well, so, everybody was take his palm leaf fan and turn out to take in the pow-wow, for maybe so they be something doing. So when Mayor Rather Ford was made 'em come to order, the city council hall was looked like a circus with three rings and lots a side shows.

"Then Mayor Rather Ford he tell City Lawyer Ram-it-in-all, 'Well, so, me and Tear Away was locked horns, and want your opinion on how to make a new city finer.'

"City Lawyer Ram-it-in-all he wrinkle his brow and act wise like the old squirrel dog. He say, 'Well, maybe so nobody else but you was think so but I was in favor of leaving it with the people 'cause they votes was worth more than Tear Away and his pikers. So that's my opinion.' "

(Tookpafka Micco and Wolf Warrior and Kono Harjo they give long grunt and about that time the women folks was holler, "Hombuxche!")

1. "Choates" refers to shoats, or young hogs.

2. A "chintz" bug is a chinch bug.

3. The Loyal Creek payment, pending since Reconstruction, had been approved by the Creek Council and payment to claimants had begun. But in the spring of 1904, the payment was held up for a month when Agent J. Blair Shoenfelt discovered a conflict in departmental regulations and laws determining heirship, a conflict between the Creek law and the Arkansas statutes, which

had applied to such cases in Indian Territory since January 1, 1898. Shoenfelt had been paying the natural guardians of minors, whereas the law required court-appointed guardians. In late June it was determined that Creek law applied to heirs of claimants who had died before January 1, 1898, and the Arkansas statutes to those who had died on that date or later. See *Muskogee Democrat*, June 21 and July 18, 1904. In the summer of 1904, it appeared that the Japanese were winning their war with Russia. Local papers depicted the Cossacks as ignorant and blindly subordinate, yet good fighters, and depicted the Japanese as intelligent, crafty, and charged with patriotism. See, e.g., *Muskogee Democrat*, June 28, 1904. Hotgun admires the "spunk" of the Japanese and compares it to Rutherford's willingness to do battle with the Muskogee Republican city councilmen. The "Flowery kingdom" was China, over which the war had started.

4. Kialegee was a Creek tribal town east of present-day Hanna, Oklahoma.

5. Hotgun refers to court costs and fines versus time in jail ("rock pile"). The recorder collected the fines, hence Hotgun's reference to the "city finer." The original reads, "The people who know who . . ."

6. "Yet do I fear thy nature. / It is too full of the milk of human kindness" (Shakespeare, *Macbeth*, act I, scene 5).

7. Morgan Caraway and other councilmen, S. A. Lanning and Benjamin Martin.

8. The spoils of office are a "pie." "Short" crust is tender and flaky—hence better than "long" crust, which is hard and tough.

9. Some Muskogee leaders believed that their town could be the capital of the new state. A group led by C. W. Turner, A. Z. English, J. W. Zeveley, C. W. Raymond, P. B. Hopkins, and Charles N. Haskell announced that they could raise the funds for a million-dollar capitol building. An artist's sketch of the proposed building appeared with an article in the *Muskogee Democrat*, June 29, 1904.

10. That is, he played with a flourish.

11. The *Muskogee Phoenix*, a Republican paper, and the *Muskagee Democrat* closely followed the story. The reference to the *Times* is unclear because no copies of that newspaper exist for this period. The *Phoenix* supported the council, whereas the *Democrat* called Caraway's motion a Republican attempt to "bunco" the public. *Muskogee Democrat*, June 24, 1904.

12. Thomas Marcum, a Muskogee attorney, had led a revolt in the territorial Democratic convention at Ardmore in 1900. Disputed were not only delegates

to the national convention in Kansas City but also the national committeeman's post for Indian Territory. Marcum, who had been committeeman, managed to retain his position, though his right to it was debated. See *Cherokee Advocate*, June 16, 1900.

13. City Attorney W. F. Rampendahl (1879–?), a native of Illinois who had come to Indian Territory in 1901, returned to Muskogee from the Louisiana Purchase Exposition at St. Louis on June 29. See *Muskogee Democrat*, June 29, 1904, and Harlow, *Makers of Government*, 429.

Letter No.51

[*Muskogee Democrat*, September 20, 1904]

Senator William M. Stewart of Nevada arrived at Muskogee unannounced on September 18. Chairman of the Senate Committee on Indian Affairs for the approaching session of Congress, Stewart had come to Indian Territory to obtain firsthand information; at least that was what he told the press. But like many politicians before him, he spent one day in Muskogee, visiting the Dawes Commission, the Indian agency, and the federal courts, before departing in the afternoon to continue a seven-day tour in Indian Territory and Oklahoma. Before leaving, however, Stewart told the press that he favored single statehood for Oklahoma and Indian Territory and, meanwhile, territorial status for Indian Territory so that taxes could be levied for schools, roads, and other public improvements. He also opposed the current system by which allotments were leased and argued that allotments should be sold only to "bona fide" settlers. Some members of the press found it difficult to take Stewart's visit seriously. Public opinion was jaded because many political notables had visited the territory and little reform had followed. The politicians made no more stir than the coming or going of summer tourists, said the *Muskogee Democrat*. They never left the railroad right-of-way to get the "real" story from the Indians and the white settlers, and the legislation they recommended was based on notes jotted down on the rear platform of a train traveling sixty miles an hour.

✍

"Well, so," Hotgun he say, "Senator Stewit of New Fodder, was in our midst prospecting for statehood."

And Tookpafka Micco he say, "Well, so a man never get too old to learn, or maybe so to be a bridegroom."

(Wolf Warrior and Kono Harjo they was brighten up and grunt and pay close attention.)

Then Hotgun he say, "Well, so Senator Stewit, of New Fodder, was no exception to that. He wasn't too old to learn or maybe so to be a widower neither."[1]

And Tookpafka Micco he smoke slow and say, "Well, must be the Senator was come down here by surprise, 'cause the Muskogee Evening Pop didn't anticipate it."[2]

Then Hotgun he go on and say, "Well, so he didn't make any noise beforehand. He come in unnoticed, like a prosperous farmer from the states and was registered at the Katy with his valet and women folks before Colonel Duglast got wind of it."[3]

"Well, so," Hotgun he go on and say, "that was last Sunday 'bout dinner time. He land in Muskogee on the Sabbath so he wouldn't have to give the sidewalk to the Creek Freedmen while he was taking in the town and prospecting for statehood."[4]

And Tookpafka Micco he say, "Well, so how he pass off the time Monday?"

"Well, so," Hotgun he say, "the Senator was call on the Dawes Commission and turn 'round and go out, 'cause the Dawes Commission maybe so be here ten years more and he could visit it some other time.

"Then he go and see the Injin agent and ask him, 'Well, so how is business?' And the Injin agent he say, 'Well, so it's mighty dull; haven't taken in much today for advertising land to sell in the Phoenix. I was had a red tag sale every week, but they was no buyers hardly.' Then the Senator he say, 'Well, so how 'bout taking off the restrictions?' And the agent he say, 'Well, so if a full-blood was made application to had his restrictions moved off, I was turned it down, 'cause he better advertise it. But, maybe so, if a white Injin was made application, I was left it to Secretary Its-cocked and that was the end of it.'⁵

"Then Senator Stewit he go and see how J. Gouge Right was making it and was found him looking grand, gloomy and peculiar. The Senator he say, 'Well, so what's the matter?' And J. Gouge Rite [*sic*] he say, 'Well, so I was feel bilious and had bad taste in the mouth. Maybe so I didn't had 'nough exercise and was falling into decay.' Then the Senator he say, 'Well, maybe so after while the Big Man at Washington was put you on the retired list.'

"Then the Senator he go and visit the new bull pen and found the prisoners was just taken a good bath and put on clean clothes. Then he go to call on the federal judge, but the bailiff was told him no one was allowed in the court room if couldn't walk on his tip-toes and stay in till court adjourned.⁶

"Then the Senator he go back to the hotel and send word to the newspaper men to come and pay they respects. When they come the Senator he say, 'Well, so you could say I was for single state-hood and put a four-decker over it.' "⁷

Tookpafka Micco he smoke slow and study long time and say, "Well, so then Senator Stewit didn't talk to the Injins that own the land, or maybe so the white men that raise the crops and build the towns?"

And Hotgun he say, "Well, so he was prospect for statehood among the politicians and office-holders."

Then Tookpafka Micco he say, "Well, so comment was unnecessary."

---

1. William Morris Stewart (1827–1909), a native of New York, had served as attorney general of California and in 1860 moved to Nevada ("New Fodder"),

The Fus Fixico Letters

where he served in the state constitutional convention in 1863. He was a U.S. senator in 1863–75, 1882, and 1887–1905. Stewart's wife died in September 1902, and in October 1903 he remarried. See *Dictionary of American Biography*, ed. Dumas Malone (New York: Charles Scribner's Sons, 1936), 18:13–14.

2. This is perhaps a reference to the *Muskogee Evening Times*, for which Posey formerly worked. The implication is that it had populist leanings.

3. Stewart arrived on Sunday, September 18, accompanied by his wife and Charles Kappler and his wife. Kappler, Stewart's "valet," was secretary of the Senate Committee on Indian Affairs. *Muskogee Democrat*, September 19, 1904. Hotgun ribs Clarence Douglas, the editor of the *Phoenix*, who considered himself on good terms with Republican politicians, because he was not notified of Stewart's intention to visit Muskogee. The party stayed at the Katy Hotel, and while the men made their rounds, Mrs. Douglas entertained the ladies in the Douglas home. Stewart is like the "prosperous farmer" because the most noticed emigrants from the states were riffraff, opportunists, or fortune seekers.

4. Saturday was the day that rural blacks came to town to do business and were visible on the streets; on Sunday, the streets would be empty.

5. Creek lands that could be sold were advertised in the *Muskogee Phoenix* and other local newspapers. Under federal law, white and freedmen citizens of the Indian nations could sell their allotments outright. Inherited land could also be sold. The owner could apply to advertise the sale. Bidders submitted sealed bids and certified checks for one-fifth of their bids. Sixty days after the land was advertised, the bids were opened; the land went to the highest bidder if the bid was at least market value and if the bidder paid the remainder of the price. Of the many tracts advertised, few sold each week. Indians could also apply for removal of restrictions on the sale of their surplus allotments. If the application was approved, the Indian could make a warranty deed. Shoenfelt believed that syndicates were operating among the Indians, negotiating purchases on removal of restrictions at prices far below market value, and he considered it his personal duty to protect the Indians. He refused to approve applications that he believed were influenced by land buyers and sent them by the hundreds for Hitchcock's determination. By the end of August, thousands were pending determination because Hitchcock was on vacation. The processes of advertising, sale, and removal of restrictions were slow, complicated, and tedious. Hence Shoenfelt's complaint that he had little to do. *Muskogee Democrat*, July 2, 16, and 18 and August 4, 20, 24, 27, and 31, 1904.

6. On September 19, 173 prisoners, including 16 women and 93 blacks, were

moved from the "old prison pen under the hill" to the new federal prison on Court Street. Each prisoner was made to take a bath and was given clean clothing before being transferred. *Muskogee Democrat*, September 19, 1904.

7. A "four-decker" was a headline in large type.

Letter No.52

[*Muskogee Daily Phoenix*, January 1, 1905; *Cherokee Advocate*, January 14, 1905]

When Congress convened in late 1904, the statehood issue revived. In mid-December, the Senate Committee on Territories reported what was known as the Hamilton bill, which had been introduced in the preceding Congress. Debate on the bill had not begun by New Year's Day, but speculation on its chances of passing and on potential office-seekers had started. One name frequently put forward in Indian Terri-tory and Washington as a Republican senatorial candidate was J. Blair Shoenfelt, the Indian agent at Muskogee. Though Posey had associated Shoenfelt with the grafters in 1903, his attitude changed when Shoenfelt appeared to be one of the few federal officials untainted by the scandal. As Hotgun and his friends take stock at the beginning of 1905, they accept the inevitability of statehood and anticipate not only the political maneuvering it will bring but also the prospects of tax-financed govern-ment. Those prospects make them nostalgic for the old days of Creek government.

✍

"Well, so," Hot Gun [*sic*] he say, "we didn't had to pay no taxes now, but maybe so this time next year they be lots a changes and we was had statehood with Oklahoma, with Quapaw Agency and Osage reservation throwed in to make it a good bargain,[1] 'sides Colonel J. Bear Showemthat for member a the House a Kings in Washington.[2] Ever'body was look for something like that and was anxious for further developments."

Tokpafka [*sic*] Micco he pay close attention and spit behind the backlog and say after 'while, "Well, so Colonel J. Bear Showemwhat he say he aint candidate for big honor like that, if he could keep from it. So, when the newspaper man was approached 'im about it, he say, 'Well, so, Colonel, how 'bout it?' the Colonel he say, 'Well, so how 'bout what?' And the newspaper man he say, 'Well, so theys a rumor ever'where you was had your pegs set to be senator and dish out lots a pie to the multitude, if Plenty Sofar wasn't flushed your game.' And the Colonel he spin 'round in his office chair like he was uneasy and say, 'Well, so that was a big lie.' And the newspaper man he say, 'Well, so you couldn't dash cold water on it like that, 'cause Colonel Clarence B. Douglast was interviewed himself in Washington and write a special and say that was the program. So what you say to that?'³ Then the Colonel he swell up big and say, 'Well, so I wouldn't stand for more talk like that and you better go off and don't monkey with me.'"

Then Hotgun he scooped up a fresh coal a fire in his pipe and say, "Well, so all candidates was talked that way. When they was say 'no' they mean 'yes,' like a woman, and was deceived nobody."

(Wolf Warrior and Kono Harjo they was inter-rested [*sic*] and listened close.)

"But," Hotgun he go on and say, "I was mighty sorry to see ever'thing change up different. It was made me homesick for old times. But Charley Curtis he say it was inevitable, and old Senator Stewit from New Fodder was sidin' with 'im. So I guess we was up agin it and had to face it, 'cause we couldn't turn our backs to it like the Rushings."⁴

Tokpafka Micco he look in the fire and study over it and say, "Well, so what was Charley Curtis done for Kansas?"

And Hotgun he close his eyes put near shut and say, "Well, so, like old Paro Bruner say, that make me scratch my head where it aint itch. But, like I start to say, I was sorry to see the change, 'cause we was better off without it."[5]

(Wolf Warrior and Kono Harjo they was give big grunt.)

Then Hotgun he go on and say, "Well, so who was paid the taxes anyhow if we was had statehood? I like to know that. The Injin couldn't 'cause the Big Man at Washington he say the Injin didn't had enough sense to know what he was doing. The white renter couldn't 'cause he didn't had nothing but a mule blind in one eye and a lot a children all about the same size to raise a mortgage on. And the business man in town couldn't 'cause he was had to vote bonds for Abe Lincoln school houses and George Washington parks and things like that 'sides going down in his jeans for money to fight tribal taxes with."[6]

(Tokpafka Micco he smoke slow and spit behind the backlog again, while Wolf Warrior and Kono Harjo they was keep on paying close attention.)

And Hotgun he put another fresh coal a fire in his pipe and go on and say, "Well, so we was in too much hurry for statehood. Look like we don't know when we was a good thing when we had it. The Government was looked after us and paid all the bills now and all we had to do was to lay in the shade and drink sofky and set on the jury. The government was appropriate money for our children to go to school on when they wasn't picking cotton. It was had deputy marshals to capture whiskey peddlers and judges to carry out Arkansas laws and take cases under advisement for twelve months and maybe so longer than that.[7] So what more we want?"

And Tokpafka Micco he say, "Well, recon [sic] so we don't want nothing more but office."

1. The Quapaw agency served a number of small tribes in the northeastern corner of Indian Territory: Seneca, Eastern Shawnee, Quapaw, Ottawa, Confed-

erated Peoria and Miami, Wyandot, and Modoc. The Osage reservation consisted of present-day Osage County, Oklahoma. The territories of those tribes and the Five Civilized Tribes composed the area in present-day Oklahoma not included in Oklahoma Territory in 1904.

2. "House a Kings" is the U.S. Senate. In earlier letters, Shoenfelt was called J. Bear Sho'-am-fat. The amelioration of his name here reflects Posey's growing regard for Shoenfelt.

3. Clarence Douglas, the editor of the *Muskogee Phoenix*, was an active Republican who had been a political associate of Pliny Soper, the Republican national committeeman from Indian Territory. They had disagreed, however, on the appointment of a postmaster at Muskogee. In mid-December, Douglas sent a telegram from Washington to his *Phoenix*, naming Shoenfelt and Bird McGuire, the territorial delegate from Oklahoma, as potential Republican candidates for the Senate from the new state, thus snubbing Soper, who had aspirations to the office. When asked by reporters about his political goals, Shoenfelt emphatically denied having any political ambitions. *Muskogee Democrat*, December 17 and 22, 1904.

4. At the end of 1904, the war with Japan was not going well for the Russians.

5. Paro Bruner, a Creek freedman, was micco of Canadian Colored Town. He had served in the Creek National Council in either the House of Kings or House of Warriors since 1870. He was a frequent visitor at the enrolling division of the Dawes Commission, where Posey worked, to identify applicants for enrollment. *Muskogee Democrat*, July 15 and August 24, 1904.

6. Lincoln schools and Washington parks represent not only the rationale of town officials to tax residents but also the Americanization of Indian Territory. The tribes had levied a tax of one-half of 1 percent on the original cost and value of goods introduced into the territory. After businessmen brought suit, one district judge ruled that the tax could be collected and another that it could not. In October 1904, the court of appeals reversed the latter opinion, but businessmen appealed to the U.S. Supreme Court, and collection was suspended once more while the appeal was in process. Businessmen complained that they paid taxes to the municipalities for services and that an added half percent was too heavy a burden. See *Muskogee Democrat*, October 20 and 22, 1904.

7. In 1904 the authority of remaining tribal laws ceased when the statutes of Arkansas were extended to Indian Territory and administered by the federal courts. See Debo, *And Still the Waters Run*, 301–2.

The Fus Fixico Letters

[*Muskogee Daily Phoenix*, January 15, 1905]

The buildings at Fort Gibson, northeast and across the Arkansas River from Muskogee, had been privately owned for a number of years. One barracks building had been bought by Tams Bixby, who in 1903 organized the Town and Country Club. The members repaired the stone building and built broad verandas around it for use as a summer clubhouse where members could enjoy the pleasant landscape and cooler temperatures and hold lavish parties. In November 1903, six hundred invitations to a ball were sent out to members and to guests in St. Louis, Kansas City, and elsewhere. A special train took partygoers from Muskogee to Fort Gibson. With Bixby as president, the organization had among its members prominent businessmen of Muskogee as well as many federal officials. It was viewed with suspicion by outsiders. In the summer of 1904, there were charges that it was really a town-lot scheme, and many believed that intoxicants were kept on the premises, in violation of the law. The Prohibition movement had become strong in Indian Territory. Antisaloon organizations were expanded. The Indian Territory pharmacy board not only prohibited druggists from selling intoxicants, a common practice, but also from drinking; some druggists were fined and sent to jail. Prohibitionists supported the Hamilton statehood bill pending before Congress because it contained a Prohibition clause, and the local church federation sent a lobbyist to Washington. The general public believed that not only the Town and Country Club but also the Wauhillau Club had been violating the law prohibiting intoxicants. After the Town and Country Club held its widely advertised New Year's Eve watch party on December 31, 1904, charges were made that intoxicants had been served. When a federal grand jury was impaneled at Muskogee on January 9, 1905, one area of investigation was the sale and introduction of illegal intoxicants. However, the grand jury returned no indictments.

🖎

"Well, so," Hotgun he say, "the evil men do[1] was leaked out before the Big Jury and start lots a talk and make prosperity for the Yellow Journal.[2] So you better be careful where you throw your Peruny bottle."

Tokpafka [*sic*] Micco he spit in the ashes and think about it and say, "Well, so you was give the Club-in-the-Country a mighty hard jolt."

"Well, so but," Hotgun he go on and say, "they was always plenty room for doubt and ever'body was had a right to his share. Maybe so the Club-in-the-Country was only had Apollinaris bottles lying 'round in the back yard."[3]

And Tokpafka Micco he say, "Well, so it was looked awful suspicious anyhow; 'cause Lieutenant Colonel Adjutant General J. Wentdressed Withem was made a weak confession to the Big Jury and try to explain how it was.[4]

"The Chief a the Big Jury[5] he ask 'im, 'Well, so how about that big blowout you give? Maybe so you call it a Kangaroo Seance?'[6]

"And Lieutenant Colonel Adjutant General J. Wentdressed Withem he smote his knees together like he was had the buck ague[7] and say, 'Well, so I wasn't the only one into it; but I couldn't remember enough to turn any states' evidence. Got so much writing to 'tend to for the Injin Agent 'sides being a lion in society I didn't had time to lay up things in my mind so I could swear to it.'

"Then the Chief a the Big Jury he look like he was crabbed and say, 'Well, so who else was you invited 'sides yourself and what did you had for the stomach's sake?'[8]

"And Lieutenant Colonel Adjutant General J. Wentdressed Withem he look like he was outflanked and say, 'Well, so I disremember maybe so I was just dreamed about it.'

"Then the Chief a the Big Jury he look awful cross and say, 'Well, so you know what kind of a oath you was under?'

"And Lieutenant Colonel Adjutant General J. Wentdressed Withem he smote his knees together again and look innocent like a calf and say, 'Well, so I couldn't recollect anything seems like.'

"So the Chief of the Big Jury was excused 'im and sent for the nigger cook. He ask her, 'Well, so, Auntie, what does the Club-in-the-Country imbibe, anyhow?'

"And the old Auntie she say, 'Well, so sometimes coffee and sometimes tea and den again sometimes pure water. But how you 'spec' I gwinter to know when de Loosetenant Colonel Stunt General Mistah Wentdressed Withem don't trust nobody with his gin but hissef?'

"So the Chief a the Big Jury was had to report he couldn't find anything against the Club-in-the-Country on that kind a evidence."

And Hotgun he smoke slow and say, "Well, so the soldier was had a close shave from the circuit riders anyhow."

(Wolf Warrior and Kono Harjo they was give big grunt.)

Then Hotgun he go on and say, "Well, so what kind of a thing is that Club-in-the-Country anyhow?"

And Tokpafka Micco he say, "Well, so it was the Muskogee Four Hundred, mostly pie eaters.[9] They was had a fine home in the country over to Fort Gibson."

1. "The evil that men do live after them; / The good is oft interred with their bones" (Shakespeare, *Julius Caesar*, act 3, scene 2, l.80).

2. Yellow journalism was characterized by sensational, exploitative reporting that was not required to be accurate.

3. "Apollinaris" bottles are wine bottles.

4. J. Fentress Wisdom (1875–?), a Tennessee native, went to Muskogee in 1892, where he was a bookkeeper. The next year he was appointed chief clerk of the Union agency, where his father, Dew M. Wisdom, was Indian agent. See Luther B. Hill, *A History of the State of Oklahoma*, 2 vols. (Chicago: Lewis Publishing Co., 1909), 2:326–27.

5. Tookpafka Micco refers here to the foreman of the grand jury.

6. Calling the New Year's Eve party a "Kangaroo Seance" is perhaps a takeoff on kangaroo court, one that is called without authority and operates outside the law.

7. Buck ague, today known as "buck fever," is the nervousness that occurs when novice hunters sight game, usually deer.

8. "Drink no longer water, but use a little wine for thy stomach's sake and thine often infirmities" (I Timothy 5:23).

9. "Pie eaters" is Hotgun and Tookpafka Micco's term for opportunists and grafters.

Letter No. 54

[*Muskogee Daily Phoenix*, April 16, 1905; *Holdenville Tribune*, April 20, 1905; *Muskogee Phoenix*, April 20, 1905]

On April 5, President Theodore Roosevelt made a sweep through Indian Territory on his way west to hunt. His train entered the territory from Parsons, Kansas, and stopped two minutes at Vinita and two minutes at Wagoner, where it was supposed to have only slowed down so that the people could wave at the president. The train arrived at Muskogee at 11:02 A.M. The president was whisked from the train to a grandstand that had been built beside the tracks; in a brief address to the crowd of fifteen hundred, he spoke in generalities to the men about statehood, the duties of good citizenship, the need to elect honest men, and decency. He did acknowledge, however, his pleasure at seeing so many women and children. After a couple of presentations and brief ado, Roosevelt was whisked back to the train, which pulled out at 11:10. Posey had often criticized politicians involved in the process of Indian legislation, men such as Hitchcock, Bonaparte, and Stewart, who made brief visits to the territory, saw few of the people, and yet claimed to know what was best for them. Roosevelt was a capital example. The man who was of key importance in the statehood issue that directly affected all of the people had spent less than ten minutes talking to them.

✍

"Well, so," Hotgun he say, "Colonel Clarence B. Duglast, he was dee-lighted and Chief P. Porter, he was dee-lighted, and Charley Gibson he was dee-lighted, and Alice M. Lobbysome[1] she was dee-lighted too."

And Tookpafka Micco he was look down his old pipe-stem and say, "Well, so what for?"

And Hotgun he go on and say, "Well, so 'cause the Great White Father from Washington was suffered 'em to come unto 'im on the grand stand, while he was showing his teeth and shaking the Big Stick before the multitude up to Muskogee."[2]

Then Tookpafka Micco he spit out in the yard and say, "Well, so what kind of a thing's the Big Stick, anyhow?"

And Hotgun he look wise, like the supreme court, and explain it, "Well so the Big Stick was the symbol of power, like a policeman's billy. In the jungles a Afriky it was called a war-club; and in the islands a the sea, like Australia, it was called a boomer-rang; and among us fullblood Injins we call it a ball-stick; and if it was fall in the hands a the women folks, it was called a rolling-pin, or maybe so, a broom-handle. It was had lots a different names, like breakfast food. Over in Europe a king was had precious stones put in it, to make it more ornamental than useful, and call it a scepter. The brass-knucks was the latest improvement on it. In olden time Samson was had a Big Stick made out of a jaw-bone of a ass, and was made a great hit with it among the Philistines.[3] Same way when the Great White Father was want to show his influence all he had to do was to flourish the Big Stick and everybody was get out from under it."

(Wolf Warrior and Kono Harjo they was grunt and Tookpafka Micco he was pay close attention and spit out in the yard again.)

Then Hotgun he smoke slow and go on and say, "Well, so, like I

203

first start to say, Colonel Clarence B. Duglast he was dee-lighted and Chief P. Porter he was dee-lighted, and Charley Gibson he was dee-lighted and Alice M. Lobbysome she was dee-lighted too. They was all butt in before the reception committee could see if they badges was on straight. They was put the Great White Father on they shoulders and histed 'im upon the grand stand, and he was made a talk to the multitude. He say, 'Well, so I was mighty glad to see you all and hope you was all well. I couldn't complain and I was left Secretary Itscocked enjoying good health. (Big cheers and somebody out in the crowd say, Bully for Itscocked!) Look like you all was had a fine country down here. You all ought to had statehood and let Oklahoma show you how to run it.[4] (Colonel Clarence B. Duglast, he pay close attention and listen for some word 'bout 'imself.) I want everybody to had a square deal down here. (Lots more big cheers and everybody smiling but the Snake Injin.) You all was had a fine town here too. You could run flat boats up to it from Ft. Smith,[5] and deliver the goods over lots of railroads, and pump out oil, and develop salt-licks and float bee-courses.[6] But I didn't had time to talk any more, 'cause I couldn't stop here but two minutes and I have been here put near five. So long.'

"Then the special train was kick up a cloud of dust and hide behind it, and the multitude was climb down off the houses and telegraph poles and go tell they neighbors 'bout it. Colonel Clarence B. Duglast he go and tell his friends the President think he was ten cents straight,[7] and Chief P. Porter he go and tell his friends the President say he was the greatest living Injin,[8] and Charley Gibson he go and write a 'Rifle Shot' 'bout giving the President a fan made out a tame turkey feathers instead of eagle plumes, and Alice M. Lobbysome she go and buy the platform the President stood on for a souvenir.[9] Maybe so she was made a bedstead out of it and distribute the sawdust and shavings among the full-bloods to look at."

And Tookpafka Micco he say, "Well, so I might need some kindling next winter and the keepsakes was come in handy."

(Wolf Warrior and Kono Harjo they was give another big grunt.)

Then Hotgun he go on and say, "Well, so the next stop the Great White Father make was out in Oklahoma in a big pasture, where they was lots of cayotes [*sic*]. He was got after one a horse-back and crowd it over the prairies till he was get good results and captured it alive. He was had lots of fun with it before he was run it down. The President was a great hunter and was kill big game well as a cayote or jackrabbit. So he was go on to the Rocky Mountains to beard the bear and lion in they den."[10]

And Tookpafka Micco he say, "Well, so this time the Lord better help the grizzly."

1. Alice M. Robertson was not on the stage at first. Roosevelt asked to be presented to her. She had won an ugly political battle over the postmaster's position at Muskogee, taking office in January. Roosevelt reportedly assured her that her job was secure as long as he was president. *Muskogee Democrat*, January 6 and April 5, 1905. There is no evidence that Charles Gibson was on the stage. His wife was, however. Clarence Douglas's *Muskogee Phoenix* was one of the leading Republican newspapers in the territory, hence his presence on the stand.

2. "But when Jesus saw it, he was much displeased, and said unto them, Suffer the little children to come unto me, and forbid them not: for of such is the kingdom of God" (Mark 10:14). "Big Stick" was the popular label for Roosevelt's heavy-handed foreign policy.

3. "And Samson said, With the jawbone of an ass, heaps upon heaps, with the jaw of an ass have I slain a thousand men" (Judges 15:16).

4. Roosevelt was on public record in favor of single statehood. One of the arguments often made for joining the two territories was that Oklahoma already had a government in place. Opponents like Posey disliked that idea because they believed it gave Oklahoma politicians an advantage.

5. Roosevelt did not touch on navigation of the Arkansas River. On the day of Roosevelt's visit, a navigation convention met at Muskogee, and the delegates from Indian Territory, Arkansas, and Kansas formed the Arkansas Valley Navigation Association, with Charles N. Haskell of Muskogee as president. Haskell was on the speaker's platform, probably at Pleasant Porter's invitation. *Muskogee Democrat*, April 5, 6, and 14, 1905.

6. The oil industry was rapidly developing in Indian Territory. Standard Oil had a pipeline and storage facility at Muskogee. *Muskogee Democrat*, January 5, 1905. Discussion of river navigation to Muskogee was common at the time. Salt licks were areas where salt deposits were found on the earth's surface. Considered valuable in the nineteenth century, they were no longer economically significant. To float a bee course is to search for colonies of wild bees by tracking their flight path (a beeline) by triangulation from a water or nectar source. Roosevelt touched generally on economic matters and did not deal in specifics and certainly did not concern himself with economic trivialities such as salt licks and bee courses.

7. The meaning of "ten cents straight" is uncertain.

8. President William McKinley was credited with labeling Porter as the greatest living Indian. *Muskogee Times-Democrat*, September 3, 1907.

9. Not Gibson but his wife presented Roosevelt with a fan that she had made from the tail feathers of an eagle that her husband had killed seven years earlier. *Muskogee Democrat*, April 5, 1905. Gibson wrote a regular column called "Rifle Shots" for the *Indian Journal*, but if he produced one for this occasion, it has not been found. There is also no evidence that Robertson bought the grandstand.

10. Roosevelt spent several days near Frederick, Oklahoma, in a pasture of 480,000 acres; the area had been reserved when the Kiowa-Comanche lands were opened to settlement and was now leased to cattlemen. A railroad siding with a telegraph office called Kingola was built to conduct national business while Roosevelt hunted coyotes on a Kentucky hunting horse behind wolf-hounds brought there especially for his use. He captured one coyote by hand, grabbing it by the jaws after the dogs had it down. From there, Roosevelt went through New Mexico, which was also seeking statehood; though large crowds had gathered, the train went through the towns without stopping. On April 15, he began his bear hunt at New Castle, Colorado, twelve miles west of Glenwood Springs. In early May he reported good luck, he and his two companions having bagged ten bears. See *Muskogee Democrat*, April 6, 7, 12, 14, and 15, and May 8, 1905; Theodore Roosevelt, "A Wolf Hunt in Oklahoma," *Scribner's Magazine* 38

(November 1905): 513–32; and idem, "A Colorado Bear Hunt," *Scribner's Magazine* 38 (October 1905): 387–408. "And dar'st thou, then, / To beard the lion in his den, / And Douglas in his hall?" (Sir Walter Scott, *Lochinvar* [1808], stanza 14).

Letter No.55

[*Muskogee Daily Phoenix,* July 30, 1905; *Dustin Dispatch,* August 5, 1905; *Muskogee Phoenix,* August 10, 1905]

Despite widespread discussion of statehood during the congressional session of 1904–5, it early became apparent that a statehood bill was unlikely to pass. In general, the Republicans were reluctant to establish a state that they feared would be Democratic. Matters were complicated by attempts to tie Oklahoma statehood to that of New Mexico and Arizona. When the Senate took up the Hamilton bill in early January, three factions emerged. Some Democrats favored joint statehood for Oklahoma and Indian Territory if New Mexico was admitted and if statehood for Arizona was delayed until the population reached half a million. Another faction favored joint statehood for Oklahoma and Indian Territory but opposed joint admission of New Mexico and Arizona unless both territories cast a majority vote for the constitution. Others opposed the Hamilton bill for certain provisions such as Prohibition, mixed schools, location of the eastern district court at Muskogee, and establishment of the capital at Guthrie.

When, as expected, a bill failed to pass, the executive committee for single statehood for Oklahoma and Indian Territory called a convention in Oklahoma City on July 12. After adopting resolutions asking Congress to consider Oklahoma statehood separately from the New Mexico and Arizona issue, the one thousand delegates selected a committee of twenty to present the resolutions and appeal to the president.

The single-statehood movement in Oklahoma caused a countermovement by separate-staters in Indian Territory. In March, J. A. Norman, a Cherokee living at Muskogee, began a series of articles calling for a constitutional convention in Indian Territory to establish a state he called "Sequoia." In early July he used the names of the Cherokee chief W. C. Rogers and the Choctaw chief Green McCurtain in a call for meetings in early August to elect delegates to the convention. After subsequent meetings in Muskogee by businessmen and Indian and white politicans, the chiefs of the Five Civilized Tribes, except Douglas H. Johnston of the Chickasaws, called for the election of delegates who would meet at Muskogee on August 21. Although some parts of Indian Territory did not show strong support for the separate-statehood movement, Hotgun correctly predicts that the location of county boundaries, seats of government, and boundaries for congressional and senatorial districts would generate interest.

✍

Well, so while the locusts was singing in the blackjack trees and the women folks was pounding sofky corn, Hotgun and Took-pafka Micco and Wolf Warrior and Kono Harjo they was held a powwow in the shade.

And Hotgun he look down his long pipe stem and smoke slow with his eyes put near shut and say, "Well, so that Oklahoma convention was put me in mind a the nigger preacher asking the blessing."

And Tookpafka Micco he say, "Well, so how the colored brother ask the blessing?"

And Hotgun he go on and say, "Well so the nigger preacher bow his head and say, 'O Lord, we was mighty thankful for this feast. Please pass the possum.' Same way Oklahoma was pray to Congress, saying, 'We be mighty thankful for statehood. Please pass the Injin Territory.'"[1]

Tookpafka Micco and Wolf Warrior and Kono Harjo they was spit in the dog-fennel and give a big grunt.

Then Hotgun he go on and say, "The prayer was short and sweet, but the chairman was had to sit on the lid to keep the speeches for the occasion from slopping over on the second page of the People's Vindicator.[2] Henry Be Lobbying he was amongst the ITS, and he get up and shove his manly bosom to the front and entertained 'em with some extracts from his graduating oration.[3] He say, 'This was a grand and glorious country. It was the land a the brave and the home a the brave. Everybody was created free and equal — subject to later developments. Greece and Rome was the greatest countries of olden times, but the United States was the grandest domain the moon or sun ever shone upon. From the dashing waves a the Atlantic to the rolling billows a the Pacific — from the icy mountains a the North Pole to the everglades a Florida the Stars and Stripes was the emblem a liberty. I was glad to stand before you today in the short-grass country. Injin Territory was clasp hands with Oklahoma. We was the cream a civilization — if you don't mind the whey. But we was not in the Union, so we better butt in.' "

And Tookpafka Micco he say, "Well, so that was the long and short a the Oklahoma convention."

(The women folks was keep on pounding sofky corn and the locusts was keep on singing in the blackjack trees and Wolf Warrior and Kono Harjo they was pay close attention.)

Then Hotgun he go on and say, "Well, so it's a long lane that don't turn.[4] The Chiefs was called a constitution convention and the boosters for single statehood was getting scarce as bald headed Injins. The politicians was crowding the band wagon like Muskogee society crowd the Hyde Park owl car."[5]

And Tookpafka Micco he ask Hotgun, "Well, so was all the chiefs favor the big powwow to make medicine for statehood separated from Oklahoma?"

And Hotgun he say, "Well, so they was all favored it but the chief a the Chickasaw nation. He was had other fish to fry, like the hundred thousand dollar warrant scandal. The grand jury was meet pretty soon and he didn't had any enemies to make. He was had friends on both sides a the statehood fence.[6] But all the same the Chickasaw nation be represented. One swallow don't make a summer."[7]

"But so," Tookpafka Micco say, "Colonel Duglast and Deacon Marrs and Governor Makefire say single statehood was inevitable."[8]

And Hotgun he say, "Well, so it was inevitable to die but the doctors was had lots a practice. It's time to had a change and shift the scenery. All the Snake Injins was rounded up in the Creek nation; Dick Adams and Bob Owens was skimmed the cream in the Cherokee nation;[9] they wasn't enough pine timber left in the Choctaw nation for a set a house logs; all the fine springs was gobbled up by the government for health resorts for retired carpet-baggers and they wasn't enough money left in the treasury to hail a bread wagon with. So the Five Civilized Tribes didn't had anything to live for but statehood and the removal a the restrictions."

And Tookpafka Micco he ask Hotgun, "Reckon so they be a big attendance at the constitution convention?"

And Hotgun he say, "Well, so bound to be. It was this way: If Okmulgee didn't want the county seat, Henryetta was take it off of her hand like a duck catching a June bug; if Wagoner didn't seek after the county seat, Coweta was willing to relieve her a the burden; if South McAlester was indifferent, Haileyville was got busy; and if Eufaula didn't had her boundary lines on straight, maybe so Dustin was profit by it.[10] When the Dawes commission was set in to wind up this country it was had to lay out section lines and township lines before it could allot the Injins. Same way the constitution convention was had to draw plans and specifications for statehood, and that was call for county lines and districts for congressmen and senators to run in. No one was opposed the move to have statehood separated from Oklahoma but railroad lawyers and well-meaning but misguided country editors and corn field statesmen with bee hives in they hats."

Tookpafka Micco and Wolf Warrior and Kono Harjo give long grunt and help theyselves to a watermelon.

1. Separate-state advocates in Indian Territory considered single-statehood efforts in Oklahoma an attempt simply to annex Indian Territory, which Oklahomans would dominate.

2. The People's Vindicator has not been identified.

3. Henry P. Robbins, the postmaster at South McAlester and clerk of the court for the Western District of Indian Territory, was one of two speakers who responded to the welcoming speech of I. N. Holcomb, former Oklahoma territorial superintendent of instruction. *Muskogee Democrat*, July 12, 1905; *Vinita Weekly Chieftain*, January 7, 1904; *Daily Oklahoman*, May 25, 1905.

4. "It's a long lane that knows no turnings" (Robert Browning, *The Flight of the Duchess*, 1845, stanza 17).

5. Hyde Park was an amusement park on the Arkansas River northeast of Muskogee with regular streetcar service from town. An "owl car" was a streetcar that ran after midnight.

6. The Chickasaw chief Douglas H. Johnston was at odds with Tams Bixby on the delivery of Chickasaw allotment deeds. Chickasaw and Choctaw deeds required the signatures of both chiefs, and Johnston refused to sign, thus holding up delivery to both Chickasaws and Choctaws. Johnston was facing an investigation of scandal involving Chickasaw school funds. But that was probably not the reason he refused to participate in the call to convention. The single-statehood issue had not been as hotly agitated in the Chickasaw Nation as it had elsewhere, and as he told the press, he felt it was too early for statehood because the allotment process was not finished. In addition, he favored single statehood with Oklahoma. *Muskogee Democrat*, July 28 and 29, 1905.

7. The adage "One swallow does not make summer" dates at least to the sixteenth century and is probably based on "One swallow does not make spring" from Aristophanes' *The Birds* (414 B.C.).

8. David M. Marrs was the editor of the *Vinita Chieftain;* Bird S. McGuire (1865–?) was a delegate to Congress from Oklahoma Territory.

9. Richard Calmit Adams, a Delaware from Fort Gibson, served as attorney for his people and had successfully pursued their claims. The Registered Delawares had joined the Cherokees in 1867. *El Reno News,* June 18, 1897; *Vinita Daily Chieftain,* July 30, 1900, and May 2, 1904. Robert L. Owen was accused by the *Cherokee Advocate* of having inflated his legal fees for pursuing Cherokee claims. See, e.g., *Cherokee Advocate,* February 4, 1905. Some fees were large because attorneys claimed a percentage of the claims award.

10. Wagoner is the county seat of Wagoner County, McAlester of Pittsburg County, and Eufaula of McIntosh County. Coweta and Haileyville are in Wagoner County and Pittsburg County, respectively, but the county line for McIntosh County was drawn east of Dustin, placing it in Hughes County. Hotgun's prediction of county line locations was surprisingly accurate.

Letter No.56

[*Muskogee Daily Phoenix,* August 20, 1905; *Dustin Dispatch,* August 26, 1905; *Muskogee Phoenix,* August 31, 1905]

During the first three weeks of August plans were made for the constitutional convention at Muskogee on the twenty-first. Members of the local commercial club organized to welcome and entertain the delegates. Charles N. Haskell, Pleasant Porter's choice to oversee the election of delegates from the tenth district, called a meeting on August 7, at which seven delegates were selected. Similar meetings occurred throughout Indian Territory. Much of the enthusiasm for separate statehood, however, was centered in Muskogee; in outlying areas, the majority of territorial newspapers editorialized against it. Though Indian leaders such as Porter argued that the Indians not only wanted but deserved separate statehood, there seemed to be little support among the white population, and blacks were generally excluded from the process. Meanwhile, some Oklahoma single-staters became concerned that the separate-statehood movement might succeed because of the strong Prohibitionist leanings of the separate-staters.

✍

"Well, so," Hotgun he say, "while the Japs and Russians was trying to smoke the pipe a peace at Portsmouth, the separate statehood delegates in Injin Territory was packing they pasteboard telescopes for Muskogee, to make a grand up-to-date constitution.[1] Newspaper reporters was already had they transportation and all the southeast rooms in the hotels engaged for the occasion. The railroads was offered half fare rates, including the plus.[2] The committee on entertainment was busy overhauling the Pike at Hyde Park and drawing up contracts with summer resort show companies, and attractions like that. The mayor was engrossed in 'Ancient and Modern Eloquence' to welcome the delegates. And everything was cocked and primed."[3]

(Wolf Warrior and Kono Harjo look 'way off over the hills and spit in the ragweeds.)

Then Tookpafka Micco, he say, "Well, so what the single staters think about it, anyhow?"

And Hotgun he go on and say, "Well, so they was looked kind a curious and act like a poor horse fenced off from the fodder stack in the winter time."

And Tookpafka Micco he say, "Maybe so the range in the Short-grass country[4] wasn't afford much picking."

Then Hotgun he go on and say, "Well, so the sentiment a the people was unanimous for the constitution convention, and they was only three country editors against it. Lamb, a Okmulgee, he keep lamming 'way every week; but he was only add to the gaity [*sic*] a the nations. All lambs like to buck around and shake they tails. And Deacon Marrs, a Vinita, he say things in his thumb paper unbecoming a true Christian and intermarried Cherokee citizen. And then there's Billy Walker, a Purcell. He never let up and was his own excuse for being. He say heap a mean things. But his editorials was too long to quote and life was too short to read them."[5]

And Tookpafka Micco he say, "Well, so we hear all time the newspaper was mould public opinion."

And Hotgun he say, "Well, so they do if the people didn't had they mind made up already."

Then Tookpafka Micco he say, "Well, so where Delegate Connie Foley stand, anyway?"

And Hotgun he say, "Well, so, that's what Henry Be Lobbying don't know.[6] He was send a telegram to Connie and say, 'Well, so if you was favored single statehood, answer and charge it to me.' But somehow he was missed connection. Maybe so the wire was down somewhere. But I think Connie was played bad politics to expose his hand for Henry Be Lobbying's benefit. We Injins was kind a raise Connie and maybe so he do what's right."

(Wolf Warrior and Kono Harjo grunt and spit in the ragweeds again.)

Then Hotgun he go on and say, "Well, so I wasn't a delegate to the constitution convention, but it was had my moral support, anyhow. Maybe so the Injin Territory wouldn't make a big state by itself like Texas, but you could set Rhode Island down in it twenty-five times and had room enough left for the floating population of Arkansaw."

And Tookpafka Micco he say, "Well, so you think we was ready for statehood?"

And Hotgun he say, "Good and ready. We was ready for the Government to keep its promise and fence us off to ourselves. We was give up all our bad habits, like wearing breech clouts and feathers on the head. We wear hand-me-downs now all the time and live in box shacks with a side room to it instead of log huts daubed with mud. We was give up the simple life, and buy fine

buggies and lightning rods and calendar clocks and had our forefathers' pictures enlarged and be civilized citizens instead common fullblood Injins. So we was ready for statehood. "

Then Tookpafka Micco he say, "Reckon so they stick in a clause
for prohibition in the constitution so we could still had our Peruna and Morning Star Bitters. "

And Hotgun he say, "Well, so that was the understanding, but
Ann Hasa-bush was take a hand in the fight for statehood and say
you better keep out everything but Budweiser, 'cause it was a soft
drink and didn't intoxicate like Oklahoma white mule.[7] But I was
in favor a the prohibition clause — I don't want to break away from
the old favorites like you mention. "

Then Tookpafka Micco he say, "Well, so what name you
reckon they give the new state?"

And Hotgun he say, "Well, so some say call it Terra-india, the
land a the Red Man; but maybe so they better name it Ta-ra-
boom-de-ay, the land a the boomer. "

1. Negotiations to bring an end to the Russo-Japanese War were going on at
Portsmouth, New Hampshire. See *Muskogee Democrat*, August 7 and 8, 1905.
"Pasteboard telescopes" are cheap suitcases.

2. "The plus" is the tax. Railroad companies in Indian Territory often offered
"excursion" rates for special events. Southeast rooms would be desirable in summer; in the days before air conditioning, those rooms would be the coolest in
Muskogee because of the direction of the prevailing winds.

3. The Muskogee Commercial Club established a hospitality committee on
August 2 to look after the comfort of the delegates and to arrange reduced
railroad fares. Hyde Park was an amusement park and picnic area opened in June
1905, replete with the Hyde Park College Inn Restaurant, an automatic vaudeville, a skating rink, a theater, and of course, a "pike," or midway. *Muskogee
Phoenix*, April 5, 1906; *Muskogee Democrat*, April 21, June 12, and August 1 and 3,
1905. The mayor of Muskogee was Francis B. Fite, who was to welcome the
delegates. Like a muzzle-loaded weapon to which powder has been applied,

Muskogee is primed, cocked, and ready to fire. "Ancient and Modern Eloquence" was perhaps a textbook.

4. The "Short-grass country" is Oklahoma Territory.

5. Sentiment was far from unanimous in favor of separate statehood, and the final analysis would show that far more newspapers favored joint statehood with Oklahoma than separate statehood for Indian Territory. In addition to the *Muskogee Phoenix*, in which Pósey published his Fus Fixico letters, the three editors named had been particularly outspoken. Frank Fenimore Lamb, of the *Capital News* in Okmulgee, argued — and to a large extent correctly — that the proposed convention was not an Indian affair but was Charles N. Haskell's; Lamb later said that the convention was "tainted by negroism," which the opposition press took as a slur on Pleasant Porter, whose ancestry was part African. D. M. Marrs, of the *Vinita Chieftain*, tended to downplay the convention preparations, calling them a "fizzle," and labeled the convention a "fly speck" in history. The Indians' speaking for statehood by calling a convention was a wail; Anglo-Saxons dominated, he claimed. W. H. Walker, of the *Purcell Register*, called the event Robert L. Owen's " 'constitutions while you wait' convention." A few people controlled the process and, through "Muskogee dictation," drummed up interest by creating contention over the location of county courthouses. The separate-statehood proponents, Walker said, were a "no state crowd." *Muskogee Democrat*, July 27 and 29 and August 4, 9, 12, 23, and 26, 1905.

6. The exchange between Foley and Robbins has not been located.

7. Ann Hasa-bush is Anheuser-Busch. As statehood approached, it appeared likely that legislation creating the state would contain a Prohibition clause. The United States Brewers' Association argued that most beer and ale contained only 3.5 percent alcohol, far less than most patent medicines such as Peruna and Morning Star Bitters. In November 1905, the organization petitioned the president not to prohibit beer and ale with less than 4.5 percent alcohol. In December, officials of the Western District of Indian Territory banned Hotgun's and Tookpafka Micco's favorite, Peruna, as an intoxicant. *Muskogee Phoenix*, November 16 and December 16, 1905.

Letter No.57

[*Muskogee Daily Phoenix*, August 27, 1905; *Muskogee Phoenix*, September 7, 1905; *Cherokee Advocate*, September 9, 1905; *Sturm's Statehood Magazine* 1 (October 1905): 90–91]

Many Indian leaders believed that agreements with the federal government had guaranteed the Five Civilized Tribes a state of their own when they were prepared for citizenship. That belief and the fear of political domination by Oklahoma in a joint statehood made them anxious to develop an acceptable constitution for the state of Sequoyah. A common belief existed that Congress had not passed a statehood bill because the Indians had not demonstrated their desire for statehood. Thus the Sequoyah convention was an opportunity for them to display not only their political know-how but also their ability to grapple with constitutional issues. The convention opened with great fanfare on August 21 and on the surface appeared to be an Indian affair. Chief Pleasant Porter was chosen president, and each of the Five Civilized Tribes had a vice president. Chief W. C. Rogers was chosen for the Cherokees, Chief John Brown for the Seminoles, and Governor Green McCurtain for the Choctaws. The Creeks and Chickasaws were represented by white men: C. N. Haskell and William H. Murray, respectively. Posey, who was not one of the 167 elected delegates, was chosen secretary, though there is little evidence that he participated in the convention. Committees were set to work at drafting a constitution and adjourned until September 5, when the draft would be discussed and adopted. Despite Hotgun's touting the convention as an Indian achievement, it was actually dominated by Haskell and Murray.

✍🏻

"Well, so," Hotgun he say, "the Injin has spoken. Long time ago he give a war whoop and go on the warpath; this time he call a convention and go on record. Instead a making medicine he make history; instead a chasing the pioneers with a tomahawk, he preside in convention and use the tomahawk for a gavel to call the pioneers to order; and instead a swearing vengeance against the pale face, he get up and make a big talk on how to make a state. The Injin is civilized and aint extinct no more than a rabbit. He's just beginning to feel his breakfast food."[1]

(Tookpafka Micco and Wolf Warrior and Kono Harjo pay close attention, and the locust was singing lonesome in the catalpa tree.)

And Hotgun he go on and say: "Well, so somebody was had to take the lead for separate statehood, and the Injin say 'might as well be me.' So he report for duty first and was immortalized himself. He wait put near a hundred years and Opportunity didn't find him asleep in the wigwam. He was watch faithful at his post and make good when the time came. You could call the movement for separate statehood bosh, or fiasco, or sentiment, and names like that if you want to, but I was call it a declaration a independence that was had its foundation on every hearthstone in Injin Territory."

(Tookpafka Micco and Wolf Warrior and Kono Harjo give a big grunt and spit in the jimpson weeds [*sic*].)

And Hotgun he go on and say, "The Injin was kicked out a his swaddling clothes a red tape and was ready to follow the flag and constitution without Oklahoma to give him encouragement with stimulants. The United States was bound by treaty and Christian duty to back the Injin up in the struggle for his rights."

Then Hotgun he light his stone pipe and give Tookpafka Micco and Wolf Warrior account a the big powwow at Muskogee. He say, "Well, so, according to arrangements, Chief Lodges, a the Cherokees, he knocked on the table with his trusty tomahawk and tell the delegates from the Creek nation and Choctaw nation and Chickasaw nation and Seminole nation and Quapaw Agency and Wyandotte reservation to pull off they hats and behave themselves, so the Lord could hear the invocation a the preacher.[2]

"Then Mayor Fight,[3] a Muskogee, he pull out his speech and say, 'Well, so I was glad to welcome you all to the magnificent city a the southwest and turn over the key to you. You could had the

Hyde Park for full measure and one fare for the round trip on the street car; and you could stay in the primeval forest till the owl car come after you. I never did see such a big powwow like this before, and I was hope you all was had good luck and hitch your band wagon to the lone star a statehood. That was a better ambition than to be a tail for Oklahoma to wag and brush the flies off. So I thank you all for your attention.'

"Then William Merry,[4] a the Chickasaws, he get up and make a response off hand. He say, 'Well, so we was thankful for the pass key to Muskogee and Hyde Park attractions. If we had come in late it was all right and no questions asked. Now, I was for separate statehood. I was for anything to promote happiness. They aint no rhyme nor reason in giving Injin Territory in marriage to Oklahoma. It was like marrying a duke or prince of a run-down royal family to the daughter of a rich trust magnate, so he could repair his ancestral home and roll in luxury. The two countries didn't had nothing in common, unless, maybe so, it was a weakness for firewater. So if you put the two together you was had a drunken brawl. When the Quakers was want statehood congress was give 'em Pennsylvania; when the Dutchman was want statehood congress was give 'em New York; when the Pilgrim fathers was want statehood congress was give 'em Massachusetts; when the Yankees was want statehood congress was give 'em Connecticut; when the gentlemen was want statehood congress was give 'em Virginia; when the Populists was want statehood congress was give 'em Kansas; when the Mossbacks was want statehood congress was give 'em Arkansaw. That's the way United States was founded. It was called the fundamental law. So when the Injins was want statehood congress ought to give 'em Sequoyah.'

"(Chief Lodges he pay close attention and spit behind the stage scenery; Chief Makecertain he fan himself with the palm leaf instead of a turkey wing and look stoical; Chief Porter he look pleasant, and Chief Brown he look like a celebrated Japanese statesman with whiskers.)

"Then the convention was made Chief Porter permanent chairman a the powwow and he was equal to the occasion. He say, 'Well, so the fullblood Injin was about to die and go to the Happy Hunting Grounds. So he was called you all together to hear his will. He want you to take his sofky patch and make a big farm out of it, and raise wheat and oats and prunes and things like that instead a flint corn and gourds. He want you to tear down his log hut and build a big white farm house with green window blinds. He want you to take his three-hundred-pound filly with the pestle tail and raise Kentucky thoroughbreds. He wants you to round up his mass-fed razorback hogs and raise Berkshires and Poland Chinas. He want you to make bulldogs and lap poodles out a his sofky curs. He want you to had no understanding with Oklahoma.'

"(C. N. Haskell he pay close attention and let his cigar go out; U. S. Russell he put near bust open with oratory; Editor Smith, a Atoka, he look like he was regenerated and the angels in Heaven was rejoicing over his repentance for past transgressions;[5] and they was lots a women present and the air was smell like cologne.)"

1. That is, he is just getting started.

2. Chief William Charles Rogers (1847–1917) gaveled the convention to order at 11:07 A.M., August 21. The Reverend A. Grant Evans, of Muskogee, gave the prayer. *Muskogee Democrat*, August 21, 1905. The Quapaw and Wyandot lands were in the extreme northeast corner of Indian Territory.

3. Francis B. Fite had been a delegate to the single statehood convention at Oklahoma City on July 12. His welcoming speech appears in *Muskogee Democrat*, August 21, 1905.

4. William H. Murray (1869–1956), acting for Governor Douglas H. John-

ston of the Chickasaws, responded to Fite's welcome. A Texan, Murray had farmed, edited newspapers, and practiced law before going to Tishomingo, Chickasaw Nation, in 1898. He married a relative of Governor Johnston's, thus becoming a Chickasaw citizen by intermarriage, and served as an assistant to Johnston. See *Who Was Who in America*, 3:628.

5. Charles N. Haskell, the dominant figure at the convention, later became the first governor of Oklahoma. An enthusiastic U. S. Russell, editor of the *South McAlester Capital*, got the floor and called for a resolution for immediate statehood before the temporary organization of the convention was completed. Paul B. Smith was the editor of the *Indian Citizen*. *Muskogee Democrat*, August 21, 1905.

Letter No.58

[*Muskogee Daily Phoenix*, date uncertain, probably September 1905. The only known copy is a newspaper clipping in the Posey Collection, Thomas Gilcrease Institute of American History and Art.]

In the wake of the Sequoyah statehood convention, supporters of the Sequoyah constitution speculated on who the officials of the new state would be. Among the many local people who had political ambitions was J. Fentress Wisdom, a petty bureaucrat at Muskogee. A native of Jackson, Tennessee, he had been named chief clerk at the Indian agency at Muskogee, where his father, Dew M. Wisdom, was agent. In June 1905, he was dismissed from government service because he had refused to enforce a tax imposed on local merchants by the Creek Nation, arguing that the tax was "un-American." That act, no doubt, garnered some favor among the businessmen. Hotgun and Tookpafka Micco contemplate not only their condition under statehood but also the prospects of Wisdom's candidacy for governor.

This was the only Fus Fixico letter to be illustrated. The cartoonist was Charles H. Sawyer, a native of Meriden, Connecticut. Sawyer had served as U.S. consul to Canada for a number of years and had gone to Indian Territory in 1900 as assistant U.S. attorney for the southern district. He was later a law clerk for the Dawes Commission. Suffering from tuberculosis, in early 1905 he went to Kerrville, Texas, for his health, returning to Muskogee in late August, where he drew cartoons for the local papers. He died in January 1906. This cartoon and the letter were probably produced sometime between his return from Texas and late October, when his last cartoon appeared.

✍

Well, so while the ducks was scooping up the juice a the watermelon rinds and the old squirrel dog was stretched out dozing in the shade a the ash hopper and the locust singing lonesome in the blackjack grove, Hotgun he was get a good holt on the bottom round a his hickory chair with his heel and lean back again the catapa tree and ask Tookpafka Micco, "Well, so what was you thought about the future state, anyhow?"

And Tookpafka Micco he shut his eyes close together and smoke slow a while and say, "Well, so I wasn't posted on the hereafter, like the circuit rider."

Then Hotgun he say, "Well, so I know you wasn't called to eat chicken in Zion instead a corn bread, with whey on the side, on a quarter section in the tall timber.[1] So I was talked to you from the stump instead a pulpit, and want to know what you think about the future state in politics, like when we was had statehood separated from Oklahoma and a million dollar headquarters in Muskogee with plank sidewalks 'round it wide enough to make a shade for the toad frog."[2]

"Well, reckon so," Tookpafka Micco he say, "everything be a whole lots different then. Maybe so when the big change was set in, in Nineteen Hundred and Six, it was continued till old Gabriel was blowed on his horn to call in the chasers after the bucks if they was not gone out a hearing."[3]

Then Hotgun he say, "Well, so everything be different then, like you say. Instead a kings and warriors in the council house, we was had boodlers and machine makers in the legislature; and instead of a chief, we was had a governor to slice the pie and call out the militia; and instead a fish frys, we was had clam bakes and free lunches; and instead a sofky and peruny, we was had the best Kentucky and Milwaukee could afford;[4] and instead a the pestle and mortar,[5] we was had goff [*sic*] sticks; and instead a sofky patches, we was had tennis courts; and instead a grassfed fillies, we was had air ships; and instead a stomp dances, we was had social functions, where the womens was wear necklaces instead a tarrapin [*sic*] shells and shirt waists, and the men was divide they hair between the eyes.

"Maybe so," Hotgun he go on and say, "if the lord was spared you from the grafter till Nineteen Hundred and Six, you was see Creek freedmen driving the automobile to Governor J. Wentdressed Withem's inaugural ball."

(Wolf Warrior and Kono Harjo was paid close attention and look curious, and the ducks was still had they bills up to the eye in the juice a the watermelon rinds and the locust keep on singing lonesome.)

Then Tookpafka Micco he was asked Hotgun, "Well, so how come you think J. Wentdressed Withem be governor instead of a dog pelter?"[6]

And Hotgun he say, "Well, so it was manifest destiny. He was had encouragement from Dam Bigpie and Bob Watson.[7] They was told him it was all right and he could go ahead."

Then Tookpafka Micco he say, "Well, maybe so J. Wentdressed Withem was had a cinch on his lofty ambition, like Caesar;[8] but I like to know if he was had the qualification, too."

And Hotgun he say, "Well, so he was a chip right off a the old block. Some a his forefathers was went in the army with muskets and come out with swords and ugly scars on they briskets. Then he was had blue blood coursing through his veins and you could see it under the skin, like violets coming up in the spring a the year. He didn't had no hair on his wrist neither, and that show he wasn't come from the monkey. Then, 'sides that, some a his ancestors, 'way back yonder, was dukes, and they was something said in the family history about a crown wrapped up in tissue paper and hid away under the rafters in the attic."[9]

Then Tookpafka Micco he say, "Well, maybe so J. Wentdressed Withem was had ancestors wounded in the brisket, but I don't think he was ever had a stone bruise on his heel;[10] and, maybe so, he was had no hair on his wrist, like he was kin to the rhinocerus [*sic*]; and, maybe so, some a his forefathers long time ago was dukes, but I don't think he was ever wrapped up anything in tissue paper except 'Duke's Mixture.' "[11]

(Wolf Warrior and Kono Harjo was grunt big.)

"Well, so then," Hotgun he go on and say, "J. Wentdressed Withem was a self-made man and didn't had to depend on his ancestors. He was had good judgment in business and had ability to execute, and, maybe so, if he was governor he could saved up lots a money for the country by his experience in economy. Then he was had book learning too 'sides that, and was burned up lots a midnight oil getting acquainted with the old masters. So, I think J. Wentdressed Withem was good timber for governor and fine prospect for the full dinner pail."

Then Tookpafka Micco he study it over and say, "Well, so but the records a the Department was showed different. When Bonyparts was weighed him in the balance he didn't pan out. He was only had a big mouth for pie with short crust. He swear to support the Constitution, but he make the Constitution take care of him.[12] He tread in the primrose path a dalliance instead of on the sands of time. Maybe so he was sit up late with rare volumes, like Decameron; but that wasn't a good recommendation for governor."[13]

"But, maybe so," Tookpafka Micco he go on and say, "I was had to agree with you about his pennywisdom,[14] 'cause one time I hear he was take two women to the soda fountain to set 'em up. 'Well, so,' he say to one, 'what you like to had?'

"And the woman she say, 'Well, so I don't know; maybe so some ice cream.'

"Then he say to the other one, 'Well, so what you take?'

"And the woman she say, 'Well, reckon so I take ice cream too.'

"Then the clerk he say to J. Wentdressed Withem, 'Well, maybe so you take the same.'

"And J. Wentdressed Withem he say, 'Well, so, I believe, I was druther had some ice water.'"

1. A quarter section is 160 acres.

2. Muskogee residents assumed that their town, the largest in Indian Territory, would become the capital if the territory achieved statehood.

3. The Five Civilized Tribes were supposed to cease to exist on March 4, 1906. The pun in this passage is elaborate. "Bucks" refers to both money and deer; the "chasers" are grafters and dogs. Gabriel's horn on Judgment Day calls the grafters to account just as the hunter's horn calls the dogs in — if they are not too far gone.

4. Kentucky and Milwaukee refer to whiskey and beer, respectively.

5. The pestle and mortar are wooden instruments used in pounding corn for sofky and other foods.

6. A "dog pelter" is a dogcatcher.

7. Tams Bixby was commissioner to the Five Civilized Tribes; Robert B. Watson was city inspector of sewer works for Muskogee. See M. R. Moore, *Moore's Directory of the City of Muskogee, Indian Territory* (Muskogee: Phoenix Publishing Co., 1904), 245.

8. That is, Wisdom had it under control.

9. The Wisdoms were a wealthy family with roots in North Carolina. Dew M. Wisdom, the father of J. Fentress Wisdom, had received severe wounds during the Civil War. See Gideon, *Indian Territory*, 210–11. The references to royal ancestry are uncertain. The popular idea that man had descended from monkeys had apparently resulted from the well-known Oxford debate in 1860 on

Charles Darwin's theory of evolution. Bishop Samuel Wilberforce, an opponent of the theory, had derisively asked whether it was through his grandmother or his grandfather that Darwin claimed to have descended from a monkey.

10. A "stone bruise" is a sore spot on the bottom of the foot. The bruise, caused by a stone or some other object, is usually the result of going barefoot.

11. Tookpafka Micco refers to mixed heritage, the opposite of a purebred or thoroughbred and implying low class. He may also refer to a hidden bottle of whiskey.

12. "Let me be weighed in an even balance, that God may know mine integrity" (Job 31:6). The suggestion is that the investigation conducted by Charles J. Bonaparte in 1903 implied that Wisdom was involved in graft.

13. The implication is that Wisdom will not contribute anything lasting. "Do not, as some ungracious pastors do, / Show me the steep and thorny way to heaven, / Whiles, like a puff'd and reckless libertine, / Himself the primrose path of dalliance treds, / And recks not his own rede" (William Shakespeare, *Hamlet*, act 1, scene 3, ll.47–51). "Lives of great men all remind us / We can make our lives sublime, / And, departing, leave behind us / Footprints on the sands of time" (Henry Wadsworth Longfellow, "A Psalm of Life," 1838, stanza 7). The *Decameron* is a collection of tales written in the fourteenth century by Giovanni Boccaccio.

14. This pun on Wisdom's name suggests that his "economy," discussed above, was a result of stinginess, as the following ancedote suggests.

Letter No.59

[*Muskogee Daily Phoenix*, October 29, 1905; *Muskogee Phoenix*, November 2, 1905; *Holdenville Times*, November 3, 1905; *Muskogee Times*, date undetermined, clipping, in Posey Collection, Thomas Gilcrease Institute of American History and Art]

The work of the Sequoyah constitutional committees was dominated by Charles N. Haskell and William H. Murray, and in later years they took credit for much of the constitution's content. As vice president of the convention, Haskell served on all of the committees, and he and Murray were apparently not above using the location of county seats to bring delegates in line with their thinking on constitutional issues. They oversaw the process, even through the editing stage. Whoever deserves the credit, the result was a document of about thirty-five thousand words, containing—among other provisions—a bill of rights with thirty-one articles, the prohibition of child labor and farming out of convicts for labor, and a provision for a vote on woman's suffrage. The convention reassembled on September 5, completed its work, and set November 7 as the date for a ratification by the people. Prominent leaders of the convention traveled throughout the territory, holding rallies and speaking in favor of ratification. The issue of locating county seats continued to be hotly debated.

✍️

"Well, so," Hotgun he say, "after all the dear people was had to settle it; an' maybe so, this time next year be lots a hamlets in the commonwealth of Sequoyah day-dreamin' roun' the court house square, waitin' for the fall trade up an' the circus calliope to come 'long an' break the mont'nd [*sic*]."[1]

An' Tookpafka Micco he look innocent at Hotgun, like he want to know what he was drivin' at, anyhow.

An' Hotgun he go on an' say, while the autum' leaves was driftin' down, "Well, so if the plans a the big constitution powwow do n't miscarry an' the machinery stay in gear, the Injins an' niggers an' the white element could exercise they great American privilege an' pile up a staggerin' majority for separate state hood November the seventh. That be a big day in the winnin' a the west an', maybe so, it be set aside so it won't get mixed up with work days.[2] After this battle a the ballots, all Injuns be constituents instead a wards a the big man at Washington. Secretary Itscocked was had to wind up his tape an' let go the scepter then an' bow to his time subjects. An' the picnic orator could climb up on the dry goods box in the shade a the scrub oaks an' talk about this great grand and glorious country!"

(Wolf Warrior and Kono Harjo they was spit in the leaves an' look troubled.)

Then Tookpafka Micco he say, "Well, so I hear heap talk all time lately 'bout county seats an' things like that. Lots a places I see renters stan'nin' in the middle a the cotton patch arguin' like they was more in it than fillin' the long sack with fleecy staple. I like to know what's a county seat anyhow, an' what make people quit work to talk about it."

An' Hotgun he look down his old pipe stem, like he was takin' sure aim, an' say, "Well, so a county seat was a kin' of a busk groun', only it was more assumin'. It was had big brick buildin's with rock posts in front instead of brush arbors, an' upholstered chairs to set on instead a split-log benches, an' waxed floors to dance on instead a the bare groun', an' whiskey to drink instead a physic.[3] They was forty-eight counties in the state of Sequoyah, but looks like they wasn't enough to go roun' an' they was heap a squabblin' between railroad flag stations an' star route postoffices an' back district neighborhoods."[4]

(Wolf Warrior an' Kono Harjo they was pay close 'tention an' dream an' sigh for old times, like when Locha Harjo was chief an' you could pick up your rifle an' kill a deer back a the sofky patch.)[5]

Then Tookpafka Micco he say, "Well, so you reckon we get statehood separate from Oklahoma? What's your honest conviction, anyhow?"

An' Hotgun he puff out big clouds a smoke an' put near shut his eyes an' say, "Well, so that depen's; it was a hard question to answer; it make wise men scratch they heads where it do n't itch, an' bring ever'body to the partin' a the ways.[6] I couldn't look far 'nough into the lobbies an' cloakroom at Washington to tell what congress was had up its sleeve, but separate statehood prospects right now look so flatterin' they was a big howl goin' up over in the Short Grass country."[7]

An' Tookpafka Micco he say, "Well, so wolves do n't howl till they was after prey, an', maybe so, this time we be the prey."

An' Hotgun he nod his head and go on and say, "Well, so the cayote with the lonesomest voice an' hungriest mouth was Delegate Makefire, an' the one next to him was Dennis Flynn, an' when these two get together with Plenty Sofar and Colonel Duglast, that constitute the pack after the fat calf.[8] An' once in a while some more cayotes howl 'way off an' you couldn't hear 'em hardly. That was Kansas congressmen and Illinois senators scentin' the air. They was all coyotes; the Lobo wolves don't go in packs an' make the night hideous."

Then Tookpafka Micco he say, "Well, so the language a the treaty was plain an' the honor a the United States was staked on it. So I vote for Sequoyah an' the nearest postoffice for county seat when the time come."

1. The *Muskogee Times* version reads "monot'ny". A line may have been omitted after "the commonwealth of Sequoyah" in this sentence.

2. That is, the day might be set aside as a holiday. "The winning of the West" was a popular expression in the nineteenth century, embodying the concept of subduing the Indian and making the West "civilized" according to Euro-American standards. It was the title of a work (1889–96) by Theodore Roosevelt.

3. The annual busk, or Green Corn Ceremony, was the major ceremony among the Creeks. The busk ground, or town square, was surrounded by four arbors, one at each cardinal direction, in which log benches provided seating for officials. The busk ground was bare and hard-packed earth. The purifying "physic," or medicine, was ritually drunk on the second day of the busk. See Frank G. Speck, *The Creek Indians of Taskigi Town* (Millwood, N.Y.: Kraus Reprint Co., 1974), 111–12, 140–41.

4. Drawing county boundaries was difficult because town boosters wanted their towns to become the county seat. Besides contention over location of county seats, people wrangled over the names of counties. Posey, for example, wanted them all to have Indian names. Some people wanted a county named for themselves. In a rhyme about county names, a local Muskogee editor suggested

that one be named for Posey. *Muskogee Democrat*, August 25, 28, and 30 and September 1, 1905.

5. Locher Harjo was elected principal chief of the Creeks in 1875 and was impeached in 1876.

6. "For the king of Babylon stood at the parting of the way, at the head of two ways, to use divination: he made his arrows bright, he consulted with images, he looked in the liver" (Ezekiel 21:21).

7. In an effort to blunt the Sequoyah statehood movement, single-state leaders from Oklahoma Territory called a convention at Tulsa, Creek Nation, in September. *Muskogee Democrat*, September 11, 18, and 21, 1905.

8. Bird S. McGuire, of Pawnee, Oklahoma, was a congressional delegate from Oklahoma. He had announced that he would reintroduce the Hamilton statehood bill in that winter's Congress and made public a letter from House Speaker Joseph Cannon, who said that the best way to obtain single-state legislation was to advocate separate statehood, as the Sequoyah convention had. Dennis Flynn, a former delegate, echoed this sentiment in his public statements. Pliny Soper was the former U.S. attorney for the Northern District of Indian Territory. Clarence Douglas, as the editor of the *Muskogee Phoenix*, was a strong voice for Republicans and apparently had political aspirations. See *Muskogee Democrat*, September 14, and October 14, 1905, and *Muskogee Phoenix*, October 26, 1905.

Letter No.60

[*Muskogee Times*, early December 1905, date uncertain. The only known copy is a clipping in Posey Collection, Thomas Gilcrease Institute of American History and Art.]

The ratification vote on the Sequoyah constitution did not reflect the widespread separate-state sentiment that its proponents had claimed. Although the constitution was ratified overwhelmingly, fewer than half of those eligible voted. Though Sequoyah supporters put the best face on it, their chances of success were small. However, the vote demonstrated the strength of the Democrats in Indian Territory, and Republicans became intent on securing as many federal political plums in Indian Territory as possible before statehood. One focus of their efforts was the replacement of C. W. Raymond, judge of the Western District of Indian

Territory, whose term ended in December. In the previous winter, Clarence Douglas had publicly challenged Raymond's fitness for office. Douglas's charges were investigated, but Raymond was exonerated. Then the Muskogee Bar Association had gone on record against Raymond's reappointment. Republican congressmen from Kansas and Missouri, Republican organizations in Oklahoma and Indian territories, Tams Bixby, Dennis Flynn, and citizens from Indian Territory extensively lobbied President Roosevelt in behalf of Luman F. Parker, Jr., to replace Raymond. Parker, whose major qualification seems to have been the favor of the railroad companies, had a singularly undistinguished record.

✍

Well, so Thanksgivin' Hotgun an' Tookpafka Micco an' Wolf Warrior an' Kono Harjo drink sofky instead a eggnog an' talk long time over they pipes by the fireside.

An' Hotgun he say, "Well, so I like to know what Plenty Sofar an' Nate Kicksome an' Cliff Jack's Son an' Colonel Clarence Duglast an' Lowman Parker was had to be thankful for, anyhow."[1]

An' Tookpafka Micco he says, "Well, maybe so this was the winter a they discontent. All they pet schemes an' plans for the future was fall flat, like a exhausted baloon [*sic*]; the people was snowed 'em under with votes for Sequoyah, an' the Man With the Big Stick at Washington was give 'em a cold deal instead of a square one."[2]

An' Hotgun he says, "Well, so the vote for Sequoyah was the irony a fate, but the experience at the White House was a stunner."

Tookpafka Micco an' Wolf Warrior an' Kono Harjo listen close an' spit behin' the backlog.

An' Hotgun he go on an' say, "Well, so it was like this: Plenty Sofar, big lawyer for the Frisco, an' Cliff Jack's Son, big lawyer for the Katy, an' Lowman Parker, close kin to the big lawyer for the Frisco, an' Nate Kicksome, big lawyer for the Muskogee street railway, was all call at the White House to pay they respects an' get out a injunction again the Judge a the Western District."[3]

"Well, so," Tookpafka Micco he says, "What about the big lawyer for the M. O. an' G., an' the big lawyer for the Fort Smith an' Western, an' the big lawyer for the Midland Valley, an' the big lawyer for the proposed route to Shawnee from Henryetta?"[4]

Wolf Warrior an' Kono Harjo grunt an' spit behin' the backlog agin.

An' Hotgun he go on an' say, "Well, so they was all there in spirit. But like I start to tell, the nigger porter was meet 'em at the White House door an' inform 'em King Manylicks, of Abysinnia, was had a man in the Blue Room makin' Christmas presents to the President. So they had to wait outside in the hall an' cool they heels till they turn come.[5] This was give Nate Kicksome a good chance to go over his forty minute masterpiece an' see if it needed any more polishin' an' he was avail himself a the opportunity. Maybe so two hours later King Manylicks' man get through presentin' elephant tusks an' rhinoceros hides an' stuffed pythons an' lion skin mats an' keepsakes like that to the President an' comes out takin' his departure. Plenty Sofar come put near shakin' hands with 'im, he looked so much like one a his constituents. Then they were ushered into the august presence. The Man With the Big Stick he look at his watch an' say, 'Well, so what you men want, anyhow, this time a day?' An' Nate Kicksome he smile weak an' say, 'Well, so Mr. President, I was the speaker for the committee on Judge Raymond's scalp.'[6] An' the Man With the Big Stick say, 'That so?' An' Nate Kicksome he nod. Then the Man With the Big Stick he say, 'Well, so I'm sorry but I got all the hides an' hair I want just now. Good day.' "

An' Tookpafka Micco he say, "Well, so what did they had agin the Judge a the Western District, anyhow?" An' Hotgun he say, "Well maybe so the most serious charge was because they couldn't had any influence with 'im, or make 'im be friends with the grafter. 'Sides that the Judge wouldn't let 'em spit on the floor an' put they feet on the bench an' clean they fingernails while court was in session. He was made 'em all behave theyselves an' treat cotton pickers same as big lawyers for the railroads an' make no distinctions between the high an' low an' the rich an' poor. A section boss was look good to him as Plenty Sofar or Cliff Jack's Son. So I like Judge Raymond for the enemies he has made."[7]

An' Tookpafka Micco he look in the fire an' spit in the ashes an' say, "Well, so now if the Man With the Big Stick at Washington was club the big life insurance companies an' corporations like that his fame was secure."[8]

1. N. A. Gibson ("Nate Kicksome") was the attorney for the Muskogee Traction Company.

2. "Now is the winter of our discontent / Made glorious summer by this sun of York" (William Shakespeare, *King Richard III*, act 1, scene 1, ll. 1–2). "Square deal" was a popular expression first used by Theodore Roosevelt on his western tour in 1903 to express what he hoped to achieve for the people of America. Frank Martin Lemon, "Square Deal," *Dictionary of American History* (New York: Charles Scribner's Sons, 1976), 6:378.

3. Luman F. Parker, Jr., had served three years as assistant district attorney under Soper. Parker's father was solicitor general for the Frisco system, with headquarters in St. Louis. *Muskogee Phoenix*, December 14, 1905. In late November, a large party had called at the White House, asking Roosevelt not to reappoint Judge Raymond. On November 27, a delegation headed by Tams Bixby, Chief W. C. Rogers of the Cherokees, Chief Pleasant Porter of the Creeks, G. W. Grayson, and J. W. Zeveley, a Muskogee attorney, called at not only the White House but the Department of Justice as well. Later that day, Pliny Soper, Zeveley, and others called on Roosevelt again on Parker's behalf. *Cherokee Advocate*, December 2, 1905.

4. The Missouri, Oklahoma, and Gulf (MO&G), the Fort Smith and Western, and the Midland Valley were other companies with railroads in Indian Territory. William Kenefick, the owner of the MO&G, was planning an extension of his line from Henryetta, just south of Okmulgee, to Shawnee, sixty miles west, in Oklahoma Territory. *Muskogee Phoenix*, December 14, 1905.

5. Menilek II was the emperor of Ethiopia from 1889 to 1913. As editor of the *Indian Journal* in 1902–3, Posey had frequently associated blacks and the Republican party and had asserted that Roosevelt gave preferential treatment to blacks over Indians.

6. Gibson had been chairman of the Muskogee Bar Association grievance committee that had drafted the resolution against Judge Raymond's reappointment. *Muskogee Democrat*, September 30, 1905; *Muskogee Phoenix*, October 5, 1905.

7. In mid-December, it was announced that Raymond would retire. Judge William R. Lawrence was moved from the northern district to replace him at Muskogee, and Parker was appointed to replace Lawrence at Vinita, where Parker had served under Soper. Before going to Indian Territory, Parker, who was not quite thirty-five, had been a stenographer in New Mexico and Oklahoma territories. After three years as assistant district attorney under Soper, he had served three years as master of the chancery in the northern district and had been a member of the law firm of Hutchings and Murphey in Muskogee. Despite his obvious connection with railroad interests, the Republican press claimed that the railroads had no influence over him. His appointment met opposition in charges against both his and Soper's integrity when they had worked in the northern district. *Muskogee Phoenix*, December 7, 16, and 21, 1905.

8. In his annual message to the Fifty-ninth Congress, Roosevelt called for antitrust legislation that would regulate corporations, including insurance companies. See Lewis L. Gould, *Reform and Regulation: American Politics, 1900–1916* (New York: Wiley, 1978), 63.

Letter No.61

[Undated fragment, perhaps March 1906, typescript in Posey Collection, Thomas Gilcrease Institute of American History and Art]

Posey had interviewed the Creek statesman Yadeka Harjo at his home near Hickory Ground in October 1905 while annotating the tribal rolls for the Dawes Commission. One of the survivors of the removal from Alabama, Yadeka Harjo had served in the Union army during the Civil War and later in Creek tribal government as a delegate to Washington, a district judge, and a member of the House of Warriors. When he died in early 1906, Posey wanted to make his death the subject of a Fus Fixico letter. Among Posey's papers is a fragment, subtitled "Hot Gun on the Death of Yadeka Harjo." The effort, however, is rather sentimental and awkward. Eventually, Posey gave his ideas poetic expression, and he published "Hotgun on the Death of Yadeka Harjo" in January 1908. Both the prose fragment and the poem appear below.

✍

So it was Hot Gun [*sic*] look 'way off, lonesome like, an' smoke slow an' tell Tookpafka Micco an' Wolf Warrior an' Kono Harjo, "Well, so my ol' time frien', Yadeka Harjo, was finished 'is days an' go to be a good Injin. It make me feel sorry to think about it. We been frien's long time. We come together from the Ol' Country, an' live close neighbor to one 'nuther. He come to my house an' I go to 'is house, an' we set down an' talk till dinner time an', maybe so, stay all night. All time we cultivate big frien'ship an' small sofky patch. We didn't visit one 'nuther 'cause we had business. He didn't had nuthin' I want to get holt of 'cept good will, an' I didn't had nuthin' he like to have 'cept the same thing. So when he see me ridin' up to 'is front gate, he wasn't 'fraid he had to go on my note or vote for me for office. Same way, when I see 'im comin', I wasn't uneasy."

(Tookpafka Micco an' Wolf Warrior an' Kono Harjo pay close 'tention an' think o' the ol' days when Checota was chief[1] an' Injin Territory was a huntin' groun' for the Five Tribes 'stead of a paradise for Illinois politicians.)

"So it was," Hot Gun he go on an' say, "when I was to Yadeka's house las' time, we had long talk. He tell me, 'Well, so my day's gettin' [few]² an' the way before me's in the shadow. I couldn't see ahead far. Maybe so nex' time you come I be gone. So I want to leave some words for you to han' down.'

"I pay close 'tention an' my ol' time frien', Yadeka Harjo, he go on an' say, 'Well, so I pass through many days; maybe so I was put near hundred years ol'; I couldn't tell.³ So what I say is ol' man talk. Long time ago He That Looks Over Us give the Injins more lan' than any other people. He put a big ocean on the east side of it an' a big ocean on the west side of it. Then he put summer on the south side an' winter on the north side. He put gold an' silver in the hills an' fishes in the streams an' game in the woods an' on the prairies. He give the Injin the bow an' arrow an' tol' 'im to be happy.' "

Hotgun on the Death of Yadeka Harjo⁴

"Well, so," Hotgun he say,
    "My ol'-time frien', Yadeka Harjo, he
Was died the other day,
    An' they was no ol'-timer left but me.

"Hotulk Emathla he
    Was go to be good Injun long time 'go,
An' Woxie Harjoche
    Been dead ten years or twenty, maybe so.⁵

"All had to die at las';
    I live long time, but now my days was few;
'Fore long, poke weeds and grass
    Be growin' all aroun' my grave house, too."

Wolf Warrior listen close
    An' Kono Harjo pay close 'tention, too,
Tookpafka Micco he almos'
    Let his pipe go out a time or two.

1. Samuel Checote was chief from 1867 to 1874. See John Bartlett Meserve, "Chief Samuel Checote, with Sketches of Chiefs Locher Harjo and Ward Coachman," *Chronicles of Oklahoma* 16 (December 1938): 401–3.

2. A word is missing here. See line ten of the poem. See also Minnie H. Posey, comp., *Poems of Alexander Lawrence Posey*, rev. ed. (Muskogee: Hoffman Printing Co., 1969), 37.

3. A news report said that Yadeka Harjo was past ninety, feeble, blind, and much loved by his neighbors, who planted and harvested crops for him in his late years. The report said, "The old man is telling his friends that he has passed through many days and that his end is near." *Muskogee Times-Democrat*, February 21, 1906.

4. The poem first appeared in *Kansas City Star*, January 19, 1908, and was reprinted in *Indian Journal*, January 24, 1908.

5. Hotulk Emathla was second principal chief in 1895, when Posey was elected to the House of Warriors. Woxie Harjoche has not been identified.

Letter No.62

[*New-State Tribune*, March 8, 1906; *Indian Journal*, March 16, 1906]

Although the Sequoyah statehood petition was introduced in the U.S. Senate, it was obvious by early 1906 that congressional sentiment favored single statehood for Oklahoma and Indian territories. What was not obvious was whether a statehood bill would pass the winter session of 1905–6, although the prospects had looked favorable at first. The Hamilton bill was reintroduced and passed in the House in early February, but bitter political wrangling ensued in the Senate over questions such as whether the admission of the territories of Arizona and New Mexico should be tied to the admission of Oklahoma Territory. By early March, no bill had passed. The tribal governments were due to expire on March 4; with statehood delayed and much tribal business still to conclude, Congress passed a resolution continuing the tribal governments. To conservative Creeks like Hotgun, the delay of statehood, though only temporary, made the future appear even more uncertain.

So it was Hotgun he set by the fire an' smoke slow an' think long time. Then he spit in the ashes an' tell Tookpafka Micco an' Wolf Warrior an' Kono Harjo, "Well, so hist'ry repeats itself, an' they was n't nuthin' new under the sun. The big progress o' modern times was only a var'ation o' ancient civilization. They was n't any difference 'tween nineteen-ought-six, A. D. an' nineteen-ought-six, B. C., only Pharoah rode in a chariot an' Roosevelt busts the bronco; an' 'stead o' the pyramids, we got the Panama canal project;[1] an' 'stead o' Moses an' the Ten Commandments, we got Thomas Lostsome an' the Frenzied Finance;[2] an' 'stead o' tyrants like Nero, we got philanthropists like John D. Rockyfeller; an' 'stead o' Solomon, we got Senator Smoot; an' 'stead o' the Parthenon, we got Tammany Hall; an' 'stead o' the Golden Age o' Pericles, we got the era o' the Big Stick, an' life insurance graft, an' coal strikes, an' railroad rebates, an' machine politics."[3]

Tookpafka Micco an' Wolf Warrior an' Kono Harjo pay close 'tention.

An' Hotgun he go an' say, "Well, so but sometime they was rare exceptions an' hist'ry do n't repeat itself. So, that's how come Injin Territory was left standin' after March[4] hunters was n't gettin' num'rous to save the pieces. Congress was take the extinction o' the Injin under advisement an' order Secretary Itscocked to fan the council fire till further notice. So it was the Five Civilized Tribes still had a habitation an' a name, an' Big Chief Porter an' Big Chief Lodges an' Big Chief Brown an' Big Chief Johnson an' Big Chief Makecertain was n't out of a job like Othello."[5]

An' Tookpafka Micco he say, "Well, so then I go to lots o' trouble an' expense for nothin', gettin' ready to take up the white man's burden an' walk off with it. I tell my wife she mus' quit huntin' wild onions in the creek bottom an' gather gossip in the womens' [*sic*] literary club, an' stop poundin' sofky corn an' subscribe for the Ladies' Home Journal, an' hire a creek freedman for a coachman an' go shoppin' in a buggy with red runnin' gears an' a high seat 'stead of on a three hundred pound filly with the colt followin' 'long behin'. Then I was go before the Injin agent an' ask 'im to take off my hobbles[6] so I could sell my land an' buy a pair o' tailor-made breeches with legs like a talkin' machine horn an' a waistcoat that look like the comic supplement o' the Sunday daily. Then I go 'mong the politicians an' help build a machine to swing the full blood vote when the time come."

An' Hotgun he say, "Well, so you better countermand your orders an' stick to your sofky patch an' die a nat'ral death with the rest o' the Injins."

---

1. The Panama Canal project had begun after the Hay-Bunau-Varilla Treaty (1903) but would not be completed until 1914.

2. Thomas William Lawson (1857–1925), a Boston stockbroker and writer, had amassed a fortune of some fifty million dollars by 1900, much of it through his alliance with Standard Oil in the reorganization of its Anaconda mine as Amalgamated Copper. Later, *Everybody's Magazine* asked him to write a history of Amalgamated Copper, which he did in a series titled "Frenzied Finance" (1904–5), later collected and published as a book (1905). His exposure of underhanded money dealings lost him friends and, ultimately, his fortune. See *Dictionary of American Biography*, ed. Malone (1933), 11:59–60.

3. The reign of Nero Claudius Caesar, emperor of Rome (54–68 A.D.), was directed by his viciousness and vanity. John Davison Rockefeller (1839–1937), oil baron, philanthropist, and titular head of Standard Oil, was criticized in the early 1900s by muckrakers like Thomas Lawson and Ida Tarbell. See *Dictionary of American Biography*, ed. Robert Livingston Schuyler (New York: Charles Scribner's Sons, 1958), Supp. 2:574–75.

Solomon, the king of Israel, was reputed for his wisdom. Reed Smoot (1862–1941) was a U.S. senator from Utah (1903–1933) and apostle in the Church of Jesus Christ of Latter-Day Saints. His right to sit in the Senate was challenged on grounds of his position in the church and of allegations that he had approved of polygamy. Democrats charged that Roosevelt supported him in return for Smoot's delivery of the Mormon vote for the Republicans. See *The National Cyclopaedia of American Biography* (New York: James T. White, 1949), 35:63–64.

The Parthenon, the temple of Athena, was built on the Acropolis at Athens (447–32 B.C.). William Marcy Tweed and others involved in New York City corruption belonged to the Society of St. Tammany. The term "Tammany Hall" became synonymous with corrupt machine politics. See Catherine O'Dea, "Tammany Hall," *Dictionary of American History*, 6:459–60.

Pericles (ca. 495–29 B.C.), eminent in Athenian civil and military affairs, was known for his honesty, intellect, and influence in strengthening the empire. See *The Oxford Classical Dictionary*, 2d ed., ed. N.G.L. Hammond and H. H. Scullard (Oxford: Clarendon Press, 1970), 800–801. "Big Stick" was a term applied to Theodore Roosevelt's nationalistic foreign policy and his willingness to use military force, if necessary, to enforce it. Thomas Lawson attacked the insurance companies in his "Frenzied Finance" articles and helped bring about an investigation of insurance companies in 1905. Coal strikes had been much in the news during the month before the publication of this letter. See, e.g., *Muskogee Democrat*, Febuary 2, 7, and 9, 1906. In an effort to strengthen the Interstate Commerce Commission, Roosevelt had worked for a year to secure legislation to regulate railroad rates. See Gould, *Reform and Regulation*, 54–58, 62–64.

4. A line was apparently omitted here.

5. That is, Congress passed the resolution extending the governments of the Five Civilized Tribes with the current chiefs at their heads: Pleasant Porter, William C. Rogers, John F. Brown, Douglas H. Johnston, and Green McCurtain. Othello, in Shakespeare's tragedy, was commander of the armed forces of Venice and led those forces against Cyprus. Othello's "job" was not threatened. Perhaps the reference is a loose comparison of the potential end of the Five Civilized Tribes to the tragic self-destruction of Othello in the play.

6. That is, Tookpafka Micco would ask the Indian agent to remove the restrictions from the sale of his allotment.

Letters No.63, No.64, and No.65

[No.63: *New-State Tribune*, March 15, 1906; *Indian Journal*, March 23, 1906. No.64: *New-State Tribune*, March 22, 1906; *Henryetta Free-Lance*,

March 23, 1906; *Indian Journal*, March 30, 1906. No.65: *New-State Tri-bune*, March 29, 1906; *Henryetta Free-Lance*, March 30, 1906]

As the statehood debate continued in Congress, the rhetoric of men such as Senator Albert J. Beveridge of Indiana heightened fears, long felt by Indian leaders, that the Indians might be left out of the political process. Conventions were held in Oklahoma to urge Congress to act, and would-be politicians mounted telegram campaigns. Hotgun concludes that Indian Territory and Oklahoma Territory, waiting for statehood, are like Chu-fee, the rabbit, who chose sycamore balls as food and nearly starved to death waiting for them to fall. Although Posey had long ago embraced the idea of progress that would come with the new state, he now believed that prospects for the "common" Indians, as Tookpafka Micco called them, looked dimmer.

✍ [No.63]

"Well, so," Hotgun he say, "if we didn't get statehood this spring, we could had poke greens an' wild onions scrambled with eggs, anyhow."

An' Tookpafka Micco he spit back in the corner o' the fire place and say, "Well, maybe so, we have greens an' statehood both. The young hoosier statesman from the banks o' the Wabash[1] was made a big spread-eagle talk in the senate chamber an' created a stir in the galleries an' lobby halls, an' politicans was hurryin' back from the capitol like bees swarmin' an' workin' overtime. So it didn't take a first-class prophet to prophesy 'bout statehood, an' you didn't had to put on your specs to see which way the wind was blowin' the straw."

Wolf Warrior and Kono Harjo grunt like they didn't welcome the news an' shake they heads like they thought the Injin was fall on evil days.

Then Hotgun he say, "Well, so I like to hear what kind o' spiel the young hoosier statesman from the banks o' the Wabash was give 'em, anyhow."

An' Tookpafka Micco he go on an' say, "Well, so he tell 'em Oklahoma an' Injin Territory make a fine lookin' couple an' ought to had they picture taken together, so congress could have it enlarged an' hang it up on the map o' our common country. Then he go on an' warm up to the occasion an' pay a glowin' tribute to the pioneers. He say they was overcome the coyote an' exterminate the beaver an' chase all the deer out o' the country with hounds. They was replace the wild animals with domestic ones, like the thrifty razorback; they was chop down saplin's an' buil' huts; they was dig in the sod an' throw up rude abodes; they was laid the foundation o' a new state, an' give civilization a home in the backwoods. An' the women folks was had a hand in it an' did most o' the work, the Lord bless 'em! They was nurse the tow-headed kid with one arm an' made butter with the other one; they was brought in the wood an' cooked; they was make the garden an' slopped the pigs an' put something to eat on the table; they was picked the cotton an' pulled the corn an' made the childrens' [*sic*] clothes an' patched the old man's overalls; they was 'tended church on Sunday while the old man went to swap horses or, maybe so, set on the damp groun' in the bush playin' poker an' caught 'is death o' cold instead o' the winnin' hand. Then he go on an' tell 'em that was the kind o' people that make the new country fit to live in. He say they was all typical Americans an' Arkansawers [*sic*], an' they was 'bout a million o' 'em ready for civilization.[2] He say they all go to the new country with nothin' but a big start o' children. Some o' them was squatters an' boomers an' sooners an' intruders with a past,[3] but they was want forgiveness now an' a chance to get back in the Union."

Then Hotgun he spit over the backlog an' say, "Well, so the

young hoosier statesman from the banks o' the Wabash wasn't up on facts an' ancient hist'ry. He was jus' puttin' words together to see how many he had. The Injin was the only bona fide pioneer in this country, an' the Injin squaw was the woman that furnish the magic an' help overcome the wild animals an' carry civilization into the waste places with her sofky pestle an' mortar."

An' Tookpafka Micco he smoke slow and study long time an' say, "Well, so the Lord helps 'em that help 'emselves — except the Injin."[4]

1. Albert Jeremiah Beveridge (1862–1927), of Indiana, had introduced the Hamilton bill in the Senate in early February and championed its cause. See *Muskogee Phoenix*, February 1 and 8, 1906. A native of Ohio, Beveridge served as senator from Indiana (1899–1905, 1905–1911) and was the author of *The Russian Advance* (1903), *The Young Man and the World* (1905), *The Bible as Good Reading* (1906), and other works. See *Who Was Who in America*, 1:91.

2. Hotgun's account of Beveridge's speech reflects Posey's view of the types of white Americans who had overrun Indian Territory during the two preceding decades. Hotgun's distinction between Americans and Arkansans reflects Posey's contempt for the latter, who to him epitomized the worst class of whites.

3. "Squatters" were people who occupied land to which they had no title. Classes of squattrs included the following: "boomers" were people who sought to have Oklahoma lands opened to non-Indians; "sooners" were those who attempted to sneak into Oklahoma lands and stake a claim before the filing period was officially opened; and "intruders" were those who entered Indian Territory and illegally squatted on the public domain of the Indian nations. These types of people either broke the law or sought to overturn laws that protected Indian rights.

4. This is Tookpafka Micco's version of a saying common in literature since the Greek writer Aeschylus but popularized in America by Benjamin Franklin in *Poor Richard's Almanack* (1732–57).

✍ [No.64]

"Well, so," Hot Gun [*sic*] he say, "Ol' Cannon wasn't no clan kin to me, but he was a man after my own heart. He stan' flat-footed an' didn't had that homely look for nothin'. He tell ol' Senator Four Acre, 'I fight you till hell froze up an' then, maybe so, monkey with you some roun' on the ice.' "[1]

An' Tookpafka Micco he say, "Well so, that look like a slippery proposition an', maybe so, Uncle Joe fall down on it if he wasn't put a keerful."[2]

An' Hotgun he go on an' say, "Well, maybe so, but his feet wasn't gone out from under 'im yet, an' waitin' for statehood to come was gettin' mighty monot-nous for the camp followers o' politics. They was gettin' excited an' keepin' the wires to Washington hot sendin' telegrams. They couldn't stan' the agony any longer. Some sign they name to the telegram Postmaster, an' some sign it Lawyer, an' some sign it Business Man, an' some sign it Editor, an' some of 'em sign it Vox Pop-a-lie. The postmaster he want to keep on cancellin' stamps an' puttin' your mail in somebody else's box; the lawyer he want no end o' law suits over cloudy titles an' a chance to take the stump for office; the business man he want to exploit the Injin an' escape the tribal tax; the editor he want the county printin' an' anything else he could lay hands on."

"But," Hotgun he go on to say, "you couldn't find no fullblood Injin's mark to any telegram to Washington, an' no farmer's John Hancock neither.[3] The telegram signed Vox Pop-a-lie was a false pretense on the face of it. The fellers that send it didn't come roun' an' say, 'Well, so, Tookpafka Micco, you want statehood?' or, maybe so, 'Bill Jones wasn't you tired o' waitin' for statehood?' "

An' Tookpafka Micco he say, "Well so, the common Injin back in the hills an' the white renter in the tall timber along the river wasn't consulted."

An' Hotgun he say, "Well, so, the common run o' Injins an' white people was more anxious for a good crop an' liftin' the mortgage off the ol' dun mule than a constitutional convention anyhow."

An' Tookpafka Micco he say, "Well so, if we happen to break into the Union they be somethin' doin'. The fullblood Injin an' his white renter maybe so come out o' the sticks an' be pall bearers at the polls for the fellers that sign the telegrams Vox Pop-a-lie."

Wolf Warrior an' Kono Harjo give a big grunt an' spit in the ashes, an' about that time Hotgun's women folks say, "Hom-bux-che!" (Come and eat.)

1. Joseph Gurney Cannon (1836–1926) had been a judge in Illinois before being elected to Congress, serving several terms (1873–91, 1893–1903, 1903–13, 1915–23). He served four terms as speaker of the House of Representatives. He had championed the Hamilton bill and used heavy-handed tactics against House members who opposed it. Senator Joseph Benson Foraker (1846–1917), of Ohio, had been a superior court judge and governor of Ohio before serving in the U.S. Senate (1897–1903, 1903–9). He had introduced the Sequoyah petition into the Senate, opposed the sections of the Hamilton bill providing for the admission of Arizona and New Mexico territories as a state, and faced fierce opposition from Senator Beveridge. Cannon at first threatened to tie up the bill in committee if it came back to the House with Foraker's amendment, but when Foraker compromised, settling for a referendum on statehood by voters of Arizona and New Mexico, Cannon agreed to accept the amendment and predicted passage of a statehood bill. *Muskogee Phoenix*, December 14, 1905, January 11 and 25, February 1 and 22, and March 15, 1906; *Who Was Who in America*, 1:190, 410. Hotgun's reference to "clan kin" with Cannon is a word play on *cannon* and *gun*.

2. "Put a keerful" means pretty careful.

3. A "John Hancock" is a signature.

✍ [No 65]

"Well, so, long time ago," Hot Gun [*sic*] he say, "all the animals was had a big powwow to settle the food question, an' Es-te Lus-te, the nigger, was preside over the meetin' an' make a suggestion like this: He say, 'Well, so, how it do if each one o' us consult 'is own taste an' take 'is choice?' All the animals was agreed to it an' give Es-te Lus-te, the nigger, the first swipe, an' he take water-melon; Sok-ha Hot-ka, the possum, he take persimmons; an' Wot-ko, the coon, he take crawfish; an' Chu-la, the fox, he take poultry; an' E-thlo, the squirrel, he take hick'ry nuts; an' Ya-ha, the wolf, he take carrion; an' Chu-fee, the rabbit, when it come 'is time, he look up a sycamore tree an' say, 'Well, so, the nice fruit hangin' up in this tree suit me all right.' So all the animals was choose what they like to eat an' scattered off except Chu-fee, the rabbit. He set under the sycamore tree, an' wait for the nice fruit to get ripe an' fall. He set there an' wait an' wait till he get so hungry an' poor he couldn't make a shadow hardly. The nice sycamore fruit jus' dry up an' float off in the air. So Chu-fee, the rabbit, had to give it up an' go an' steal some green peas."

Tookpafka Micco an' Wolf Warrior an' Kono Harjo like to hear ol' time Injun stories an' pay close 'tention.

An' Hot Gun he smoke an' go on an' say: "Well so, same way like the animals, all the politicians was hold big powwow in Wash-ington to settle the mighty issues o' the day. Uncle Joe, the big man o' the house, was preside over the meetin', an' Oklahoma an' Injin Territory was the rabbit after the nice fruit o' statehood on the sycamore tree."[1]

1. Equating Joseph Cannon, Speaker of the House, with Es-te Lus-te may be a reference to the link between the Republican party and blacks, a topic Posey often harped on in his days as an editor. The implication is made stronger by Hotgun's stereotyping of blacks by having Es-te Lus-te choose watermelon.

Letter No.66

[*Muskogee Daily Pheonix*, June 24, 1906; *Kansas City Star*, June 24, 1906; *New-State Tribune*, June 28, 1906; *Holdenville Times*, June 29, 1906; *Daily Oklahoman*, July 1, 1906]

The statehood bill, known to Oklahomans as the Enabling Act, was finally passed by Congress and approved by the president on June 16. It established the legal framework for drafting a constitution and electing public officials. In the wake of its passage, local politicians began to publicize, often in an inflated manner, the importance of their roles in gaining passage of the legislation. For the Indian citizens, who had for the most part been left out of the political process of the proposed state, the Enabling Act was a major social, economic, and cultural turning point. Where they would fit in the political scheme was uncertain, but Hotgun warns of the pitfalls of becoming embroiled in party politics.

✍

"Well, so," Hotgun he say, "I like to know who done it, anyhow."

An' Tookpafka Micco he smoke 'is ol' hatchet-pipe slow an' say, "Well, so, in olden times, seven cities want to be Homer's birthplace;[1] an', same way, all the politicians claim the credit for statehood an' dispute with one 'nother. Delegate Makefire he say he done it an' couldn't tell a lie 'bout it.[2] He say if the fight he put up for statehood wasn't worth a decent burial in the Statesman's corner o' the capitol buildin' it wasn't worth takin' the Father o' His Country's example in vain. Clarence Duglast he say he done it — with Washington Post interviews written by 'imself — an' he want a outside lot facin' the main aisle in the Poet's Corner;[3] also 'is statue, with a sword buckled on, standin' 'straddle o' lot o' carpetbaggers. An' they was some commissioner court lawyers an' not'ry publics claim the honor, too, but they wasn't entitled to it no more than Crazy Snake."

Then Hotgun he say, "Well, so Delegate Makefire an' Clarence Duglast was imposin' on that razorback the statehood rooters take to congress last winter an' someone ought to report 'em to the humane society."[4]

(Wolf Warrior an' Kono Harjo give big grunt an' spit in the ragweeds an' pay close 'tention.)

Then Hotgun he go on an' say, "Well, so before statehood they was too much sentiment mixed up in the Injin problem. The missionary he tell the Injin he must lay up treasures in Heaven, but didn't show 'im how to keep body an' soul together on earth and lay by for the rainy day; an' the school teacher he learn 'im how to read an' shade 'is letters when he write, but didn't teach 'im how to make two blades o' grass grow out o' one; an' the philantropist [*sic*] remind 'im o' the century o' dishonor instead o' the future individual responsibility;⁵ an' the government dish out beef an' annuity to 'im instead of a mule an' a plow. Everything like that make the Injin no count, except give jobs to government clerks."

An' Tookpafka Micco he say, "Well so the ol' order was passed away. Maybe so now the politician tell the Injin how to win salvation in the Democrat party, or Republican party, an' party bosses teach 'im how to put in two votes instead o' one."

Then Hotgun he go on an' say, "Well, so if the Injin know 'is business, he was better off than before. All he had to do was be a Injin an' stay to 'imself like an ol' bull in the winter time. He don't want to be Democrat or Republican. Maybe so 'is hair was long enough for a Populist, but he better not. If he take sides he wont 'mount to nothin' an' couldn't be dog pelter."

An' Tookpafka Micco he say, "Well so I was raised on Democrat sofky an' don't care who find it out, but I don't vote for yellow dogs on 'count o' the color."⁶

(Wolf Warrior an' Kono Harjo grunt an' spit in the ragweeds ag'in an' move further in the shade.)

Then Hotgun he go on an' say, "Well, so we was all one people now an' neighbors, anyhow, regardless o' race or politics or re-

ligion. Instead o' Choctaws an' Chickasaws an' Seminoles an'
Creeks an' Cherokees an' Boomers an' Osages an' Sequoyahans,
we was all Oklahomans. Muskogee wasn't in Injin Teritory an'
Oklahoma City wasn't in the Short Grass Country. You didn't had
to slip over the line for the stomach's sake now. You could be at
home in Beaver county same as at Hickory Ground.[7] You could
say, 'I'm from Oklahoma' an' be proud of it same as if you was
from Ol' Dominion."

1. Homer's birthplace has been disputed since antiquity, with Chios and
Smyrna the best supported. In 1897, Posey read Denton J. Snider's *Homer in
Chios* (1891), which remains in his personal library maintained at Bacone Col-
lege.

2. Bird S. McGuire, Oklahoma's territorial delegate to Congress, had worked
relentlessly for statehood. He had drafted a statehood bill in 1905, and Republican papers had argued that he deserved the credit if statehood was achieved. By
early 1906, he was a national figure, quoted frequently in the papers. See *Muskogee Phoenix*, December 7 and 28, 1905, January 25, 1906.

3. Clarence Douglas, the editor of the *Muskogee Phoenix*, spent April and May
1906 in Washington, reporting on the statehood bill debates and working with
others in lobbying for removal of restrictions on the sale of allotments. Douglas
gave interviews to not only the *Washington Post* but also other papers, in which he
made himself appear a central figure in the struggle for statehood. McGuire, a
fellow Republican, also sang Douglas's praises on the House floor. See *Muskogee
Phoenix*, April 19 and 26 and May 3, 1906. Douglas's April 13 interview with the
Post was reprinted in the *Muskogee Phoenix* on April 19. In celebrating the statehood bill, Douglas and McGuire heaped praise on one another for their respective roles in the lobbying effort. See *Indian Journal*, July 6, 1906. Douglas was not
elected to office in Oklahoma, but McGuire served in Congress as a representative from the first district, 1907–13.

4. In December 1905, single-statehood supporters paraded the streets of
Washington, D.C., with a razorback hog they had acquired in Missouri. They
kept the animal in their hotel and decorated it with a placard that said "Statehood." Some Oklahomans and residents of Indian Territory were outraged
because the popular concept of "razorback country" was that its people were

"ignorant, indolent and contemptible." See *Cherokee Advocate*, December 16, 1905.

5. *A Century of Dishonor* is the title of Helen Hunt Jackson's 1881 exposé of the federal government's handling of Indian affairs. It was influential in the reformist debate that led to the Dawes Act of 1887.

6. A "yellow dog" Democrat is one who will vote for the party's candidate regardless of the person's qualifications.

7. Beaver County is the easternmost county in the Oklahoma panhandle; Hickory Ground, the meeting place of the Snakes, is south of Henryetta.

Letter No.67

[*Muskogee Daily Phoenix*, November 25, 1906; *Holdenville Tribune*, November 29, 1906; *Sturm's Oklahoma Magazine* 4 (July 1908): 16]

The Enabling Act had provided that an election of delegates to a constitutional convention occur within six months of June 16, the date of the act's approval. The convention would consist of 112 delegates, 55 from each territory and 2 from the Osage Nation. Election districts were established during the summer, and November 6 was set as election day. Although the many candidates varied in backgrounds and brought forth a number of issues, the Democratic press continued to hammer away at certain issues. The Democrats accused the Republicans, who had been in power in Washington, D.C., and Oklahoma Territory, of being responsible for the hold that corporations such as Standard Oil and the railroads had on the proposed state and for "Hitchcockism" — the graft and complex legalities that fostered restrictions on land sales. But most important, the Democrats accused the Republicans of supporting social and political equality for blacks. When the votes were counted, the Republicans won only twelve seats. Posey had for some time expressed doubts concerning the Indian's role in shaping the new state. In October he had told the press that the Indian would be apathetic, viewing politics as a "white man's business." The election of delegates seemed to bear him out. Only ten men of part-Indian heritage were elected. Like Posey,

The Fus Fixico Letters

Hotgun and Tookpafka Micco believe that the Indian has become a political pawn who will be left without political power.

✍

So it was Hotgun he sat on his ol' split-log bench under the brush arbor at Oche Apofa,[1] an' smoke slow an' look 'way off in the Injin summer long time. Then he was spit ag'in' a scrub-oak an' tell Tokpafka Micco[2] an' Wolf Warrior an' Kono Harjo, "Well, so the Great Spirit was manifest 'imself in lots o' different ways. In olden times in Israel, he was showed 'imself in the burning bush, and in Babylon, he was showed himself in handwriting on the wall, an' in Egypt, in a pillar o' fire by night.[3] He was appeared in different ways in different lan's to suit the occasion, an' he was appeared nowadays same as in the days o' Moses an' Pharoah an' Bill Shazzer. So Tuesday, November 6, 1906, He was manifest 'imself in Injun Territory an' Oklahoma in the ballot box, an' dumfounded the carpetbaggers an' put an end to their iniquity. The mighty chiefs o' the pie counter an' the high priests o' Mammon was seized with big consternation, an' the people was delivered from the bondage o' Hitchcockism."

(Tokpafka Micco an' Wolf Warrior an' Kono Harjo they was paid close attention an' put near let their pipes go out.)

Then Tokpafka Micco he speak up an' say, "Well, so I think it was a Democratic cyclone, for they was lots o' dead timber in the senatorial forest. Giant Plenty Sofar an' Monarch Duglast was uprooted an' prostrated an' they was no sturdy tree left standin' but Sequoia Haskell."[4]

An' Hotgun he go on an' say, "Well, so statehood was a sad thing for the Injin, but I didn't had no tears to shed over lost tribal rule, like Crazy Snake; for the new state politician was my shepherd an' I got all I want. He was tolled me off to one side an' had business with me for my local influence. He was cultivated my acquaintance for his party's sake. He was prepared the table before me in the presence o' the bartender an' hol' up two fingers an' call for a couple o' small ones. He was tell me, 'Eat, drink an' be game, for, maybe so, to-morrow I want you to vote for me.' "[5]

Then Tokpafka Micco he speak up ag'in. He say: "Well, so long time ago the white man was put his arm 'roun' the Injin's neck an' give whiskey an' big treaty medals for his lan'.[6] But now it come to pass the white man was had ever'thing the Injin's got but his vote. So he was tolled him back in the alley, if it was in Muskogee, or to the corner saloon, if it was in Shawnee,[7] an' set 'em up to him an' give him entertainment an' try to trade him out of it. The pale face was too cunning an' the red man was too easy. He was sell his birthright for a nip. You hear lots o' talk about William Buzzabee, the coal baron, for senator, an' Bird Makefire for running mate, but if you was listened right close to hear what my ol' time friend Nokos Elle an' my ol' time friend Hotulk Emartha was running for, you could heard a pin drop. The news gatherers wasn't lying in wait for ol' Cho Eka to interview him about his chances for congress, an' my ol' time friend Chepon Holata wasn't livin' in retirement like John D. Rockyfeller, an' dodgin' the kodak fiends an' stayin' out o' the lime-light."[8]

(Wolf Warrior an' Kono Harjo give big grunt an' Hotgun he look 'way off in the Injin summer ag'in an' smoke slow.)

1. "Oche Apofa" is Hickory Ground.

2. Posey uses this spelling in subsequent letters.

3. "And the Angel of the Lord appeared unto him in a flame of fire out of the midst of a bush: and he looked, and, behold, the bush burned with fire, and the bush was not consumed" (Exodus 3:2). Belshazzar, the king of Babylon (550– ca. 540 B.C.), held a great feast at which the party drank wine from vessels taken out of the temple of God at Jerusalem and praised the gods of gold, silver, brass, iron, wood, and stone. "In the same hour came forth fingers of a man's hand, and wrote over against the candlestick upon the plaister of the wall of the king's

palace: and the king saw the part of the hand that wrote" (Daniel 5:5). "And the Lord went before them by day in a pillar of a cloud, to lead them the way; and by night in a pillar of fire, to give them light; to go by day and night" (Exodus 13:21).

4. Pliny Soper and Clarence Douglas were not delegates to the Oklahoma constitutional convention. The election was a major defeat for their Republican party. Charles N. Haskell, for his work in the Sequoyah statehood effort, had been dubbed "Cequoyah N. Haskell" by single-staters. See, e.g., *Muskogee Phoenix*, April 5, 1906. Haskell was chosen as a delegate and would prove to be the dominating force at the constitutional convention.

5. The *Indian Journal* reported on October 5, 1906, that Posey was engaged in "paraphrasing" Psalm 23 "from the Indian's point of view in regard to present federal officials." His parody ends with a variation on Isaiah 22:13: "And behold joy and gladness, slaying oxen, and killing sheep, eating flesh, and drinking wine: let us eat and drink; for to morrow we shall die." See also Ecclesiastes 8:15: "Then I commanded mirth, because a man hath no better thing under the sun, than to eat, and to drink, and to be merry: for that shall abide with him of his labour the days of his life, which God giveth him under the sun."

6. A conspicuous aspect of federal relations with Indian tribes was to present tribal leaders with special medals struck by the U.S. mint. For a century after the nation's founding, the medals were presented on special occasions, such as the signing of a treaty.

7. Intoxicants, though illegal in Indian Territory, were easily obtained in towns like Muskogee. Shawnee was in Oklahoma Territory, where intoxicants were legal.

8. Hotulk Emartha (or Edward Bullette) was second principal chief of the Creek Nation when Posey was elected to the House of Warriors in 1895. Cho Eka has not been identified. There were Creeks named Nokus (or Nocus) Elle and Chepon Holata (or Cheparn Holahta). See Creek Census Cards 2733, 2845, and 1138, Enrollment Cards for the Five Civilized Tribes, 1898–1914 (Microcopy M1186), National Archives Microfilm Publications. Whether these are the persons referred to is uncertain. John D. Rockefeller had retired as president of Standard Oil in 1897 but remained titular president until 1911. As such, he received more press notice than he apparently wanted, tending as he did to lead a personal life that was quiet and rather austere, given his wealth. See *Dictionary of American Biography*, ed. Schuyler Supp. 2:568–76.

The Fus Fixico Letters

Letter No.68

[*Muskogee Daily Phoenix*, January 6, 1907; *Indian Journal*, January 11, 1907]

The Oklahoma constitutional convention began its work at Guthrie on November 20, 1906. The work went slowly. By year's end, despite the political wrangling, a number of proposed provisions had been introduced, county lines had been laid out, and a general framework for the document had been established. However, to the general public it appeared that the delegates had done little, and some feared that what they incorrectly perceived as a sixty-day limit on the convention work— required by the Enabling Act— would not be met. The convention was dominated by delegates from Indian Territory, particularly William H. Murray, who was chosen president, and Charles N. Haskell, who manipulated delegates just as he had at the Sequoyah convention in 1905. Hotgun and his friends reflect the public concern that preoccupation with trivial matters — like how to name the deity in the preamble — was delaying the work at hand. The convention would not complete its work until March 15, 1907. The delegates would reconvene in April and July to make adjustments in the document, and the work would formally end on July 16.

✍

So it was Hotgun he had the women folks make some sour bread an' some blue dumpling an' some hick'ry nut sofky an' some good sak-ko-nip-kee an' lots o' ol' time dishes like that for New Year. Then he was invite his frien's to come an' feast with him. Tokpafka Micco he was there, an' Wolf Warrior he was there, an' Kono Harjo he was there. They was all come soon an' bring their folks an' dogs an' stayed till put near sun down. Hotgun he was had a little white jug sittin' back under the bed to 'liven the conversation.

"Well, guess so," Tokpafka Micco he say, "Alfalfa Bill an' Boss Haskell was put near ready to let their work so shine."[1]

An' Hotgun he spit in the ashes an' say, "Well, so, not hardly. It was slow business to get started out right. It was take lots o' time to draw up the plans an' specifications. So, they didn't had none o' the immortal document written yet but the scare headlines,[2] an' they was had a big confusion o' tongues before they get that far."[3]

An' Tokpafka Micco he say, "Well so, what was the trouble anyhow?"

An' Hotgun he go on an' say, "Well, so, they couldn't decide what name to give the Great Spirit, an' that bring up lots o' talk an' extra expense. Look like the Great Spirit was a stranger in the convention, an' none o' the delegates could remember His name. Boss Haskell he think it was God, but no one was second his motion. An' Henry Asp he think it was the Supreme Ruler o' the Universe, but no one was agreed with him.[4] An' Alfalfa Bill he say he believe it was Divine Providence, but there was no second to his motion neither. They was all three right; but they didn't know how to go ahead. So, while they was lockin' horns with one another, lot o' outsiders butt in with long petitions an' throw fat in the flames. There was a long petition from the unbelievers saying, 'Leave the Lord out.' An' there was another long petition from the pawn-brokers[5] saying, 'Don't put Christ in it.' An' there was still another long petition from Zion City sayin' 'Dowie's the gen-u-wine article; beware of imitations.'[6] Guess so, the petition about Misses Eddy was delayed."[7]

Then Tokpafka Micco he smoke an' look under the bed an' say, "Well so, Alfalfa Bill an' Boss Haskell an' Henry Asp could settled their differences an' saved lots o' work for the printer an' give general satisfaction if they had recognized Confucius for the Chinaman, an' Bhudda for the Hindu, an' Mohamet for the Turk, an' Saint Patrick for the Irishman, an' the totem pole for the Eskimo, an' the almighty dollar for the American." (Wolf Warrior an' Kono Harjo give big grunt.)

An' Hotgun he say, "Well, so, otherwise the delegates was worked like one man an' head off lots o' future legislation for the new state. If a delegate was kicked over the trace chains an' tried to be insurgent Boss Haskell was named a new townships after him an' all was serene along the Potomac.[8] Boss Haskell was a big medicine man an' had mighty influence. If he could make his men shovel dirt like he makes them vote ag'in their conscience, he could had the Panama canal dug maybe so in six weeks an' had time enough left to run for office on the independent ticket."[9]

Then Tokpafka Micco he glanced his eye under the bed ag'in an' say, "Well, so, anyhow I druther kill time in the chimney corner an' spit over the backlog an' worry about what is goin' to become o' me than risk my political future in a one man powwow like that up to Guthrie."

1. William H. Murray and Charles N. Haskell had demonstrated their abilities as party bosses not only during the Sequoyah convention in 1905 but also in the campaign to elect constitutional delegates to establish the organization of the constitutional convention itself.

2. That is, they had decided on the general concepts to be included such as Prohibition, railroad regulation, sale of school lands, Jim Crow provisions, etc. See *Indian Journal*, December 7, 1906.

3. Perhaps this is a comparison of the drafting of the constitution to the plan, in the Bible, of Noah's descendants to construct a tower that might reach to heaven. See Genesis, chapter 11.

4. Henry Asp (1856–?), a native of Ohio, had resided in Guthrie, Oklahoma Territory, since 1889. He was an attorney for the Santa Fe Railroad. He and Haskell had been at odds on a number of issues, but being one of only twelve Republicans at the convention, his influence was limited. See *Indian Journal*, October 19 and December 14, 1906, and Joseph B. Thoburn, *A Standard History of Oklahoma* (Chicago: American Historical Association, 1916), 836, 843, 922, 924, 1134.

5. Hotgun refers to Jews.

6. John Alexander Dowie (1847–1907), the founder of the Christian Catholic

Church, had been much in the news in recent months. In December 1904, he claimed that the church's enterprises at Zion City, Illinois, were worth an estimated thirty million dollars. But the organization was apparently in financial difficulties. In April 1906, while he was on vacation in Mexico for his health, he was deposed by the Zion City overseer, Wilbur G. Voliva, who charged him with mismanagement of Zion City affairs. See *Muskogee Phoenix*, December 3, 1903, December 19, 1904, and April 5 and 19, 1906, and *Muskogee Daily Phoenix*, April 13, 1906.

7. Mary Baker Eddy (1821–1910) founded the Christian Science Church.

8. "Trace chains" were part of the harness for draft animals. To "kick over" the traces was to refuse to work as part of a team, to be at odds with prevailing opinion. The reference to the Potomac probably means more than peace. The framers of the constitution were conscious of a potential rejection of the document by President Roosevelt if it contained provisions he especially disliked.

9. Haskell used the same kind of strong-arm tactics that had marked the Sequoyah convention. The public perception was that the constitution was in a large measure his work. His opponents called him a "rank demagogue" and a friend to big business. See *Indian Journal*, April 19, 1907.

Letter No.69

[Indian Journal, April 10, 1908]

C. N. Haskell's political machine kept rolling after the constitution was framed. In the Democratic primary in May 1907, he defeated Lee Cruce and became the party nominee for governor. The vote for ratification and election of public officers occurred on September 17. The constitution was adopted, and Haskell defeated Frank Frantz, the territorial governor of Oklahoma. Oklahoma entered the Union on November 16. Transition to statehood was not altogether smooth. The constitutional convention had established county lines and had determined county seats. The choice for the McIntosh County seat had been between Checotah and Eufaula, with the latter winning. The seats were fixed for four months, at which time a number of seats were contested. Checotah challenged the McIntosh County decision and exercised its right, under a constitutional provision, that said the county seat could be moved by a two-thirds majority vote of the people. In March 1908, Governor Haskell issued an election proclamation for the county. Posey became editor of the *Indian Journal* in Eufaula as the debate heated up in April, and he used the Fus Fixico letters in behalf of his town. Hotgun and Tookpafka Micco recognized, as did all the county residents, the economic implications of the county seat location.

"Well, so," Hot Gun[1] he say, "near's I could come at it, a county seat was a sort of a busk groun' an' it take lots o' natural advantages, like plenty scrub-oak shade an' fine pickin' for the grass fillies an' a strong flow o' water, to make a good one. So a place that didn't had these blessin's o' the Great Spirit was already defeated for the county seat."

Then Tokpafka Micco he say, "Well, so, 'cordin' to that argument, Checotah didn't had no show to experience a real estate boom." (Wolf Warrior an' Kono Harjo give big grunt.)

An' Hot Gun he look 'way off down the creek where wild onions was growin' an' go on an' say, "Well, so I concede Checotah was had some pickin' for the grass filly, but its flow o' water was weak an' uncertain, an' scrub-oak shade was scarce in its vicinity. It was had abundance o' high winds an' horizontal zyphyrs an' distant prospects, but things like that wasn't solid advantages."

1. In subsequent letters, Posey made the name two words.

Letter No.70

[Indian Journal, April 17, 1908]

The first legislature of Oklahoma was long and raucous and fraught with power politics. To the onlooker, it also had its ridiculous side. Its work was prolonged by debate on frivolous issues and attempts to pass what the press called "freak" laws, such as a ban on parlor games and the establishment of the office of state inspector of hotels, whose duties included making certain that bed sheets were a certain length. During debate on the latter, Senator Clifford Russell was reported to have offered the following as an amendment:

> Now I lay me down to sleep,
> The fleas and lice begin to creep.
> If one should bite me before I wake,
> I pray the Lord his jaws to break.

Such goings-on were enough to make the citizenry cynical about politics.

✍🏻

So it was Hot Gun he look 'way off to the backside o' the sofky patch an' give his ol' pipe a good start an' talk wisdom like this to Tokpafka Micco an' Wolf Warrior an' Kono Harjo:

"Well, so they was no political bee buzzin' 'roun' in my warbonnet. I got no aspiration for office an' no hide like a rhinoceros or C. N. Has Skill.[1] So no rival candidate could say, 'Well, so long time ago Hot Gun he was cut up at a stomp dance'; or, may be so, 'Long time ago Hot Gun he was get drunk an' break up a big campmeetin',' an' spread evil report about me like that.

"The Injin was civilized—he buy drop-stitch hose for the squaw an' teddy bear for the papoose. He was the only bonyfied [*sic*] pioneer in Oklahoma—all the rest was Arkansawyers an' Illinois politicians. He could touch the pen better'n anybody.

"May be so, the buddin' statesman tell the people in the shade o' the scrub-oaks next summer, 'This was a great an' gran' an' glorious country.' But no one was take him serious except the ones that didn't had the combination to the back door.

"So it was they was lots a talk about freak laws, like Bosco must not eat snakes, an' the women folks must not straddle o' the bronco, an' hotel guests must not do battle with bugs under short bed sheets.² Them kind o' laws was proposed to turn the 'tention o' the small fry legislators from laws that was goin' on the statute book."

1. During the campaign for governorship, Charles N. Haskell's opponents had delved into his personal background, and he answered in kind. He charged Frantz with drunkenness, infidelity, and breaking the laws of God and country, saying that Frantz had "invited a comparison of reputations." See *Indian Journal*, April 19, 1907, and *Shawnee Daily Herald*, September 3, 1907.

2. Posey's reference to "freak" laws was probably an intentional play on words. "Freak" bills introduced in the first legislature prohibited not only snake eating but also exhibitions of mesmerism or hypnotism, cracked dishes or sheets shorter than nine feet in hotels, cigarette smoking within the boundaries of Oklahoma, riding horses astride (by women), films depicting prize fights or bullfights, and getting drunk, even at home. *Shawnee Daily Herald*, March 1 and 15, 1908.

Letter No.71

[Indian Journal, April 24, 1908)

In an earlier letter (No.65), Hotgun had used the tale about the animals' choosing their favorite foods to illustrate Indian Territory's wait for statehood. Posey had told a reporter for the *Muskogee Times-Democrat* that an "old Indian" had told the same story in response to the work of the Oklahoma constitutional convention. In his version, the people of Indian Territory were like Chu-fee, the rabbit. Here, Hotgun finds the story pertinent to the McIntosh county seat contest. This time, the foolish rabbit is Checotah. Checotah obtained more votes than Eufaula, but because of votes for other towns, it failed to get the majority necessary to capture the county seat. Posey did not live to see the voting results.

✍

"Well, so," Hot Gun he say, "Checotah in the county seat fight was put me in mind o' Chu-fee, the rabbit, sittin' under the cyca-more [*sic*] tree." (Tokpafka Micco an' Wolf Warrior an' Kono Harjo get ready to pay close 'tention.)

An' Hot Gun he go on an' say, "So it was long time ago all the animals was had a big council to settle the food question. Es-te Lus-te, the nigger, was chairman o' the meetin', an' he make suggestion like this: 'Well, so,' he say, 'each animal could choose for himself what he like to eat.' All the animals was agreed to that an' give Es-te Lus-te, the nigger, first choice, an' he take yams an' watermelon. Sok-ha Hot-ka, the 'possum, he take the wild apple, or persimmon; Woht-ko, the raccoon, he take crawfish; Chu-la, the fox, he take birds; Eth-thlo, the squirrel, he take nuts; Ya-ha, the wolf, he take meat been dead long time; an' so on like that till ever' animal had his bill o' fare but Chu-fee, the rabbit. When it come his time to pass his plate, he look up in a cycamore tree an' say, 'Well, so, the nice fruit hanging up in this tree look like it suit my taste all right.' So, all the animals was choose what they want to eat an' scatter off. Chu-fee, the rabbit, he sat roun' under the cycamore tree an' wait for the nice fruit to get ripe an' fall. But the cycamore fruit just dry up an' the wind come 'long an' blow it 'way like mist. Chu-fee, the rabbit, he sat there an' wait an' wait till he put near starve to death. He get so poor an' weak he look like he had bad consumption. His eyes stick out o' his head an' his nose get sharp. After while he had to give it up an' go steal something to eat, like green peas out o' people's gardens. Checotah was Chu-fee, the rabbit, in the county seat fight. It look up in the cycamore tree o' politics an' get hungry for county seat fruit." (Tokpafka Micco an' Wolf Warrior give big grunt an' Kono Harjo he spit in the tall weeds.)

The Fus Fixico Letters

Letter No.72

[*Indian Journal*, May 8, 1908; *Muskogee Daily Phoenix*, May 1908, date uncertain, clipping, in Posey Collection, Thomas Gilcrease Institute of American History and Art; *Shawnee Daily Herald*, May 17, 1908]

The Oklahoma constitution (article 1, section 7) prohibited, for twenty-one years, the selling or trading of intoxicating liquors from that part of the state that had formerly been Indian Territory, except through a state dispensary. It charged the legislature with establishing one agency in each incorporated town of two hundred or more population and one agency in counties that had no town of that size. The agencies could sell liquor for medicinal, industrial, and scientific purposes and to apothecaries who filed a bond of one thousand dollars on the condition that the liquors they obtained be used to fill prescriptions or to compound medicines. The buyer had to file a statement, swearing to the use of the liquor, and each sale was to be registered. Throughout the spring of 1908, the legislature tried to draft legislation but failed to agree on a law. The lawmakers did agree, however, to admit the dispensary question to the voters and to allow the provisions of the constitution to remain in effect. Druggists were to become agents for each town of two hundred or more or for anywhere else that had "apparent demand." The state bought the liquor. It was taken to Guthrie, the capital, where state labels and seals were put on the bottles before they were shipped to the druggists. To the cost were added handling expenses and a profit for the state. In April, the state dispenser, Robert Lozier, made a contract with Sunnybrook Distillery Company of Louisville for a three-month supply of rye whiskey. Posey wrote on April 17, " 'Sunnybrook' is not a new whiskey and has a wide circle of acquaintances." The system was fraught with problems. Druggists complained that they could buy whiskey at lower prices outside the state, and by late May, only about one hundred had filed the necessary bond. The conclusion drawn by Posey and others was that the druggists either were not dispensing liquor or were doing so illegally.

✍

So it was Tokpafka Micco want to know if Sunnybrook was any kin to Senator Brook,[1] an' Hot Gun he tell 'im, "Well, so they was no kin to one 'nuther; but, maybe so, they was good frien's socially."

Tokpafka Micco he didn't know no better an' think Sunnybrook was a man, an' Hot Gun was had lots o' fun out o' him before he get wise. An' Wolf Warrior an' Kono Harjo didn't know no better neither, an' think Sunnybrook was a young boy from Kentucky, like Hot Gun say. When they find out different they smoke slow an' look 'way off an' don't see nothin' to laugh at. But the women folks was fixin' dinner an' Tokpafka Micco an' Wolf Warrior an' Kono Harjo wasn't offended long. You can't make a Injin mad when the smoke is comin' out o' the chimney an' the dog is lookin' in the kitchen door.

"Well, so," Hot Gun he go on an' say, "ever'thing was different since statehood. Instead o' busk groun's we got county seats; instead o' stomp dances, we got rallies; instead o' green corn feasts, we got primaries; instead o' fish frys we got the initiative and referendum; an' instead o' fifty lashes on the bare back we got sixty days on the rock pile.[2] So, instead o' the ol' time whiskey peddler that stayed in the woods till after dark, we got a dispensary agent. This new kind o' whiskey peddler was come out of the pulpit, an' you couldn't see the back o' his knee for the tail o' his coat.[3] He was peddle Sunnybrook, an' it was put' near good as 'white mule' mixed with branch water, or the new kind o' peruny.[4] He was handle no other bran' of firewater but this Sunnybrook. If you was drink any of it you wasn't accountable for your misdemeanors. It was the kind o' strong drink Solomon tackled in olden times an' called a mockery."[5] (Tokpafka Micco an' Wolf Warrior an' Kono Harjo pay close 'tention an' look dry.)

An' Hot Gun he go on an' say, "The peddler o' this Sunny-brook stuff was a preacher, like I say, an' he was had lots o' other peddlers under him, an' some o' them was women. Guess so that make the business more interestin'. You couldn't get any Sunnybrook if you didn't know how to tell big lie an' swear it was the truth. Makes no difference how husky you was you had to make a oath you was puny an' wasn't long for this world!"

Then Tokpafka Micco he say, "Well, so I think the new state whiskey law was breed lots o' graft an' cheerful liars, an' make me sorry for religion an' womanhood."

1. Eck E. Brook was a state senator from Muskogee and a good friend of Posey's.

2. The Creeks had no jails; tribal law prescribed corporal punishment for noncapital offenses.

3. The churches had played a large role in the temperance lobby for Prohibition in Oklahoma. The "dispensary agent" was Robert Lozier, of Blackwell. He was a native of Missouri, where for six years he had been a member of the state central committee of the Anti-Saloon League. He was currently head of the Kay County, Oklahoma, league. *Shawnee Daily Herald*, March 27, 1908.

4. "White mule" was homemade grain alcohol.

5. "Wine is a mocker, strong drink is raging; and whosoever is deceived thereby is not wise" (Proverbs 20:1).

Letter No.73

[*Indian Journal*, May 22, 1908]

The first legislature of Oklahoma had among its members some who had little legislative skill and less statesmanship. Quite often decorum failed, and debate degenerated to name-calling and personal violence. Tookpafka Micco and Hotgun find these actions a contrast to the Creeks' former way of deliberation. Thus in Posey's last letter, his characters reflect on the vast changes that had occurred in Creek society during his short life.

So it was while the rain was comin' down on the clapboards an' Shell Creek was gettin' out o' its banks an' the cocklebur was gettin' a good start in the sofky patch,[1] Hot Gun an' Tokpafka Micco an' Wolf Warrior an' Kono Harjo was sit roun' the fireplace an' smoke slow an' spit in the ashes an' talk. What a Injin say on a rainy day was had meanin'. Fruit an' things like that get ripe in the sun, but a scrub Injin's thought don't get ripe till it rains.

"Well, so," Tokpafka Micco he say, "I think we need some fullblood Injins in the legislature. They could give the law-makin' body more dignity an' less insurrection. If the fullblood solon didn't had any gray matter, that don't make no difference–C. N. Has Skill could give 'im all he need."

An' Hot Gun he say, "Well, maybe so, the fullblood could borrow 'nough gray matter to get 'long with, but he was no John L. Sullivan or Hercules.[2] A nimble mind don't count for anything in the Oklahoma legislature an' couldn't get any emergency bills passed. You couldn't cover yourself with glory in Squirrel Rifle Bill's prize ring if you wasn't handy with your fists an' had lots o' hard muscle.[3] The noble art o' self-defense was better than great knowledge o' Blackstone in the Oklahoma legislature. Roberts' [sic] Rules o' Order was a classic you didn't had to know anything about. The only thing you had to be up on was Marquis o' Queensberry rules.[4] So, before you run for the legislature you better consider how hard you could lan' on the enemy with your fist or how straight you can hurl the ink bottle."[5]

Then Tokpafka Micco he say, "Well, so I don't think my long experience in Creek council was train me for strenuous work like that. In the Creek council all I had to do was smoke an' spit an' hol' up my han' to vote if I was awake."

1. The comments on flood are poignant. Posey drowned in the floodwaters of the North Canadian River less than a week after this letter appeared.

2. John Lawrence Sullivan (1858–1918), of Boston, won the heavyweight pugilist championship in 1882 and lost it in 1892. See *Webster's Biographical Dictionary* (Springfield, Mass.: G. & C. Merriam Company, 1972), 1430. Hercules, a Roman cult hero, was reputed for his great strength and courage. See *The Oxford Classical Dictionary*, ed. M. Cary et at., 413–14, 416.

3. Speaker of the House William H. Murray organized his hangers-on into what he called the Squirrel Rifle Brigade, issuing commissions as officers to newspapermen and dignitaries. The commission had a cartoon of Murray and a cocklebur for a seal. See *Indian Journal*, May 15, 1908.

4. Sir William Blackstone (1723–80) was an English jurist whose *Commentaries on the Laws of England* (1765–69) became a standard work on English law. Henry Martyn Robert (1837–1923), an army engineer, first published *Robert's Rules of Order* in 1876. The work became a standard for parliamentary procedures. Sir John Sholto Douglas (1844–1900), the eighth marquis of Queensberry, was a patron of boxing. With John Graham Chambers, he devised the Marquis of Queensberry Rules (1867) for the sport. See *Webster's Biographical Dictionary*, 155, 1266, and 434.

5. "It is a dull day in the state legislature when a fight is not pulled off. In a mixup Tuesday Senators [Emory D.] Brownlee and [A. E.] Agee hurled ink wells and such epithets as 'brainless, braying jackass' at each other" (*Indian Journal*, May 1, 1908).

Key to Names in the
Fus Fixico Letters

A. Tall Bush = Adolphus Busch
Aggy'll Not Do = Emilio Aguinaldo
Albert Gallop = Albert McKellop
Alfalfa Bill = William H. Murray. *See also* William Merry
Alice M. Lobbysome = Alice Mary Robertson
Ann Hasa-bush = Anheuser-Busch
Ben Called Burt = Benjamin Colbert
Ben Lay For It = Ben F. Lafayette
Big Man at Washington = Ethan Allen Hitchcock. *See also* Secretary Itscocked
Bill Shazzer = Belshazzar
Billy Make Combs = William McCombs
Bob Willing = Robert Lee Williams
Bonyparts (Bony Parts) = Charles J. Bonaparte. *See also* Charley Bony Parts
Boss Haskell = Charles N. Haskell. *See also* C. N. Has Skill
Break in Rich (Break-in-rich) = C. R. Breckenridge
C. B. Stew It = C. B. Stuart. *See also* Judge Stew It
C. N. Has Skill = Charles N. Haskell. *See also* Boss Haskell
Charley Bony Parts = Charles J. Bonaparte. *See also* Bonyparts
Charlie Divide Some = Charles A. Davidson
Cheesie Mac Aint Flush = Albert Gallatin (Cheesie) McIntosh
Chief Lodges = William Charles Rogers
Chief Make Certain (Makecertain) = Green McCurtain
Chief Mostly = Palmer Mosely
Chief Puffingtown = Thomas M. Buffington
City Lawyer Ram-it-in-all = W. F. Rampendahl

Key to Names in the Letters

Clarence Dug Last (Duglast; Clarence Bee Dug Last; Clarence B. Douglast) = Clarence B. Douglas

Cliff Jack's Son = Clifford L. Jackson

Corner It = Melvin Cornish

Cry For The Cobb = Guy P. Cobb

Dam Big Pie (Bigpie) = Tams Bixby. *See also* Tams Big Pie

Delegate Makefire = Bird S. McGuire

Editor Rustle = U. S. Russell. *See also* Rustle; Us Rustle

Frank See Cupboard = Frank C. Hubbard

Gay Blair Shoenfelt = J. Blair Shoenfelt. *See also* J. Bear Sho'-am-fat; J. Bear Showemthat; Shoamfat

General Cussed Her = George Armstrong Custer

Governor Makefire = Bird S. McGuire

Grand Pa Harry's Son = William H. Harrison

Henry Be Lobbying = Henry P. Robbins. *See also* Henry Be Robbing

Henry Be Robbing = Henry P. Robbins. *See also* Henry Be Lobbying

Henry Fur Man = Henry M. Furman

J. B. Stump Some = J. B. Thompson

J. Bear Sho'-am-fat = J. Blair Shoenfelt. *See also* Gay Blair Shoenfelt; J Bear Shoemthat; Shoamfat

J. Bear Showemthat (Showemwhat) = J. Blair Shoenfelt. *See also* Gay Blair Shoenfelt; J. Bear Sho'-am-fat; Shoamfat

J. Gouge Right (Jay Gouge Right) = J. George Wright

J. Wentdressed Withem = J. Fentress Wisdom

Jimmy Eats Huckleberries = James H. Huckleberry

Jim Misgivings = James M. Givens. *See also* Jim's Living

Jim's Living = James M. Givens. *See also* Jim Misgivings

John D. Bend A Stick = John D. Benedict

John D. Rockyfeller = John D. Rockefeller

Judge My Fee = Arthur P. Murphy. *See also* See My Fee

Judge Stew It = C. B. Stuart. *See also* C. B. Stew It

Kid Morgan = Gideon (Gid) Morgan

King Manylicks = Menilek II

Lead Better = Walter A. Ledbetter

Lick's Broke = Eck E. Brook

Lilly Suky Annie = Lydia Kamekeha Liliuokalani

Key to Names in the Letters

Lowman Parker = Luman F. Parker, Jr.

Mad Mule = Mulai Ahmedes-Raisuli

Make Merry = J. F. McMurray

Mallet = William H. Mellette

Matthew Whey = Matthew Quay

Mayor Fight = Francis B. Fite

Mayor Rather Ford = Samuel M. Rutherford. *See also* Sam Rather Ford

Mayor Sick = Robert W. Dick

Nate Kicksome = N. A. Gibson

Nute Brewery = Isaac Newton (Newt) Ury

Plenty Soap = Pliny Leland Soper. *See also* Plenty So Far

Plenty So Far (Sofar) = Pliny Leland Soper. *See also* Plenty Soap

President Rooster Feather = Theodore Roosevelt

Ridge Pasture = Ridge Paschal

Rob It Owing (Robit Owing; Rob It L. Owing) = Robert L. Owen

Russell Steal Well = Stillwell H. Russell

Rustle = U. S. Russell. *See also* Editor Rustle; Us Rustle

Sam Rather Ford (Same Rather Ford) = Samuel M. Rutherford. *See also* Mayor Rather Ford

Secretary Itscocked (It's Cocked; Its Cocked) = Ethan Allen Hitchcock. *See also* Big Man at Washington

See A Castle = C. E. Castle

See A Loon = Charles A. Looney

See My Fee (See-my-fee) = Arthur P. Murphy. *See also* Judge My Fee

Senator Four Acre = Joseph Benson Foraker

Senator Stewit = William M. Stewart

Shoamfat = J. Blair Shoenfelt. *See also* Gay Blair Shoenfelt; J. Bear Sho'-am-fat; J. Bear Showemthat

Tams Big Pie = Tams Bixby. *See also* Dam Big Pie

Tear Away = Morgan Caraway

Thomas Lostsome = Thomas William Lawson

Tight Tuttle = Dwight Tuttle

Tom Bark Some = Thomas Marcum

Tom Needs It (Needsit) = Thomas B. Needles

Tommy Owing = Tom Owen

Us Rustle = U. S. Russell. *See also* Editor Rustle; Rustle

Key to Names in the Letters

W. W. Has Stings = William W. Hastings

William Buzzabee = William V. Busby

William Ginning Bran = William Jennings Bryan. *See also* William J. Brian

William J. Brian = William Jennings Bryan. *See also* William Ginning Bran

William Merry = William H. Murray. *See also* Alfalfa Bill

Notes for the Introduction

1. "From Fus Fixico," *Indian Journal*, October 24, 1902.

2. The historian James Axtell, in a style befitting his subject, has recently examined some of the historical evidences revealing this sense of humor during the American colonial period. See his "Humor in Ethnohistory," *Ethnohistory* 37 (Spring 1990): 109–25.

3. Despite massive literary production by Indian humorists before 1900, scholars in the field of American humor have ignored them. One scholar has, however, noted the Indians' exclusion: "Some scholars have pursued American humor's native strains (though not among the truly Native Americans, the Indians) for indications of the frontier nation's cultural emergence." See Arthur Power Dudden, ed., *American Humor* (New York: Oxford University Press, 1987), xi. Part of the credit for documenting the body of pre-1900 Indian humor goes to James W. Parins, who with Daniel F. Littlefield, Jr., did the basic bibliographic work that led to their *A Biobibliography of Native American Writers, 1772–1924* (Metuchen, N.J.: Scarecrow Press, 1981) and *A Biobibliography of Native American Writers, 1772–1924, Supplement* (Metuchen, N.J.: Scarecrow Press, 1985). Parins also presented a paper with Littlefield on "Dialect Writers of the Indian Territory" at the Western Literature Association annual meeting, St. Louis, Missouri, October 2–4, 1980.

4. For a good overview of acculturation among these people, see W. David Baird, "Are There 'Real' Indians in Oklahoma? Historical Perceptions of the Five Civilized Tribes," *Chronicles of Oklahoma* 68 (Spring 1990): 4–23.

5. The following biographical sketch is based on Daniel F. Littlefield, Jr., *Alex Posey: Creek Poet, Journalist, and Humorist* (Lincoln: University of Nebraska Press, 1992), especially chapters 1–7.

6. Much of the argument and some brief passages in the following section have appeared in ibid., chapter 7, and Daniel F. Littlefield, Jr., "Evolution of Alex

Posey's Fus Fixico Persona," *Studies in American Indian Literatures* 4 (Summer/ Fall 1992): 136–44, though subsequent research has caused revision of some minor points in the latter.

7. Littlefield, *Alex Posey*, chapter 2.

8. See, e.g., Posey's Journal (pp.5, 17, 19, and 41), item 3826.183a, Alexander L. Posey Collection, Thomas Gilcrease Institute of American History and Art, Tulsa, Oklahoma.

9. See, e.g., ibid., p.19; "Died in the River He Loved," *Kansas City Star,* June 7, 1908; "Was the Poet Laureate," *Indian School Journal* 10 (April 1910): 29.

10. Frank G. Speck, *The Creek Indians of Taskigi Town*, Memoirs of the American Anthropological Association, no. 2 (Millwood, N.Y.: Kraus Reprint Co., 1974), 119–20; Posey's Journal, p.5.

11. For journalists' comments, see, e.g., *Indian Journal*, July 11 and 18 and September 19, 1902, and January 16, 1903, which reprinted them. For Posey's humor, practically any issue will serve, but see especially various items in *Indian Journal*, March 14, April 25, August 1 and 22, and September 19, 1902.

12. *Muskogee Daily Phoenix*, July 17, 1902.

13. *Fort Smith Times*, October 15, 1903.

14. *Indian Journal*, April 4, 1902.

15. Ibid., June 20, July 4 and 18, and August 15, 1902.

16. According to William Elsey Connelley, all of these tales were printed as pamphlets at Bacone. See Connelley, "Memoir of Alexander Lawrence Posey," in Minnie H. Posey, comp., *The Poems of Alexander Lawrence Posey* (Topeka: Crane and Co., 1910), 56. No copies of the first and the last — "Chinnubbie Harjo, the Evil Genius of the Creeks" and "Chinnubbie's Courtship" — have been found. A pamphlet version of "Chinnubbie and the Owl" is in Scrapbook, item 4627.33, Posey Collection, Thomas Gilcrease Institute of American History and Art. A copy of "Chinnubbie Scalps the Squaws" as it appeared in the *B.I.U. Instructor* 2 (May 20, 1893), is in Littlefield's files. Posey's description of Chinnubbie appears in "Chinnubbie Scalps the Squaws."

17. *Indian Journal*, May 18, 1894.

18. "Joe Harjo Writes Again," *Indian Journal*, September 4, 1902. The headline indicates that there was an earlier letter, but it has not been found. A number of summer 1902 issues of the newspaper are unavailable.

19. "Joe Harjo Again," *Indian Journal*, October 10, 1902.

20. Nearly all issues of February 1902 carried stories of Chitto Harjo's

Snakes, but see especially *Indian Journal,* February 28, 1902. See also issues for March 7, April 11, August 1, and October 3, 1902. Accounts of Chitto Harjo appear in John Bartlett Meserve, "The Plea of Crazy Snake (Chitto Harjo)," *Chronicles of Oklahoma* 11 (September 1933): 899–911; Eleanor Patricia Atwood, "The Crazy Snake Rebellions: A Study in the Breakdown of Tribal Government," *Vassar Journal of Undergraduate Studies* 15 (May 1942): 44–60; Mel H. Bolster, "The Smoked Meat Rebellion," *Chronicles of Oklahoma* 31 (Spring 1953): 37–55; Daniel F. Littlefield, Jr., and Lonnie E. Underhill, "The 'Crazy Snake Uprising' of 1909: A Red, Black, or White Affair?" *Arizona and the West* 20 (Winter 1978): 307–24.

21. *Indian Journal,* October 24, 1902.

22. Ibid., November 7, 1902.

23. Ibid., March 20, 1903.

24. This quartet may have been a parody of the Informal Club, which consisted of Posey, G. W. Grayson, George Riley Hall, and John N. Thornton, who met for talk, drink, and fellowship, much as Fus Fixico's friends do.

25. Charles Gibson, "Este Charte," *Indian Journal,* May 1, 1908.

26. *Indian Journal,* May 1, 1908.

27. "Fus Fixico Jr.," *Checotah Enquirer,* April 17, 1908.

28. "Fus Fixico No.Two," *Checotah Enquirer,* May 1, 1908, reprinted from *Hoffman Herald.*

29. "Another Full-Blood Writes," *Checotah Enquirer,* April 24, 1908.

30. These quotations, respectively, are from Fus Fixico's letters in *Indian Journal,* April 24, 1903, March 20, 1903, June 26, 1903, March 20, 1903, and October 31, 1902, and *Muskogee Daily Phoenix,* July 17, 1903.

31. Correspondence concerning this interest in Posey is in Scrapbook, item 4627.32, Posey Collection, Thomas Gilcrease Institute of American History and Art; see also *Kansas City Journal,* July 19, 1903, and *New York Times,* September 1, 1903, 2:6.

32. *Kansas City Journal,* July 19, 1903; *South McAlester Capital,* July 16, 1903; and G. R. Rucker to Posey, June 20, 1903, J. F. Henry to Posey, October 14, 1903, R. Ingalls to Posey, July 32, 1903, and J. O. Brant-Sera to Posey, August 3, 1903, in Scrapbook, item 4627.32, Posey Collection, Thomas Gilcrase Institute of American History and Art.

33. *Indian Journal,* October 31, 1902.

34. Ibid., April 3, 1902.

35. *Muskogee Daily Phoenix*, April 21, 1903, reprinted with changes in *Indian Journal*, April 24, 1903.

36. *Indian Journal*, May 8 and June 26, 1903, quoting *Wagoner Record*, *Kansas City Star*, and *Kansas City Times*.

37. *Muskogee Daily Phoenix*, June 3, 1903.

38. Posey's Journal (pp.5, 34), item 3826.183a, Posey Collection, Thomas Gilcrease Institute of American History and Art.

39. Posey's library is maintained by the library of Bacone College, Muskogee, Oklahoma.

40. Posey's Journal (pp.5, 34), item 3826.183a, Posey Collection, Thomas Gilcrease Institute of American History and Art.

41. *Fort Smith Times*, September 30–December 27, 1903, for example; *Indian Journal*, January 3 and March 7, 1902, and September 14, 1903.

42. On the other hand, Posey's fables could be considered his beast fables in slang, in the sense that Ade attached to the term. "When I used the word 'slang,'" Ade said later, "I meant 'vernacular'. . . . I tried to make playful use of the vernacular — which is really another way of saying 'unconventional Americanisms' — rather than out-and-out slang." The latter changed rapidly, he said, and after nearly fifty years his prose was not "flagrantly dated" but seemed "more natural than one might suppose, because it is written in the common, everyday vernacular." Quoted from J. Franklin Meine, introduction to *Chicago Stories by George Ade* (Chicago: Henry Regnery Co., 1963), xxiv.

43. See *Cherokee Advocate*, November 16, 1852, July 8, 1871, February 9, May 18, August 3, 10, 17, and 31, November 9 and 23, 1878, December 24, 1879, March 30, 1881, and February 17, 1882; *Indian Arrow*, February 24, 1888; *Muskogee Phoenix*, October 6, 1892; *Indian Journal*, August 30, November 22, and December 27, 1883; *Arkansian*, April 2, 1859, and April 13, 1860; *Fort Smith New Era*, September 17, 1867, May 6 and November 4, 1874; *Wheeler's Western Independent*, February 7, 1877, May 1 and August 7, 1878. The *Arkansian* was co-owned and edited in 1859 and 1860 by E. C. Boudinot, the son of the well-known Cherokee editor and politician Elias Boudinot. *Wheeler's Western Independent* was owned and edited by John F. Wheeler, one of the first printers of the *Cherokee Phoenix* and the husband of Nancy Watie, a sister of Elias Boudinot. Thus both border newspapers had close ties to, and enjoyed circulation in, the Cherokee Nation.

44. *Cherokee Advocate*, March 28, 1884.

45. Ibid., April 11, 1884. Other Unakah letters appear November 2, 1878, January 11, February 19, October 29, and December 17, 1879, January 21 and 28, February 11 and 18, March 24 and 31, June 2 and 23, October 13, and December 13, 1880, March 30, 1881, September 12, 1884, and February 26, 1886.

46. *Indian Chieftain*, May 28, 1885. An Ole Si letter is in *Indian Journal*, August 23, 1883. For Joner Slimkins, Cyrus Leondus Blackburn, and Big Creek Scribe letters, see *Indian Chieftain*, April 21, 1887, January 26, 1888, and July 31, 1890, respectively.

47. See, e.g., *Wheeler's Western Independent*, May 22 and August 7, 1878; *Cherokee Advocate*, May 18, June 1, August 3, and September 21, 1878; *Atoka Independent*, November 23, 1877; *Indian Journal*, June 24, 1880.

48. *Indian Chieftain*, December 31, 1885.

49. *Indian Arrow*, July 11, 1889. A second installment appeared on June 13. The first of the series has not been found.

50. For discussions of the "misspellers" or "phunny phellows" whom these writers imitated, see Brom Weber, "The Misspellers," in Louis D. Rubin, Jr., ed., *The Comic Imagination in American Literature* (New Brunswick, N.J.: Rutgers University Press, 1973), 127–37, and Walter Blair and Hamlin Hill, *America's Humor: From Poor Richard to Doonesbury* (New York: Oxford University Press, 1978), 274–99.

51. David B. Kesterson, "Those *Literary* Comedians," in William Bedford Clark and W. Craig Turner, eds., *Critical Essays on American Humor* (Boston: G. K. Hall, 1984), 167–83.

52. *Cherokee Telephone*, July 17, 1890.

53. Ibid., May 18, 1893. Other Choo-noo-lus-ky letters appeared December 18, 1890, and January 21 and March 5, 1891.

54. Ibid., June 4, 1891.

55. Choonstootee letters appeared in *Telephone*, February 22 and May 16, 1888, and April 5 and May 24, 1889; in *Arrow*, May 24 and 31, June 14, July 5, August 2, and October 5, 1895, and June 13, 1896; and in *Tahlequah Arrow*, May 7, 1898. Oo-law-nah-stee-sky's letter appeared in *Afton News*, March 1, 1895. Chu-nul-lun-sky's letters appeared in *Vinita Leader*, April 28 and June 9, 1898, and March 29, 1900. Chun-chustie's letters appeared in *Vinita Leader*, September 8, 1898, and September 27, 1900. A Kingfisher letter appeared in *Vinita Leader*, June 2, 1898, a Jeem Featherhead letter in *Vinita Leader*, May 19, 1898, and Too-

stoo letters in *Vinita Leader*, January 5 and May 4, 1899. Arnawaky's letter appeared in *Wagoner Record*, December 7, 1899. For Mary Jane Bramble's letters, see *Weekly Indian Chieftain*, May 4 and 18 and June 15, 1899. And for Lee Allen's "Grindstone Club" and "Possum Bend" letters, see *Muskogee Phoenix*, March 5 and 12, April 16, May 7, 14, and 28, June 11 and 25, July 2 and 16, August 6 and 13, September 17 and 24, and October 8, 1896.

56. See Choonstootee's letters: *Telephone*, February 22, 1888, and April 5, 1889, and *Arrow*, October 5, 1895, respectively. Choonstootee was already known to Indian Territory readers when he adopted dialect humor as a vehicle for his views in 1888. As early as 1882, in serious letters to the editor, he had addressed the issues facing the Cherokees. See *Cherokee Advocate*, February 24 and April 14, 1882, and March 30, 1883.

57. Some of the latter are attempts by the Cherokees to represent the absence of an *r* sound in their language: "plomises," "lail load," etc.

58. "Athome Writes Again," *Cherokee Advocate*, October 8, 1904. See also "Don't Like the Way Things Look," *Cherokee Advocate*, October 1, 1904.

59. "Letter of Woochee Ochee to Editor Sallisaw Star," *Sallisaw Star*, July 17, 1903, reprinted in *Tahlequah Arrow*, July 21, 1903.

60. *Adair Weekly Ledger*, July 24, 1904; see also August 18, 1905.

61. "Cherokee Full Blood Airs Political Views," *Muskogee Times-Democrat*, September 14, 1906.

62. "Creek Politics by a Fullblood," *Muskogee Times-Democrat*, August 10, 1906.

63. See *Indian Journal*, March 20 and 27 and April 10, 1903.

64. Posey published "The Alabama Prophet" while he was a student at Bacone, probably in 1893; a copy is in item 5326.441, Posey Collection, Thomas Gilcrease Institute of American History and Art. "Two Famous Prophets" appeared in *Twin Territories* 2 (September 1900): 180–82.

65. "Fus Fixico's Letter," *Indian Journal*, October 31, 1902.

66. *Indian Journal*, June 13, 1902; "Choela Is Dead," *Indian Journal*, March 30, 1903.

67. Ibid., February 28, 1902.

68. Ibid., April 11, 1902. The quotation is from "A Creek Philosopher Dead," *Kansas City Star*, January 19, 1908.

69. *Holdenville Tribune*, August 2, 1906.

70. *Kansas City Star*, June 19, 1908; *Muskogee Times-Democrat*, January 15,

Notes to Pages 35–43

1908. The quotation is from Alex Posey to F. S. Barde, January 24, 1904, in Frederick S. Barde Collection, Poets and Poetry — Oklahoma File, Archives and Manuscripts Division, Oklahoma Historical Society, Oklahoma City. It was reprinted in *Kansas City Star,* June 24, 1906.

71. *Muskogee Democrat,* May 8, 1905. The quote is from "Tokpafka Micco Visits in Town," *Indian Journal,* April 17, 1908.

72. *Indian Journal,* June 26, 1903.

73. Eufaula District Court, 1890–1898, Creek vol.12, pp.1 and 2, Creek National Records, (Microfilm CN19), Record Group 75, National Archives, maintained by Oklahoma Historical Society.

74. *Home Mission Monthly* 4 (May 1890): 165 and 5 (June 1891): 185.

75. *Muskogee Democrat,* January 2, 1906; "An Indian's Opinion about Whiskey," *Indian Journal,* July 3, 1903. The quotation is from "Sunday Ball Playing," *Indian Journal,* June 26, 1903.

76. William Leslie Clark and Walker D. Wyman, *Charles Round Low Cloud: Voice of the Winnebago* (River Falls: University of Wisconsin, River Falls Press, 1973), 6–7; Rudolph Flesch is cited from his *Art of Plain Talk* (New York: Harper and Brothers Publisher, 1946), 182. Credit for the lead to Flesch's quotation on Low Cloud goes to Clark and Wyman.

77. C. Carroll Hollis, "Rural Humor of the Late Nineteenth Century," in Louis D. Rubin, Jr., ed., *The Comic Imagination in American Literature* (New Brunswick, N.J.: Rutgers University Press, 1973), 170.

78. *Philadephia Press,* November 4, 1900, clipping, in Scrapbook, item 4627.32, Posey Collection, Thomas Gilcrease Institute of American History and Art; *South McAlester Capital,* July 16, 1903.

79. See Lawrence E. Mintz, *Humor in America: A Research Guide to Genres and Topics* (Westport, Conn.: Greenwood Press, 1988), 7–10.

80. Hollis, "Rural Humor of the Late Nineteenth Century," 171.

81. Quoted in Laura Coltelli, ed., *Winged Words: American Indian Writers Speak* (Lincoln: University of Nebraska Press, 1990), 192.

82. Norris W. Yates, *The American Humorist: Conscience of the Twentieth Century* (Ames: Iowa State University Press, 1964), 27–28.

83. "Mus Nixico's Letter," *South McAlester Capital,* January 7, 1904; "'Fus Fixico' Again," *Bartlesville Weekly Examiner,* April 28, 1906; "Some Dialect," *Muskogee Daily Phoenix,* January 17, 1904; "Fus Fixico Jr.," *Checotah Enquirer,* April 17, 1908; "Fus Fixico No.Two," *Checotah Enquirer,* May 1, 1908, reprinted

from *Hoffman Herald*; "Another Full-Blood Writes," *Checotah Enquirer*, April 24, 1908.

84. *Muskogee Daily Phoenix*, June 7, 1908.

85. Ibid., August 5, 1908, and March 22, 1910; *Muskogee Times-Democrat*, November 10 and 20, 1909, and January 27 and March 15, 1910.

86. *Muskogee Times-Democrat*, January 27, 1910.

87. Ibid., November 26, 1913.

88. Ibid., April 20, 1916.

89. William Harjo [Thomas E. Moore], *Sour Sofkee* (Muskogee: Hoffman Printing, 1983), iii, iv; telephone interview with Thomas E. Moore, January 7, 1992.

90. Harjo, *Sour Sofkee*, 1.

91. Acee Blue Eagle, "Turkey Eggs" and "Wild Onions," in *The Creek Nation Journal Centennial Edition* (Okmulgee, Okla.: N.p., 1967); telephone interview with Moore, January 7, 1992.

92. Elias McLeod Landrum was educated at Emory College in Georgia and served as district judge and senator in the Cherokee Nation before Oklahoma statehood. He later served as an Oklahoma state senator and as deputy state examiner and inspector. See D. C. Gideon, *The Indian Territory* (New York: Lewis Publishing Co., 1901), 271–72; Joseph B. Thoburn, *A Standard History of Oklahoma* (Chicago: American Historical Society, 1916), 1434–35. For examples of Landrum's dialect speeches, see Oleta Littleheart, *The Lure of Indian Country* (Sulphur, Okla.: A. Abbott, 1908), 133–38; *Renfrew's Record*, August 1, 1919.

93. *Tahlequah Arrow*, May 30, 1903; R. Roger Eubanks, "Nights with Uncle Ti-ault-ly: How the Terrapin Beat the Rabbit," *Osage Magazine* 1 (May 1910): 72–74; idem, "Nights with Uncle Ti-ault-ly: The Ball Game of the Birds and Animals," *Osage Magazine* 2 (September 1910): 45–47; Eubanks to Posey, May 1, 1908, Scrapbook, item 4627.32, Posey Collection, Thomas Gilcrase Institute of American History and Art.

94. Bertrand N. O. Walker, *Tales of the Bark Lodges, by Hen-Toh, Wyandot* (Oklahoma City: Harlow, 1919); idem, *Yon-doo-shah-we-ah (Nubbins) by Hen-Toh (Wyandot)* (Oklahoma City: Harlow, 1924).

95. *American Indian* 1 (April 1927): 9; "Capt. Ben Locke, Noted Indian Soldier-Writer, Passes Away," *American Indian* 2 (January 1928): 6.

96. Dan M. Madrano, *Heap Big Laugh* (Tulsa: Western Publishing Co., 1955), 4.

97. Joseph Bayhylle Shunatona, *Skookum's Laugh Medicine* (Tulsa: N.p., 1957), 10.

98. Quoted in Coltelli, *Winged Words*, 192.

99. Tim Giago, "Celebrating 'Grass Roots' Indian Humor," *Char-Koosta News*, May 18, 1990.

100. Angie Debo, *And Still the Waters Run: The Betrayal of the Five Civilized Tribes* (Princeton, N.J.: Princeton University Press, 1972).

Headnote Sources

No.1 and No.2: *Indian Journal*, May 2 and 16, 1902.

No.3: Ohland Morton, "Government of the Creek Indians," *Chronicles of Oklahoma* 8 (June 1930): 189–225.

No.4 and No.5: *Indian Journal*, March 7, April 11, September 19 and 26, October 3 and 24, November 7, 14, and 21, and December 5, 1902. Daniel F. Littlefield, Jr., "Utopian Dreams of the Cherokee Fullbloods: 1890–1934," *Journal of the West* 10 (July 1971): 404–27, deals with not only the Cherokees but other groups as well.

No.8: *Indian Journal*, December 26, 1902, and January 1 and 9, 1903.

No.10: *Indian Journal*, January 9 and 20, 1903.

No.11: *Indian Journal*, February 20, 1903.

No.12: John D. Benedict, *Muskogee and Northeastern Oklahoma*, 2 vols. (Chicago: S. J. Clarke Publishing Co., 1922), 1:397; Joseph B. Thoburn and Muriel H. Wright, *Oklahoma: A History of the State and Its People*, 4 vols. (New York: Lewis Historical Publishing Co., 1929), 3:253.

No.13: *Indian Journal*, March 20, 1903.

No.14: *Indian Journal*, March 20, 1903.

No.15, No.16, and No.17: *Indian Journal*, March 27 and April 17, 1903.

No.18: *Indian Journal*, April 10, 1903.

No.19, No.20, and No.21: *Indian Journal*, May 1, 1903.

No.22: *Indian Journal*, March 20 and May 22, 1903.

No.23, No.24, and No.25: *Indian Journal*, June 5, 1903.

No.26: *Indian Journal*, June 26, 1903.

No.27: *Indian Journal*, June 26, 1903.

No.28: *Indian Journal*, June 26 and July 10, 1903.

No.29: *Indian Journal*, July 11, 1902, June 26 and July 3 and 10, 1903.

No.30: *Indian Journal*, July 10 and 24 and August 14, 1903; *Vinita Daily Chieftain*,

Headnote Sources

August 15, 1903, clipping, in Ethan Allen Hitchcock Papers, Box 43, Scrapbook, 1:66, Record Group 200, National Archives, Washington, D.C.

No.31: *Indian Journal*, August 28, 1903; *Leavenworth Times*, August 18, 1903, clipping, in Hitchcock Papers, Box 43, Scrapbook, 1:3; U.S. Congress, Senate, 58th Cong., 2d sess., S. Doc. 189, 5, 7, 9, 12–15.

No.32: *Indian Journal*, August 14 and September 4 and 11, 1903.

No.33: *Indian Journal*, September 25, 1903; *Fort Smith Times*, October 25, 1903.

No.34, No.35, and No.36: *Muskogee Phoenix*, September 29, 1903; *Fort Smith Times*, November 1, 1903.

No.37 and No.38: *Muskogee Phoenix*, November 26, 1903; *Tahlequah Arrow*, December 19 and 26, 1903, and January 2, 1904.

No.39 and No 40: *Indian Journal*, April 17, 1908.

No.41: *Muskogee Daily Phoenix*, January 26, 1904.

No.42: *Vinita Weekly Chieftain*, February 25, March 17 and 31, and April 7 and 21, 1904.

No.43, No.44, No.45, No.46, and No.47: *Vinita Weekly Chieftain*, March 10 and April 7 and 14, 1904.

No.48: *Vinita Weekly Chieftain*, May 19, 1904.

No.49: *Muskogee Democrat*, June 17 and 18, 1904; *Purcell Register*, June 25, 1904; *Vinita Weekly Chieftain*, June 23, 1904.

No.50: *Muskogee Democrat*, June 24, 25, and 28 and July 1, 1904.

No.51: *Muskogee Democrat*, September 19, 1904.

No.52: *Muskogee Democrat*, December 15, 16, and 22, 1904.

No.53: *Muskogee Phoenix*, November 12, 1903; *Vinita Weekly Chieftain*, January 28, July 21, October 4 and 27, and November 17, 1904; *Muskogee Democrat*, October 27 and December 29 and 30, 1904, and January 3, 9, 11, and 12, 1905.

No.54: *Muskogee Democrat*, April 5, 1905.

No.55: *Muskogee Democrat*, December 10, 15, and 16, 1904, January 4, 6, 9, 10, and 12, April 15 and 20, May 5, June 3 and 30, and July 11, 12, 13, 14, 15, 20, 22, and 26, 1905.

No.56: *Muskogee Democrat*, July 26 and August 1, 3, 5, 7, and 8, 1905.

No.57: Angie Debo, *And Still the Waters Run: The Betrayal of the Five Civilized Tribes* (Princeton, N.J.: Princeton University Press, 1972), 162–63; H. Wayne Morgan and Anne Hodges Morgan, *Oklahoma: A Bicentennial History* (New York: W. W. Norton and Co., 1977), 77–78; *Muskogee Democrat*, August 5, 1905.

Headnote Sources

No.58: *Muskogee Daily Phoenix*, June 15 and 26, 1905, and January 18, 1906; *Muskogee Democrat*, August 28 and October 6, 7, 23, 25, and 28, 1905; Luther B. Hill, *A History of the State of Oklahoma*, 2 vols. (Chicago: Lewis Publishing Co., 1909), 2:326–27.

No.59: *Muskogee Democrat*, August 23, 28, 29, 30, and 31, September 2, 5, 8, 21, 22, 26, and 30, and October 4, 6, 9, 13, 14, 16, 19, 20, and 21, 1905; *Muskogee Phoenix*, August 24 and 31, September 7, 14, and 28, and October 5, 1907; *Constitution of the State of Sequoyah* (Muskogee: Phoenix Printing Co., 1905); Morgan and Morgan, *Oklahoma*, 79–80; William H. Murray, "The Constitutional Convention," *Chronicles of Oklahoma* 9 (June 1931): 129–30; Amos D. Maxwell, "The Sequoyah Convention," Parts 1 and 2, *Chronicles of Oklahoma* 28 (Summer, Autumn 1950): 161–92, 299–340.

No.60: *Muskogee Phoenix*, August 24, October 5, November 9 and 16, and December 7 and 16, 1905; *Muskogee Democrat*, September 30, 1905.

No.61: *Muskogee Phoenix*, March 20, 1890; *Muskogee Times-Democrat*, February 21, 1906; *Kansas City Star*, January 19, 1908; *Indian Journal*, January 24, 1908; Creek Records 25560, 32563, and 32955, Record Group 75, National Archives, maintained by Oklahoma Historical Society.

No.62: *Muskogee Phoenix*, November 2, December 7, 14, and 28, 1905, January 11 and 18, February 1, 8, 22, and 25, and March 1 and 8, 1906.

No.67: *Indian Journal*, August 31, September 7, 21, and 28, October 5, 19, and 26, and November 2 and 9, 1906.

No.69: *Indian Journal*, January 4 and 18, 1907, January 17, March 20, and April 17, 1908; *Shawnee Daily Herald*, March 1 and 15, 1908.

No.70: *Indian Journal*, April 10 and May 8 and 15, 1908.

No.71: "Story by an Indian Raconteur," *Indian Journal*, February 22, 1907, reprinted from *Muskogee Times-Democrat*; *Indian Journal*, May 29, 1908.

No.72: *Shawnee Daily Herald*, April 14, 1908; *Indian Journal*, April 17, 1908.

Bibliography

ARCHIVAL MATERIALS AND UNPUBLISHED SOURCES

Bacone College, Muskogee, Oklahoma
  Alexander L. Posey's Personal Library
Moore, Thomas E. Telephone interview, January 7, 1992.
National Archives, Washington, D.C.
  Ethan Allen Hitchcock Papers (Record Group 200)
  Records of the Bureau of Indian Affairs (Record Group 75)
    Creek National Records (maintained by Archives and Manuscripts Division, Oklahoma Historical Society)
National Archives Microfilm Publications, Washington, D.C.
  Enrollment Cards for the Five Civilized Tribes, 1898–1914 (Microcopy M1186)
  1910 Census Schedule (Microcopy T624)
Oklahoma Historical Society, Archives and Manuscripts Division, Oklahoma City
  Creek National Records (National Archives, Record Group 75)
  Frederick S. Barde Collection
  Indian-Pioneer History
Smithsonian Institution, National Anthropological Archives, Washington, D.C.
  File 1806 Creek
Thomas Gilcrease Institute of American History and Art, Tulsa, Oklahoma
  Alexander L. Posey Collection

GOVERNMENT PUBLICATIONS

U.S. Congress. Senate. 58th Cong., 2d sess., S. Doc. 189.
———. 59th Cong., 2d sess., S. Rep. 5013.

285

Bibliography

NEWSPAPERS AND MAGAZINES

Adair Weekly Ledger (Adair, Cherokee Nation), 1904, 1905.

Afton News (Afton, Cherokee Nation), 1895.

American Indian (Tulsa, Oklahoma), 1927, 1928.

Arkansian (Fayetteville, Arkansas), 1859, 1860.

Arrow (Tahlequah, Cherokee Nation), 1895, 1896.

Atoka Independent (Atoka, Choctaw Nation), 1877.

Bartlesville Weekly Examiner (Bartlesville, Cherokee Nation), 1906.

Checotah Enquirer (Checotah, Oklahoma), 1908.

Cherokee Advocate (Tahlequah, Cherokee Nation), 1852, 1871, 1878, 1879, 1880, 1881, 1882, 1883, 1884, 1886, 1903, 1904, 1905.

Cherokee Telephone (Tahlequah, Cherokee Nation), 1890, 1891, 1893.

Claremore Messenger (Claremore, Cherokee Nation), 1903.

Claremore Progress (Claremore, Cherokee Nation), 1903.

Daily Oklahoman (Oklahoma City, Oklahoma Territory [later Oklahoma]), 1903, 1904, 1905, 1906, 1907, 1916, 1920, 1922, 1942.

Dustin Dispatch (Dustin, Creek Nation), 1905.

El Reno News (El Reno, Oklahoma Territory), 1897.

Eufaula Tribune (Eufaula, Creek Nation), 1904.

Fort Smith New Era (Fort Smith, Arkansas), 1867, 1874.

Fort Smith Times (Fort Smith, Arkansas), 1903.

Henryetta Free-Lance (Henryetta, Creek Nation), 1906.

Holdenville Times (Holdenville, Creek Nation), 1905, 1906.

Holdenville Tribune (Holdenville, Creek Nation), 1905, 1906.

Home Mission Monthly (New York, New York), 1890, 1891.

Indian Arrow (Tahlequah, Cherokee Nation), 1888, 1889.

Indian Chieftain (Vinita, Cherokee Nation), 1885, 1887, 1888, 1890.

Indian Citizen (Atoka, Choctaw Nation), 1904.

Indian Journal (Eufaula, Creek Nation [later Oklahoma]), 1880, 1883, 1894, 1901, 1902, 1903, 1906, 1907, 1908.

Kansas City Journal (Kansas City, Missouri), 1903.

Kansas City Star (Kansas City, Missouri), 1906, 1908.

Kingfisher Free Press (Kingfisher, Oklahoma Territory), 1900.

Muskogee Daily Phoenix (Muskogee, Creek Nation [later Oklahoma]), 1902, 1903, 1904, 1905, 1906, 1907, 1908, 1910.

Muskogee Democrat (Muskogee, Creek Nation), 1904, 1905, 1906, 1907.

Bibliography

Muskogee Evening Times (Muskogee, Creek Nation), 1903.

Muskogee Phoenix (Muskogee, Creek Nation), 1890, 1892, 1896, 1899, 1903, 1904, 1905, 1906, 1907.

Muskogee Times-Democrat (Muskogee, Creek Nation [later Oklahoma]), 1906, 1907, 1908, 1909, 1910, 1913, 1916.

New-State Tribune (Muskogee, Creek Nation), 1906.

New York Times (New York, New York), 1903.

Purcell Register (Purcell, Chickasaw Nation), 1904.

Red Man and Helper (Carlisle, Pennsylvania), 1904.

Renfrew's Record (Alva, Oklahoma), 1919.

Sallisaw Star (Sallisaw, Cherokee Nation), 1903.

Shawnee Daily Herald (Shawnee, Oklahoma), 1907, 1908.

South McAlester Capital (South McAlester, Choctaw Nation), 1903, 1904.

Sturm's Oklahoma Magazine (Oklahoma City, Oklahoma Territory [later Oklahoma]), 1905, 1908.

Tahlequah Arrow (Tahlequah, Cherokee Nation), 1898, 1903, 1904.

Telephone (Tahlequah, Cherokee Nation), 1888, 1889.

Times-Record (Oklahoma City, Oklahoma), 1911.

Twin Territories (Muskogee, Creek Nation), 1899, 1900, 1902, 1903.

Vinita Daily Chieftain (Vinita, Cherokee Nation), 1900, 1903, 1904.

Vinita Leader (Vinita, Cherokee Nation), 1898, 1899, 1900.

Vinita Weekly Chieftain (Vinita, Cherokee Nation), 1903, 1904, 1908.

Wagoner Record (Wagoner, Creek Nation), 1899.

Weekly Indian Chieftain (Vinita, Cherokee Nation), 1899.

Wheeler's Western Independent (Fort Smith, Arkansas), 1877, 1878.

BOOKS

Avery, Catharine B. *The New Century Classical Handbook.* New York: Appleton-Century-Crofts, 1962.

Baird, W. David, ed. *A Creek Warrior for the Confederacy: The Autobiography of Chief G. W. Grayson.* Norman: University of Oklahoma Press, 1988.

Benedict, John D. *Muskogee and Northeastern Oklahoma.* 2 vols. Chicago: S. J. Clarke Publishing Co., 1922.

Blair, Walter, and Hamlin Hill. *America's Humor: From Poor Richard to Doonesbury.* New York: Oxford University Press, 1978.

Clark, William Leslie, and Walker D. Wyman. *Charles Round Low Cloud: Voice of the Winnebago.* River Falls: University of Wisconsin, River Falls Press, 1973.

Bibliography

Coltelli, Laura, ed. *Winged Words: American Indian Writers Speak*. Lincoln: University of Nebraska Press, 1990.

Constitution of the State of Sequoyah. Muskogee: Phoenix Printing Co., 1905.

The Creek Nation Journal Centennial Edition. Okmulgee, Okla.: N.p., 1967.

Debo, Angie. *And Still the Waters Run: The Betrayal of the Five Civilized Tribes*. Princeton, N.J.: Princeton University Press, 1972.

——. *The Road to Disappearance*. Norman: University of Oklahoma Press, 1941.

Dictionary of American Biography. Ed. Dumas Malone. New York: Charles Scribner's Sons, 1929, 1933, 1934, 1935, 1936.

——. Ed. Robert Livingston Schuyler. New York: Charles Scribner's Sons, 1958.

——. Ed. Harris E. Starr. New York: Charles Scribner's Sons, 1958.

——. Ed. John A. Garraty. New York: Charles Scribner's Sons, 1977.

Dictionary of American History. 8 vols. New York: Charles Scribner's Sons, 1976–78.

Dudden, Arthur Power, ed. *American Humor*. New York: Oxford University Press, 1987.

Emery, Jones Gladstone. *Court of the Damned: Being a Factual Story of the Court of Judge Isaac C. Parker and the Life and Times of the Indian Territory and Old Fort Smith*. New York: Comet Press Books, 1959.

Flesch, Rudolph. *The Art of Plain Talk*. New York: Harper and Brothers Publishers, 1946.

Foreman, Carolyn Thomas. *Oklahoma Imprints, 1835–1907*. Norman: University of Oklahoma Press, 1936.

Gatewood, Willard B., Jr. *Theodore Roosevelt and the Art of Controversy: Episodes of the White House Years*. Baton Rouge: Louisiana State University Press, 1970.

Gideon, D. C. *The Indian Territory*. New York: Lewis Publishing Co., 1901.

Gould, Lewis L. *Reform and Regulation: American Politics, 1900–1916*. New York: Wiley, 1978.

Harjo, William [Thomas E. Moore]. *Sour Sofkee*. Muskogee: Hoffman Printing, 1983.

Harlow, Rex, comp. *Makers of Government in Oklahoma*. Oklahoma City: Harlow Publishing Co., 1930.

Hill, Luther B. *A History of the State of Oklahoma*. 2 vols. Chicago: Lewis Publishing Co., 1909.

Littlefield, Daniel F., Jr. *Alex Posey: Creek Poet, Journalist, and Humorist*. Lincoln: University of Nebraska Press, 1992.

Bibliography

Littlefield, Daniel F., Jr., and James W. Parins. *A Biobibliography of Native American Writers, 1772–1924.* Metuchen, N.J.: Scarecrow Press, 1981.

———. *A Biobibliography of Native American Writers, 1772–1924, Supplement.* Metuchen, N.J.: Scarecrow Press, 1985.

Littleheart, Oleta. *The Lure of Indian Country.* Sulphur, Okla.: A. Abbott, 1908.

Madrano, Dan M. *Heap Big Laugh.* Tulsa: Western Printing Co., 1955.

Mintz, Lawrence E. *Humor in America: A Research Guide to Genres and Topics.* Westport, Conn.: Greenwood Press, 1988.

Moore, M. R. *Moore's Directory of the City of Muskogee, Indian Territory.* Muskogee: Phoenix Publishing Co., 1904.

Morgan, H. Wayne, and Anne Hodges Morgan. *Oklahoma: A Bicentennial History.* New York: W. W. Norton and Co., 1977.

National Cyclopaedia of American Biography. Vol. 35. New York: James T. White, 1949.

O'Beirne, H. F., and E. S. O'Beirne. *The Indian Territory: Its Chiefs, Legislators, and Leading Men.* St. Louis: C. B. Woodward Co., 1892.

Posey, Minnie H., comp. *Poems of Alexander Lawrence Posey.* Rev. ed. Muskogee: Hoffman Printing Co., 1969.

Shunatona, Joseph Bayhylle. *Skookum's Laugh Medicine.* Tulsa: N.p., 1957.

Speck, Frank G. *The Creek Indians of Taskigi Town.* Memoirs of the American Anthropological Association, no. 2. Millwood, N.Y.: Kraus Reprint Co., 1974.

Thoburn, Joseph B. *A Standard History of Oklahoma.* Chicago: American Historical Association, 1916.

Thoburn, Joseph B., and Muriel H. Wright. *Oklahoma: A History of the State and Its People.* 4 vols. New York: Lewis Historical Publishing Co., 1929.

Walker, Bertrand N. O. *Tales of the Bark Lodges, by Hen-Toh, Wyandot.* Oklahoma City: Harlow, 1919.

———. *Yon-doo-shah-we-ah (Nubbins) by Hen-Toh (Wyandot).* Oklahoma City: Harlow, 1924.

Webster's Biographical Dictionary. Springfield, Mass.: G. & C. Merriam Co., 1972.

Who Was Who in America. 9 vols. to date. Chicago: Marquis—Who's Who, 1942–.

Yates, Norris W. *The American Humorist: Conscience of the Twentieth Century.* Ames: Iowa State University Press, 1964.

Bibliography

ARTICLES

Atwood, Eleanor Patricia. "The Crazy Snake Rebellions: A Study in the Break-down of Tribal Government." *Vassar Journal of Undergraduate Studies* 15 (May 1942): 44–60.

Axtell, James. "Humor in Ethnohistory." *Ethnohistory* 37 (Spring 1990): 109–25.

Baird, W. David. "Are There 'Real' Indians in Oklahoma? Historical Perceptions of the Five Civilized Tribes." *Chronicles of Oklahoma* 68 (Spring 1990): 4–23.

Belcher, Wyatt W. "Political Leadership of Robert L. Owen." *Chronicles of Oklahoma* 31 (Winter 1953–54): 361–71.

Blue Eagle, Acee. "Indian Poetry." In *The Creek Nation Journal Centennial Edition*. Okmulgee, Okla.: N.p., 1967.

Bolster, Mel H. "The Smoked Meat Rebellion." *Chronicles of Oklahoma* 31 (Spring 1953): 37–55.

Connelley, William Elsey. "Memoir of Alexander Lawrence Posey." In Minnie H. Posey, comp., *The Poems of Alexander Lawrence Posey*. Topeka: Crane and Co., 1910.

"Cutting Indians' Hair." *Harper's Weekly* 46 (March 22, 1902): 357.

Eubanks, R. Roger. "Nights with Uncle Ti-ault-ly: How the Terrapin Beat the Rabbit." *Osage Magazine* 1 (May 1910): 72–74.

———. "Nights with Uncle Ti-ault-ly: The Ball Game of the Birds and Animals." *Osage Magazine* 2 (September 1910): 45–47.

Evans, Charles. "The Robert Lee Williams Memorial Dedication." *Chronicles of Oklahoma* 31 (Winter 1953–54): 375–77.

Foreman, Carolyn Thomas. "Fishertown." *Chronicles of Oklahoma* 31 (Autumn 1953): 247–54.

Foreman, Grant. "Frank C. Hubbard." *Chronicles of Oklahoma* 8 (December 1930): 454–56.

———. "J. George Wright." *Chronicles of Oklahoma* 20 (June 1942): 120–23.

"George Alfred Mansfield." *Chronicles of Oklahoma* 7 (December 1929): 491–92.

Giago, Tim. "Celebrating 'Grass Roots' Indian Humor." *Char-Koosta News*, May 18, 1990.

Gibson, Charles. "Ah-pus-kee." *Indian Journal*, May 8, 1908.

———. "The Creek Roll." *Indian Journal*, July 3, 1903.

———. "Este Charte." *Indian Journal*, May 1, 1908.

Grayson, G. W. "With Secretary Hitchcock." *Indian Journal*, May 15, 1903.

Bibliography

Hollis, C. Carroll. "Rural Humor of the Late Nineteenth Century." In Louis D. Rubin, Jr., ed., *The Comic Imagination in American Literature*. New Brunswick, N.J.: Rutgers University Press, 1973.

Kesterson, David B. "Those *Literary* Comedians." In William Bedford Clark and W. Craig Turner, eds., *Critical Essays on American Humor*. Boston: G. K. Hall, 1984.

Littlefield, Daniel F., Jr. "Evolution of Alex Posey's Fus Fixico Persona." *Studies in American Indian Literatures* 4 (Summer/Fall 1992): 136–44.

——. "Utopian Dreams of the Cherokee Fullbloods: 1890–1934." *Journal of the West* 10 (July 1971): 404–27.

Littlefield, Daniel F., Jr., and Lonnie E. Underhill. "The 'Crazy Snake Uprising' of 1909: A Red, Black, or White Affair?" *Arizona and the West* 20 (Winter 1978): 307–24.

——. "Renaming the American Indian: 1890–1913." *American Studies* 12 (Fall 1971): 33–45.

Maxwell, Amos D. "The Sequoyah Convention." Parts 1 and 2. *Chronicles of Oklahoma* 28 (Summer, Autumn 1950): 161–92, 299–340.

Meine, J. Franklin. Introduction to *Chicago Stories*, by George Ade. Chicago: Henry Regnery Co., 1963.

Meserve, John Bartlett. "Chief Samuel Checote, with Sketches of Chiefs Locher Harjo and Ward Coachman." *Chronicles of Oklahoma* 16 (December 1938): 401–9.

——. "The MacIntoshes." *Chronicles of Oklahoma* 10 (September 1932): 310–25.

——. "The Plea of Crazy Snake (Chitto Harjo)." *Chronicles of Oklahoma* 11 (September 1933): 899–911.

Morton, Ohland. "Government of the Creek Indians." *Chronicles of Oklahoma* 8 (June 1930): 189–225.

Murdock, Victor. "Dennis T. Flynn." *Chronicles of Oklahoma* 18 (June 1940): 107–13.

Murray, William H. "The Constitutional Convention." *Chronicles of Oklahoma* 9 (June 1931): 126–38.

Posey, Alexander L. "Chinnubbie Scalps the Squaws." *B. I. U. Instructor* 2 (May 20, 1893): unpaged.

——. "Mose and Richard." *Twin Territories* 2 (November 1900): 226–28.

——. "Two Famous Prophets." *Twin Territories* 2 (September 1900): 180–82.

Bibliography

——. "Uncle Dick's Sow." *Twin Territories* 1 (December 1899): 20.

"Reverend William McCombs." *Chronicles of Oklahoma* 8 (March 1930): 137–40.

Roosevelt, Theodore. "A Colorado Bear Hunt." *Scribner's Magazine* 38 (October 1905): 387–408.

——. "A Wolf Hunt in Oklahoma." *Scribner's Magazine* 38 (November 1905): 513–32.

Taylor, Baxter. "Robert Lee Williams as I Knew Him." *Chronicles of Oklahoma* 31 (Winter 1953–54): 378–80.

Trickett, Dean. "The Civil War in the Indian Territory, 1861." *Chronicles of Oklahoma* 18 (June 1940): 142–53.

"Was the Poet Laureate." *Indian School Journal* 10 (April 1910): 29.

Weber, Brom. "The Misspellers." In Louis D. Rubin, Jr., ed., *The Comic Imagination in American Literature*. New Brunswick, N.J.: Rutgers University Press, 1973.

Wright, Muriel H. "John D. Benedict: First United States Superintendent of Schools in Indian Territory." *Chronicles of Oklahoma* 33 (Winter 1955–56): 472–508.

Index

Abdul Aziz IV, 92 n.5
Abraham Linkum Jones, 24–25
Adams, Richard Calmit, 210, 212 n.9
Ade, George, 20, 41
Africa, 67 n.6
Agee, A. E., 266 n.5
Aguinaldo, Emilio, 84 n.4
Ah-sto-la-ta, 26, 27
Ainsworth, Tom, 185 n.12
Alcoholic beverages, 100 n.3, 126 n.7,
    153 n.7; law regulating, 262–64
Allen, Lee, 27
Allotment, 3–4, 53 n.4; Creek, 51, 54–
    55, 69, 70–71, 74, 86–87, 119–24,
    127, 140, 164–65; Grayson on, 71;
    Posey on, 51, 70, 86, 153 n.2
Allotments: restrictions on, 153 n.2;
    sale of, 194 n.5
Apusky, 111
Ardmore, Chickasaw Nation, 163 n.7
Arkansans, Posey on, 67 n.5, 162 n.1,
    243 n.2
Asp, Henry, 255, 256 n.4
Athome, 30

Bacone Indian University, 7, 12
Bald Hill, 74 n.3
Ball play of the Creek, 67 n.7
Bangs, John Kendrick, 21
Barde, Frederick, 183, 185 n.11

Barnett, James, 36
Barrett, Charlie, 135 n.9
Bartlesville, Cherokee Nation, 106 n.4
Baseball, 77 n.8
Beaver County, Oklahoma, 250 n.7
Benedict, John Downing, 82 n.6
Berry, E. L., 186
Beveridge, Albert J., 143 n.1, 241
Big Creek Scribe, 24–25
Big Stick policy, 240 n.3
Bill Kantfraid (Elias M. Landrum):
    humor of, 45; style of, 30–31
Bingham, G. W., 175 n.9
Bixby, Tams, 72, 73, 92 n.1, 101 n.7,
    121, 122 nn.6, 9; 128, 130 n.5, 131–
    33, 136, 150, 199, 225 n.7, 231,
    233 n.3; accusations against, 132,
    135 n.8
Blacks: in Creek Nation, 66, 67 n.6,
    159 n.5; dialect of, 25; in Indian
    Territory, 4–5, 61; legislation con-
    cerning, 256; at Muskogee, 62;
    Posey's views on, 74, 157; and Re-
    publican party, 74, 157, 174 n.5,
    234 n.5, 246 n.1. See also Creek
    freedmen
Blackstone, Sir William, 266 n.4
Blanton, J. T., 185 n.12
Blowguns, 70 n.1
Blue dumplings, 153 n.1

Blue Eagle, Acee (A. C. McIntosh), 43
Bonaparte, Charles J., 149 n.2, 164; as
fraud investigator, 136–37, 147–51,
152
Boudinot, E. C., 274 n.43
Boudinot, Elias, 274 n.43
Boxing, 266 n.4
Boynton, Creek Nation, 96, 97 n.6
Brant-Sera, J. Ojijatekha, 19
Breckenridge, C. R., 128
Brook, Eck E., 174, 175 n.10, 263,
264 n.1
Brosius, S. M., 163 n.5; investigation
by, 127–28
Brown, John F., 217, 238, 240 n.5
Browne, Charles Farrar, 23
Brownlee, Emory D., 266 n.5
Bruner, Paro, 198 n.5
Bryan, William Jennings, 82 n.4, 113,
115 n.6, 144, 145 n.6
Buffington, Thomas M., 77, 78, 98–
99
Bunny, George, 52 n.1, 59 n.4, 68 n.2
Busby, William V., 252
Busk, 54 n.1, 229 n.3. *See also* Green
Corn Ceremony

Canadian Valley Trust Company, 128,
132
Cane Creek, 76 n.4, 159 n.5
Cannon, Joseph, 230 n.8, 243–44,
245 n.1, 246 n.1
Caraway, Morgan, 186, 188–89,
190 nn.7, 11
Castle, C. E., 102, 106–7, 108 n.1,
112, 114 n.1, 140, 141, 142 n.3
Chalogee, 72 n.2
Chambers, John Graham, 266 n.4
Checotah, Creek Nation, 6, 53 n.6,
106 n.4, 257, 260

Checote, Samuel, 237 n.1
Chimney Mountain, 122
China: and Russia, 90, 91; U. S. policy
toward, 85 n.4, 92 n.5
Chinnubbie (Thomas E. Moore), 43;
humor of, 44–45
Chinnubbie Harjo, 7, 12–13
Chitto Harjo, 13–14, 16, 33, 56, 57,
60, 60 n.5, 86, 94 n.2, 109, 111, 116,
118 n.2, 126 n.7, 143–44, 152, 154–
55, 156 nn.5, 6, 161, 164, 170,
171 n.5, 251; and allotment, 140;
arrest of, 55, 57–58, 88 n.1; as can-
didate, 102, 134 n.2; humiliation of,
88 n.1; as Snake leader, 55
Choela, 16, 52, 68; character of, 14,
32–33; death of, 75
Choo-noo-lus-ky, 26–27
Choonstootee, 27; letters of, 28–29;
style of, 29
Choska, Creek Nation, 76 n.4
Christianity, 176–77
Chun-chustie, 27
Cicero, Marcus Tullius, 147 n.2
Clark, Charles Heber, 22
Cobb, Guy P., 128, 130 n.6
Colbert, Benjamin, 132, 133
"Cold Pistol," 42
Colombia, 147 nn.6, 7
Concharty Micco, 134 n.2
Conlan, Mike, 182, 184 nn.1, 2
Coon Creek, 82 n.3
Cornish, Melvin, 184 n.3
County names, 229 n.4
County seats, 228, 257–58; contests
over, 260–61; location of, 210–11,
212 n.10
Cowee Harjo, 84 n.3
Crackling, 84 n.6

Creek freedmen, 56n.2, 82n.3, 159n.5, 174n.3, 198n.5; allotments of, 171n.2, 194n.5. *See also* Blacks

Creek National Council, 52

Creeks: acculturation of, 5–6; allotment of lands to, 6, 12; humor among, 10, 42; judiciary of, 95n.4; laws of, 264n.2; racial views of, 56n.2; social change among, 152. *See also* Snake faction

Cruce, Lee, 257

Curtis, Charles, 140, 145, 146n.1, 161, 163n.4, 196

Curtis Act, 5, 14, 51, 57

Custer, George Armstrong, 89n.3

Cyrus Leondus Blackburn, 24

Darrough, W. H., 175n.9

Davidson, Charles A., 128, 130n.6

Dawes, Henry L., 4

Dawes Commission, 53n.4, 72, 73; accusations against, 119, 120, 122n.8, 127; creation of, 4; Posey's work for, 8, 177–78

Debo, Angie, 48

Deeds, allotment, 51–52, 54–55, 61, 63, 65, 66

Deere, Lawyer, 98

Democratic party. *See* Politics

Denison, Texas, 92n.3

Dialect, Indian: characteristics of, 56n.1; in serious prose, 46–47. *See also* Humor

Dialect, Posey and, 16–17, 21

Dick, Robert W., 173, 175n.6

Diogenes, 130n.1

Dogtown, 64n.6

Douglas, Clarence B., 106, 108n.3, 119, 120, 121n.1, 131, 140, 141,

142n.5, 149n.1, 150, 151nn.3, 5, 159nn.1, 6; 179, 180n.3, 182, 185n.3, 192, 194n.3, 196, 198n.3, 203, 204, 229, 230n.8, 231, 247, 249n.3, 251, 253n.4; and Hitchcock, 125n.1

Douglas, Sir John Sholto, 266n.4

Dowie, John Alexander, 256n.6

Dunne, Finley Peter, 22, 41

Eddy, Mary Baker, 257n.7

Effa Ematha (Efi Emarthla), 156n.4

Elections: Creek, 68–69, 75–76, 79–80, 83, 85, 94, 95n.3, 103–4, 104n.4, 109–11, 115–18, 123–24, 125, 131, 132; presidential, 157, 173–74, 181–84

English, A. Z., 190n.9

"Este Charte," 43

Eubanks, Royal Roger, 45

Eufaula, Creek Nation, 6, 52n.2, 257, 260

Evans, A. Grant, 220n.1

Fisher, Henry Clay, 126n.4

Fite, Francis B., 215, 218, 220n.2

Five Civilized Tribes, 3; acculturation of, 4–5; racial makeup of, 4–5

Flesch, Rudolph, 36

Flynn, Dennis Thomas, 93, 94n.2, 229, 230n.8, 231

Foley, C. E., 142n.5, 154–55, 155n.1, 156n.5, 163n.4, 214

Foraker, Joseph Benson, 244, 245n.1

Fort Gibson, Cherokee Nation, 106n.4

Fort Smith, Arkansas, 92n.3

Foster, David Johnson, 163n.4

Frantz, Frank, 257, 260n.1

Furman, Henry, 106, 108n.2
Fus Fixico: and American humor, 20–23; character of, 31–32; creation of, 8; first letter from, 1; and Indian humor, 23–31
"Fus Fixico" (imitator), 42
"Fus Fixico, Jr.," 17, 43
Fus Fixico letters: characters in, 15–16, 32–35, 37–38; development of, 8–16; dialect in, 16–18, 20; as editorials, 11–12; language in, 38–39; literary allusions in, 39–40; and local color, 40–41; political satire in, 37–39; popularity of, 18–20; sources of humor in, 37–39; style of, 35–37
"Fus Fixico No. Two," 17, 43
Fus Harjo, 43; humor of, 44

Garland, Hamlin, 88n.2
Geeks, 145n.7
General Allotment Act: Five Civilized Tribes and, 4; implementation of, 3–4
Giago, Tim, 47–48
Gibson, Charles, 27, 69, 71, 72n.4, 79, 79n.3, 95, 109, 110, 111, 203, 204, 205n.1, 206n.9; as candidate, 79–80, 83, 91, 93n.7, 94, 95n.3, 102, 103–4, 104n.5, 115–17, 118n.3; on dialect, 16–17; Posey's support for, 79–80; as writer, 53n.7, 60, 122n.8
Gibson, N. A., 231–33, 233n.1, 234n.6
Givens, James M., 174, 175n.10, 182, 184n.3, 186n.12
Goat, John, 59n.3, 75, 76n.1, 85, 85n.2

Graft: by federal officials, 119–24, 164; investigation of, 127–30, 131–34, 136–38, 147–51; by land speculators, 119–24, 165–70; Posey on, 119
Grayson, Dick, 118, 118n.7
Grayson, George W., 35, 72n.3, 85n.3, 87, 109, 233n.3, 273n.24; as candidate, 102, 118n.3; and Hitchcock, 90, 95–97, 97nn.3, 6, 7
Green Corn Ceremony, 54n.1. *See also* Busk
Green Peach War, 6, 117
Greer, Bert, 179, 181n.7
Gregory, James Roane, 134n.2

Hailey, D. M., 173, 174n.6, 183, 185n.5
Hall, George Riley, 21, 273n.24
Hamilton, Edward L., 160
Hamilton Bill, 207, 237
Harjo, H. Marcey, 110, 111n.1
Harjo, Joe, 13
Harkins, Lee, 45
Harris, Joel Chandler, 23
Harrison, William Henry, 89n.3
Haskell, Charles N., 190n.9, 212, 216n.5, 217, 220, 221n.5, 259, 260n.1, 265; at Oklahoma constitutional convention, 254–56, 256n.1, 257n.9; as Oklahoma governor, 257–58; and Sequoyah constitution, 226
Hastings, William Wirt, 182, 185n.3
Hearst, William Randolph, 140, 145, 146n.1, 186n.15
Henry, Patrick, 147n.2
Hercules, 265
Hickory Ground, 13–14, 55, 250n.7

Hillabee town, 63 n.6
Hitchcock, Ethan Allen, 78, 86,
92 n.4, 115 n.9, 119, 120, 125, 128,
131, 133, 136; in Indian Territory,
90–91, 93, 95–97; Posey on, 123
Holcomb, I. N., 211 n.3
Holden, J. S., 179, 180 n.2
Hollis, C. Carroll, 39–40, 41
Homer, 249 n.1
Hopkins, P. B., 190 n.9
Hotgun, 16; arrest of, 73, 74 n.1,
88 n.1; character of, 14, 33–34
Hot Springs, Arkansas, 163 n.9
Hotulk Emathla, 237 n.5, 252, 253 n.8
House of Kings, 5
House of Warriors, 5
Hubbard, Frank C., 102, 105, 106 n.3
Huckleberry, James H., 128, 131 n.6
Hulbutta Micco, 77, 78, 98–99
Humor, dialect: characteristics of, 26–
27; Cherokee, 24–31; in Indian
Territory, 23–31; style of, 26
Humor, Indian, 1, 41–42; in Indian
Territory, 21–22

Indian Journal, 8–9
Indian Territory: Democratic politics
in, 65; history of, 3–6
Indian Territory Press Association,
178, 179
Informal Club, 273 n.24
Ingersoll, Robert Green, 87, 89 n.5
Isparhecher, 118 n.5

Jacks, R. K., 181 n.8
Jackson, Clifford L., 106–7, 108 n.5,
113, 115 n.6, 174, 175 n.10, 182,
183, 184 n.3, 231, 233
Jackson, Helen Hunt, 250 n.5

Jeem Featherhead, 27
Jerome, Jerome K., 21
Johnston, Douglas H., 208, 211 n.6,
238, 240 n.5
Joner Slimkins, 24–25
Josh Billings, 26
Josiah Snooper, 27

Kappler, Charles, 194 n.3
Kenefick, William, 234 n.4
Keokuk Falls, Oklahoma Territory,
66, 67 n.3
Kesterson, David B., 26
Kialegee, 190 n.4
Kingfisher, 27
Kono Harjo, 35

Lafayette, Ben F., 182, 183, 185 n.3
La Flesche, Francis, 47
Lamb, Frank Fenimore, 143 n.7, 213,
216 n.5
Land, restrictions on, 126 n.3
Landrum, Elias McLeod, 278 n.92;
humor of, 45
Latah Micco, 60, 61 n.5
Lawrence, William R., 234 n.7
Lawson, Thomas William, 238,
239 nn.2, 3
Leahy, T. J., 67 n.4
Leases, 68 n.1
Ledbetter, Walter A., 184, 185 n.7
Lewis, C. B., 22
Lighthorse police, 64 n.4
Liliuokalani, Queen Lydia Kamekeha,
84 n.4
Little Frog, 30, 31
Little River, 76 n.3
Locher Harjo, 230 n.5
Locke, Ben, 45

Locke, David Ross, 23
Locke, Victor E., 175 n.9
Looney, Charles A., 183, 185 n.11
Louisiana Purchase Exposition, 105,
    106 n.3
Low Cloud, Charles Round, 36–37,
    47
Loyal Creek Claim, 74, 75, 102,
    171 n.1, 189 n.3; payment of, 104–
    5, 105 n.1
Lozier, Robert, 262, 264 n.3

McCombs, J. W., 126 n.6
McCombs, William, 85 n.3
McConkey, Ed M., 185 n.12
McCoy, Joseph, 132, 135 n.6
McCurtain, Green, 57, 77, 78, 84,
    115 n.9, 208, 217, 219; as statehood
    leader, 98–100, 102–3
McDermott, Jesse, 43–44
McGuire, Bird S., 198 n.3, 212 n.8,
    229, 230 n.8; 249 nn.2, 3; 252
McIntosh, A. C. *See* Acee Blue Eagle
McIntosh, Albert Gallatin (Cheesie),
    98, 100 n.1, 126 n.3
McIntosh, Daniel N., 100 n.1
McIntosh, Roley, 69, 70; as candidate,
    104 n.4
McKellop, Albert Pike, 86 n.5
McMurray, J. F., 184 n.3
Madrano, Daniel M., 45–46
McMurray, J. F., 184 n.3
Mansfield, George Alfred, 184 n.4
Marcum, Thomas, 182, 184 n.3,
    190 n.12
Marrs, David M., 212 n.8, 213,
    216 n.5
Mary Jane Bramble, 27
Mathews, John Joseph, 47

Medals, 253 n.6
Medicine: Creek, 68 n.2, 142 n.4; pat-
    ent, 216 n.7
Mellette, William, 123, 125 n.2,
    159 n.1
Menilek II, 234 n.5
Mexico: emigration to, 57, 58, 60;
    Snake delegations to, 61 n.5
Micco Hutka (Hutke), 62, 63, 63 n.5
Momaday, N. Scott, 47
Moore, Thomas E. *See* Chinnubbie
Morgan, Gideon, 66, 67 n.4, 112
Morgan, Tom P., 22
Morris, E. E., 175 n.9
Mosely, Palmer, 98–99
Mugwumps, 159 n.7
Mulai Ahmed-es-Raisuli, 92 n.5
Murder, 64 n.7
Murphy, Arthur P., 119, 120, 121 n.2,
    150, 151 n.4, 173, 174 n.3
Murray, William H., 217, 219,
    220 n.4, 266 n.3; and Oklahoma
    constitution, 254–56, 256 n.1; and
    Sequoyah constitution, 226
Muskogee, Creek Nation, 66, 67 n.6,
    154 n.4, 171 n.4, 190 n.9, 225 n.2;
    federal jail at, 194 n.6; political con-
    troversy in, 186–89
Muskogee Commercial Club, 213
"Mus Nixico," 42

Names, Indian, 87, 88 n.2
Nation, Carry Amelia, 144 n.5
Needles, Thomas B., 130 n.5, 159 n.6
Nero Claudius Caesar, 239 n.3
Nocose Emarther (Nocus Emarthlar),
    64, 64 n.8
Nocos Yahola, 156 n.4

Norman, J. A., 207
Nye, Edgar Wilson, 23

Oil, 206n.6
Oklahoma: constitution of, 257; first
   legislature of, 258–59, 264–65;
   "freak" laws of, 259–60, 260n.2
Oklahoma constitutional convention,
   254–56; election of delegates to,
   250; Indians at, 250
Oklahoma Territory, Republican poli-
   tics in, 65
Okmulgee, Creek Nation, 52n.3
Old Si, 25
Ole Si, 24
Open Door Policy, 172n.6
Ortiz, Simon J., 47
Osage reservation, 197n.1
Owen, Robert L., 80, 81n.1, 93,
   94n.2, 150, 151n.3, 183, 185n.10,
   210, 212n.9, 216n.5

Palmer, John, 67n.4
Panama, 147nn.6, 7
Panama Canal, 239n.1
Parker, Luman F., Jr., 231, 233n.3,
   234n.7
Paschal, Ridge, 112, 113, 114n.1,
   115n.7
Paullin, Lewis, 181n.8
Pericles, 240n.3
Perryman, Legus C., 86n.5, 118n.4;
   as candidate, 94, 95n.3, 102,
   104n.4, 109, 110, 115–16, 118n.4,
   123–24, 125, 131; as chief, 116,
   118n.1; Posey's dislike of, 109,
   123–24, 131
Pewter Dick, 25
Philippine Islands, 76n.6, 84n.4

Phillippi, M., 181n.8
Phillips, John, 10
Phillips, Johnson J., 15
Phillips, Pahosa Harjo, 85
Platt, Thomas, 139n.5
Poe, L. M., 185, n.12
Pokeweed, 94n.1
Politics: Democratic party, 173, 181–
   84, 250; and Indians, 241, 247, 250;
   Republican party, 172–73, 230–31,
   250
Porter, Pleasant, 51, 56, 56n.3, 64, 69,
   70, 75, 77, 78, 90, 98–99, 109, 110,
   126n.5, 203, 204, 206n.8, 212,
   216n.5, 217, 220, 233n.3, 238,
   240n.5; and allotment deeds, 61; as
   candidate, 79–80, 83, 85, 85n.2,
   86n.7, 94, 95n.3, 102, 115–27, 123,
   125, 126n.6; election of, 131; in
   Green Peach War, 118n.5; and
   Hitchcock, 95; marriage of, 171n.3
Posey, Alexander L.: biographical
   sketch of, 6–9; as creator of Fus
   Fixico, 1; as Creek legislator, 118;
   death of, 9; early reading of, 7, 21;
   early writing of, 7; as editor, 180n.1;
   as fabulist, 22–23; and Hitchcock,
   90, 95, 97nn.5, 7; as humorist, 40–
   41; humorous bent of, 9–10; imitators of, 42–43; and Indian dialect
   humor, 29–30; journalistic career
   of, 8; journalistic style of, 10–11;
   linguistic skill of, 35–36; literary
   legacy of, 42–45; national reputation of, 19–20; poems by, 89n.5,
   92n.2, 126n.2, 172n.7; poetry of, 7;
   political career of, 7; political views
   of, 130n.3; and progress, 126n.7,
   152; racial attitudes of, 56n.2, 61,

Posey, Alexander L. (*cont.*)
109, 118n.4, 123–24, 131; story by,
72n.2; works by, 118
Posey, Lewis Henderson, 10
Posey, Minnie Harris, 7
Posey, Nancy, 10
Progress: and Chitto Harjo, 86;
Grayson on, 87; Posey on, 86
Prohibition, 65, 99, 100n.3, 102, 199,
212, 216n.7, 256n.3, 262, 264n.3

Quapaw Agency, 197n.1
Quapaws, 3
Quay, Matthew Stanley, 86n.7, 161,
162n.4

Railroads, 6, 256n.2
Rampendahl, W. F., 186, 189,
191n.13
Raymond, C. W., 175n.9, 190n.9; at-
tempts to unseat, 230–31
Read, Opie, 23
Reed, Robert, 186n.12
Reed, Thomas Bracket, 143n.6
Republican party. *See* Politics
Robbins, Henry P., 112, 113, 114n.1,
211n.3, 214
Robert, Henry Martyn, 266n.4
Robertson, Alice Mary, 76, 77n.7,
203, 204, 205n.1, 206n.9
Robinson, James M., 163n.4
Rockefeller, John Davison, 238,
239n.3, 252, 253n.8
Rogers, W. C., 185n.12, 208, 217–19,
220n.1, 233n.3, 238, 240n.5
Roosevelt, Theodore, 16, 57, 76n.2,
151n.6; hunting trip of, 206n.10; in
Indian Territory, 202–5, 206n.5;
and Oklahoma constitution,

257n.8; western tour of, 81–82,
84n.1; writings of, 229n.2
Russell, Clifford, 259
Russell, Stillwell H., 182, 184n.3
Russell, U. S., 140, 142n.5, 179,
180n.5, 220, 221n.5
Russia, 90, 91
Russo-Japanese War, 92n.5, 190n.3,
198n.4; end of, 213, 215n.1
Rutherford, Samuel M., 174,
175n.10, 182, 183, 184n.3,
185n.12, 186, 187–89
Ryan, Thomas, 90, 93, 123

Sak-ko-nip-kee, 54,n.2
Sapulpa, Creek Nation, 163n.7
Sawyer, Charles H., 221
Senecas, 3
Sequoyah constitution, 221; contents
of, 227; ratification of, 227, 230;
writing of, 226
Sequoyah convention, 207–20
Shaw, Henry W., 23
Shawnee, Oklahoma Territory, 66,
67n.3; statehood meeting at, 112–
14
Shell Creek, 58, 59n.1
Shepherd, Mollie, 47
Shoenfelt, J. Blair, 119, 121, 122n.6,
148, 150, 159nn.1, 6; 189n.3,
194n.5, 195–96, 198nn.2, 3
Shunatona, Joseph B., 46
Sitting Bull, 89n.3
Skeen, C. A., 185n.12
Skiatook, 25–26
Smiser, Norma Standley, 184n.2
Smith, Charles Henry, 22, 23
Smith, Paul B., 220, 221n.5
Smith, Seba, 23

Index

Smoot, Reed, 238, 239n.3
Snake faction, 6, 57, 72, 73, 171n.5;
    and allotment, 54–55, 152; and
    American culture, 65; emigration
    discussed by, 57; Posey on, 13–14,
    72, 87; and statehood, 237
Sofky, 54n.2, 56n.4, 84n.6, 126n.7,
    153n.1, 225n.5
Solomon, 239
Soper, Pliny Leland, 127, 128,
    130n.5, 136, 172, 173, 174n.2,
    175n.9, 230n.8, 233, 233n.3,
    234n.7, 251, 253n.4
South McAlester, Choctaw Nation,
    106n.4
Stanley, H. J., 185n.12
Stanley, W. E., 127
Statehood, 69, 84, 93–94, 191, 195–
    97, 237–49; agitation for, 140–46,
    160–62; congressional bills for, 65,
    101n.6, 160n.8, 195, 217, 237;
    council to discuss, 57; debate over,
    57; enabling act for, 247; party poli-
    tics and, 101n.5, 207; Posey and,
    77, 79n.2, 101–2; separate, 57, 77,
    101–3, 207; single, 65, 66, 106–8,
    112–14, 140, 207–8, 230n.7, 237.
    See also Sequoyah convention
Sterrett, John A., 139n.3
Stewart, William M., 191–93,
    193n.1, 194n.3, 196
Stidham, George W., 126n.3
Stuart, C. B., 109n.6, 174, 175n.10,
    182, 184n.3
Suggs, Sidney, 179, 180n.4
Sullivan, John L., 265, 266n.2
Sweet, Alex E., 22

Takosar Harjo, 85

Tallassee Canadian town, 63n.5
Taxation, 198n.6
Tecumseh, 89n.3
Territory of Jefferson, 101n.6
Thompson, J. B., 182, 184n.3
Thornton, John N., 273n.24
Tiger, Joe, 81, 82n.5
Tiger, Moty, 71, 72n.4, 126n.6
Tobler, Sam, 118, 118n.7
Tookpafka Micco, 34–35
Tookpafka town, 54n.3
Too-stoo, 27, 30
Town and Country Club, 122n.9,
    127n.7; investigation of, 199–201
Tribal Development Company, 127,
    132
Tucker, Hampton, 101n.6
Tulmochess Yohola, 43
Turner, C. W., 190n.9
Tuskegee town, 81n.2
Tuttle, Dwight, 136, 137–38,
    139nn.3, 5
Tweed, William, 135n.8, 238, 240n.3

Unakah, 24, 25, 26
Uncle Remus, 25
Ury, Isaac Newton, 159n.6

Voliva, Wilbur G., 256n.6

Wacache, 57, 58, 59n.2, 70, 72, 73
Wade, T. L., 185n.12
Wagoner, Creek Nation, 6
Walker, B. N. O. (Hen-toh), 45
Walker, W. H., 213, 216n.5
Washington, Booker T., 76n.2
Watie, Nancy, 274n.43
Watson, Robert B., 225n.7
Watts, Thomas J., 185n.12

Index

Wauhillau Club, 158n.1

Welch, James, 42, 47

Wheeler, John F., 274n.43

White, William Allen, 20

Whitmore, Kirt, 179, 180n.6

Wildcat, Creek Nation, 66, 67n.6, 159n.5

Williams, Robert L., 173, 175n.6, 185nn.5, 9, 10; 186n.13

Wisdom, Dew M., 201n.4, 221

Wisdom, J. Fentress, 159n.1, 200–201, 201n.4; political aspirations of, 221–25

Wisdom family, 225n.9

Wolf Warrior, 35

Woochee Ochee, 30

Woodruff, Clinton Rogers, 148, 152, 164

Woxie Harjoche, 237n.5

Wright, J. George, 119, 120, 121n.2, 128, 150, 151n.4, 193

Wybark, Creek Nation, 159n.5

Yadeka Harjo, 234–36, 237n.3

Zeveley, J. W., 190n.9, 233n.3